D1557250

struggles
for
the human

**global &
insurgent
legalities**

a series edited by
Eve Darian-Smith and
Jonathan Goldberg-Hiller

struggles
for
the human

Violent Legality and the Politics of Rights

LARA MONTESINOS COLEMAN

Duke University Press Durham and London 2024

© 2024 Duke University Press
All rights reserved
Printed in the United States of America on acid-free paper ∞
Project Editor: Michael Trudeau
Designed by Aimee C. Harrison
Typeset in Portrait Text and Anton by
Westchester Publishing Services

Library of Congress Cataloging-in-Publication Data
Names: Coleman, Lara, author.
Title: Struggles for the human : violent legality and the politics of
rights / Lara Montesinos Coleman.
Other titles: Global and insurgent legalities.
Description: Durham : Duke University Press, 2024. |
Series: Global and insurgent legalities | Includes bibliographical
references and index.
Identifiers: LCCN 2023015281 (print)
LCCN 2023015282 (ebook)
ISBN 9781478025566 (paperback)
ISBN 9781478020820 (hardcover)
ISBN 9781478027683 (ebook)
Subjects: LCSH: Human rights. | Human rights—Political aspects. |
Human rights—Moral and ethical aspects. | Protest movements. |
Neoliberalism. | BISAC: LAW / International | SOCIAL SCIENCE /
Ethnic Studies / Caribbean & Latin American Studies
Classification: LCC JC585 .C58345 2024 (print) | LCC JC585 (ebook) |
DDC 323—DC23/ENG/20230731
LC record available at https://lccn.loc.gov/2023015281
LC ebook record available at https://lccn.loc.gov/2023015282

Cover art: Annabel Wyatt, *Figures against Dark Pink*, September 2017. Oil and acrylic
on canvas. Courtesy of the artist.

Dedicated to the memory of Álvaro Marín (1958–2021),
poet, essayist, beekeeper, loving human

We sing so that the light may be
The light too has its kin
The light, it has been said, is the daughter of words
But it is also the daughter of song, and of dance.
We sing to light the flame at the end of the night.
—ÁLVARO MARÍN, *Song for Eliana*

contents

acknowledgments

For all that has been written in criticism of modern/colonial conceptualizations of the human, the figure of the isolated, rational individual still pervades images of the writing process. Writing is rarely talked about in its entanglements with relationships of care and with the material conditions of everyday life. Still less do we tend to regard writing as embodied practice, involving joints and connective tissues that are vulnerable to injury. When a book is the product of almost two decades of thinking in conversation, it is impossible not to approach acknowledgments in a way that does not recognize writing as a practice undertaken in relationship. So, too, when those years have encompassed a period of physical disablement, solo parenting, and navigating violences of a more intimate nature than those I address in this book, it is necessary to acknowledge that its completion would have been impossible without the community of friends, family, colleagues, and *compañerxs* that has sustained me throughout.

This book has emerged from years of thinking and acting in the company of others, through my involvement with la Red de Hermandad and a wider network of social movement struggles in Colombia. Although I reflect at length in the introduction on the complexities of learning about a situation by living it, it is important to acknowledge just how much I have learned from these relationships: emotionally and spiritually, as well as politically and intellectually. Although I thank some specific interlocutors later, I want to give collective acknowledgment to la Red, to the members of the Corporación

Social para la Asesoría y Capacitación Comunitaria (Social Corporation for Community Advice and Training) and the social organizations of Casanare, to the Sindicato Nacional de Trabajadores de la Industria de Alimentos (National Union of Food Industry Workers), and to all the survivors of state- and corporate-sponsored terror who shared stories and reflections. I do not seek to speak for anyone involved in these struggles. On the contrary, I write in keen awareness of my current distance, without expectation of their endorsement of the analysis here. Nevertheless, I offer this contribution in the spirit of ongoing dialogue, with the acknowledgment that I have a great deal more to learn. I am also grateful to the Economic and Social Research Council and the Independent Social Research Foundation (ISRF) for research funding, without which it would have been impossible to spend this time in Colombia.

Alongside the two anonymous reviewers, whose painstaking and thoughtful feedback has greatly strengthened this book, there are four people to whom I owe the greatest thanks. My favorite child, Sophie, has spent the first thirteen years of her life enduring my pontifications about law, capitalism, and political struggle. She also did me the honor of being the first person to cite an earlier draft, in her Year 7 Religious Studies and Citizenship assignment. Being the only child of a solo parent who is trying to juggle finishing a book with the other demands of an academic job is not always easy, and I am grateful for Sophie's ceaselessly entertaining company and ability to ensure that I never lose my sense of humor, as well as for her kindness, house-cleaning rotas, and intermittent reminders that I have been writing this book in one way or another for longer than she has been alive and that I really ought to get a move on if I want to avoid posthumous publication.

Gilberto Torres, whose case against London-based oil and gas multinational BP for kidnapping and torture I discuss in this book, has been a presence throughout the writing process, even at a distance from his exile in Venezuela, in ways of which he is probably unaware. Gilberto's years of accumulated youth have made him a wellspring of insight, wisdom, and encouragement to keep fighting. Without his political leadership, the exercise in building collective critical thought around the strategic use of law that I discuss in chapter 4 also would not have been possible.

In Colombia, the author and investigative journalist Gearóid Ó Loingsigh accompanied this project from its inception and has been immensely generous in his provision of contacts, primary source material, and—on several occasions—accommodation in Bogotá. While I cite a number of the books that Gearóid has written on behalf of Colombian social organizations, it is difficult to overstate the importance of his contribution to the analysis of the links between capitalist "development" and state-sponsored terror in Colombia, and the empirical aspects of this book owe much to the rigor, courage, and commitment with which he has carried out his work (although he will no doubt take issue with parts of my argument).

Finally, my friend and sometimes coauthor Doerthe Rosenow has not only been a source of constant encouragement and steadfast kinship but has also helped shape my ideas in ways that I cannot acknowledge through the conventions of citation. Chapters 5 and 6, in particular, are much richer for her careful reading, as well as for our ongoing conversations and heated discussions over the years.

For the past ten years, I have had the privilege of being part of the International Relations Department at the University of Sussex. The intellectual environment at Sussex has had a deep impact on my writing, but particular thanks—for feedback on parts of this work, friendship, and solidarity in various combinations—go to Nadya Ali, Alice Corble, Jane Cowan, Ida Danewid, Demet Dinler, Julian Germann, Beate Jahn, David Karp, Zdenek Kavan, Peter Newell, Louiza Odysseos, Stefanie Ortmann, Patricia Owens, Ben Rogaly, Jan Selby, Ben Selwyn, Bal Sokhi-Bulley, Cindy Weber, and Louise Wise, as well as to all the members of the Global Studies Collective Writing Group. I am also grateful to all my colleagues in University and College Union Sussex for their collective efforts for our working conditions, which are also our students' learning conditions, as well as for solidarity sea swimming.

Outside of Sussex, the following colleagues and collaborators in Britain, Colombia, and beyond provided valued input on parts of the argument, either through conversation or by reading and commenting on parts of the text: Marianne Aeberhard, Leonie Ansems de Vries, Martín Ayala, Mareike Beck, Louise Braddock, Roddy Brett, Ian Bruff, Gustavo Córdoba, Lars Cornelissen, Javier Correa, Sam Corry, Nicholas Csergo, Paul Dowling, André Drainville, Mark Duffield, Robin Dunford, Bruno Federico, Henrique Furtado, Bruce Heagerty, Deana Heath, Jakob Horstmann, Fabian Laverde, Nivi Manchanda, Isaac Marín, Juan Moncayo, Helena Mullenbach, Carlos Olaya, Sebastian Ordóñez, Tom Osborne, Jenny Pearce, Colin Perrin, Alex Prichard, Pacho Ramírez, Gustavo Rojas-Páez, Chris Rossdale, Mirian Ruíz, Barry Ryan, Cristobal Silva, Owen Thomas, Karen Tucker, Michael Uebel, Manuel Vega, Illan rua Wall, David Whyte, Jutta Weldes, Sue Willman, Ben Witham, Elisa Wynne-Hughes, and Euripides Yance. Thanks also to Courtney Berger at Duke University Press and to Jon Goldberg-Hiller and Eve Darian-Smith for their support of this project, and to Courtney for advice and guidance in the final stages.

While many of those I have mentioned are also friends whose contribution has been far more than intellectual, there are others who must be acknowledged simply for being there in the darkest moments. I am profoundly grateful to Kia and Paul Armstrong, Michael Buick, Mia Eisenstadt, Anna Maria Friis, and Jonathan James for dropping everything when Sophie and I needed it the most, as well as to Refuge, Information, Support, and Education (RISE) in Brighton and to the anonymous group of colleagues whose crowdfunding efforts helped to keep us safe. The writing of this book also coincided with diagnosis of a disabling physical condition and would have ground to a halt without Britain's beleaguered National Health Service, especially the general practitioners Rebecca Jarvis and Fiona Rumboll at St. Peter's Medical Centre, and the team of specialist physios and occupational therapists at the Royal National Orthopedic Hospital who kept me writing, walking, swimming, and dancing. It would likewise not have been possible without the tenacious advocacy of Mike Moran and the ISRF's Stuart Wilson. I am also grateful to my parents, Rosemary and Iden Coleman, for their ongoing support. The discussion of wave-particle duality in chapter 6 owes much to conversations with my father, and I am grateful to my mother for proofreading an earlier draft of the introduction (although I am glad that her appraisal—"It's terribly upsetting, and I'd much rather read a novel"—did not make it onto the cover).

There is one person who is no longer here for me to thank but whose influence nevertheless permeates these pages. Álvaro Marín was not only a wonderful poet, thinker, and writer but also the person who taught me perhaps more than anyone about the hope that can unfold from devastation and the love that can endure and deepen in the face of intolerable loss. While I do not pretend that it can do him justice, it is to his memory that this book is dedicated.

introduction | Human Rights in Struggle

In an ominously titled book that best translates into English as *Biodiversity Is the Horseman of Death*, the Colombian poets Humberto Cárdenas and Álvaro Marín mention a conversation in which a well-known lawyer and sociologist described human rights as "the opium of the people."[1] Through their foray into investigative journalism, the two poets document how, in their own country, international support for human rights and "sustainable development" has gone alongside a brutal imposition of policies designed to benefit multinational corporations. Massacres of populations occupying sites targeted for resource extraction and selective assassinations of trade unionists, community leaders, and human rights activists have become normalized within this repertoire of repression. "The fact that the worst displays of cruelty are accompanied by a humanist and environmentalist discourse," Cárdenas and Marín write, "has enabled us to glimpse through lived experience the true intentions of the policies" promoted by international institutions.[2] The reference to "the opium of the people" expresses a widespread sentiment on the left that all human rights can provide in such contexts is a diversion, a sedative, a degree of analgesia in an intolerable situation. Worse, they may anesthetize us completely or provoke memory loss and confusion about what is really happening.

Cárdenas and Marín's Colombian readers would, however, immediately notice a subtext to this assessment of human rights. Their interlocutor was the late Eduardo Umaña Luna, a sociolegal thinker whose own son, Eduardo Umaña Mendoza, had been killed because of his work as a prominent human rights lawyer defending the rights of left-wing dissidents, trade unionists, and rural populations who were, in turn, being killed and threatened because of their resistance to a neoliberal economic model or because they inhabited territories lucrative for foreign investment. This is a familiar pattern across much of the world. Today, a vast proportion of victims of assassination and forced disappearance are those defending the rights of populations contesting the social and environmental costs of the predominant approach to development, focused on industries such as oil and mining, agroindustry, and other enterprises that appropriate nature for the accumulation of capital.[3]

Given this scenario, can we do without human rights? Certainly, many social movements would say that they have no option but to appeal to rights, but what are we to make of human rights as a vocabulary of opposition to the dynamics of plunder, exploitation, dispossession, and armed repression that constitute contemporary capitalism? What do we make of human rights as an expression of ethical commitment or of solidarity with others? For many, the answer would be "not much." In her book *The Shock Doctrine*, Naomi Klein denounces the international human rights movement along lines that resonate with Cárdenas and Marín's critique. The Pinochet dictatorship in Chile was, Klein argues, not only the laboratory of what was to become a global drive to restructure economy and society along neoliberal lines. It was also the laboratory for an international human rights movement whose advocacy served to detract from the fact that torture and forced disappearance were central to the process of neoliberal restructuring.[4] Even if human rights campaigners are not considered complicit with the economic policies generating premature death and misery for much of the world's population, they are often said to divert attention from the real source of the evils they so vocally deplore. Human rights, critics remind us, come burdened with the moral-political baggage of liberal individualism. They naturalize a concept of "the human" (sovereign, self-interested, and ruling over nature) that is inextricably linked to the rise of modern capitalism and shaped through the exploitation and dehumanization of colonized peoples.

Nevertheless, the routine killing of human rights defenders in many parts of the world points us to another side of the story. Whatever the critique of human rights from the left, the assault from the right is even more fervent and sustained. Right-wing authoritarians and xenophobic populists typically revile human rights, and these forces are on the rise, even in the former heartlands of liberal internationalism. "The endtimes of human rights" have even been prophesied in the face of an increasingly multipolar world order marked by conservative religious influence.[5] In 2019, the British human rights organization Liberty distributed fliers decrying politicians' attacks on the Human Rights Act and inviting readers to "tear off the rights you're happy to throw away." The list of rights under that headline (not to be tortured, not to be a slave, to have a fair trial if accused) were, by implication, rights that no one could not want. Yet, might appealing to human rights not end up foreclosing on other possibilities: forms of political economy that may be more liberatory, gentler, more enabling of human and nonhuman flourishing or even of our collective survival?

This book offers a fresh approach to the politics and ethics of human rights by way of an ethnographically infused blend of political philosophy and critical theory based on years of engagement with peasant, worker, Black, and Indigenous movements in Colombia. It is the product of almost two decades of dialogue and relationship, as well as direct involvement in struggle. When scholars refer to the "violence of development," or to synergies between neoliberalism and authoritarianism, Colombia often features as an emblematic example, in part because of the extent to which it sustains the contradictions between a formally liberal-democratic polity and a political economy that generates death on an enormous scale. This is not, however, a book about Colombia; unlike an anthropological study, it is not primarily concerned with how human rights culture is manifest in that context.[6] Rather, this is a political inquiry into human rights as a vocabulary of resistance, as well as an ethical inquiry concerned with human possibilities and political imaginations in the face of atrocity and devastation. What is most distinctive about the approach here is that it puts struggles against extractivist capitalism at the forefront of ethical and political reflection.

In Colombia, as in many other parts of the world, human rights are harnessed by social movements steeped in decolonial, Marxist, feminist, and Indigenous thought. As in many other parts of the world, too, a major focus of these struggles has been on multinational corporations, both as direct accomplices in human rights abuse and as authors and beneficiaries of a legal order that enables plunder at immense human and ecological cost. "If you were to stop and ask someone to name a human rights abuse," Stéfanie Khoury and David Whyte begin their book on corporate human rights violations, "whether they realised it or not, chances are it would include corporate involvement in one form or another."[7] There is a burgeoning literature on prospects for legal action against companies, as well as on problems with the very idea that corporations—as legal structures designed as the engine of capital accumulation—can be meaningfully held to account for the harm they generate.[8] Yet scholars have paid scant attention to how social movements use human rights in struggles against the violence of capital or to how these efforts may be focused on multinational corporations *precisely because* the corporation is the machinery of a global political economy bringing devastation and death. Nor, I should add, have existing studies considered such struggles as a lens into an appraisal of human rights more widely. While much has been written in critique of the "international human rights movement," critics rarely interrogate the profound differences between some international nongovernmental organizations (NGOs) advocating for human rights and the politics of rights within struggles at companies' sites of operation.

This book traces the trajectories of some of these struggles over years and across continents, as they have been taken up within transnational campaigns and legal actions, sparking policy initiatives on the part of global elites.[9] It is, at one level, an interdisciplinary study that engages literatures in critical legal studies, international political economy, intellectual history, and philosophy. Yet in its very method, this book can also be considered an antidisciplinary work in that it draws much of its intellectual and political inspiration from the lived thought developed within these struggles themselves. As Lewis Gordon reminds us, all disciplines and fixed conceptual frameworks risk enclosing the world within boundaries that occlude this lived dimension to thought. "Any discipline or generated system for the organization of reality faces the problem of having to exceed the scope of its object of inquiry," Gordon writes. "There is, in other words, always more to and of reality. Failure to appreciate reality sometimes takes the form of recoiling from it. . . . The discipline becomes, in solipsistic fashion, the world."[10]

As a result, *Struggles for the Human* tells a different story, both from those who embrace human rights and from critics who consider human rights inherently complicit with capitalism and neocolonialism. We should not assume in advance that rights talk constrains emancipatory change or that human rights operate only within the confines of hegemonic political horizons. Indeed, the very idea that we should decide "for" or "against" human rights only really makes sense when we bypass the politics of struggle. What I seek to show here is that, when human rights are most tightly yoked to existing structures of power, this is not because they are inextricably tied to liberal individualism or because they serve to inculcate docile forms of subjectivity, but because they are taken up as abstract values that can then be fixed neatly within an existing order of things. The predominant approach to ethics at this juncture—as a "feel-good" enterprise based on a fetishism of abstract values—has led to human rights' becoming mere add-ons to the tyranny of a "rule of law" designed to facilitate plunder. One key contribution of this book is what we might call a diagnosis of this scenario. As changes to economic policy and law slowly erase the rights of citizenship, human rights have been, in effect, "privatized." Since the second half of the 1990s, when the Washington Consensus gave way to the post-Washington era of "development with a human face," ethical discourse has become a core feature of neoliberal business as usual. In this context, a series of interventions for "corporate social responsibility" and "decent work" have made human rights entirely contingent on the profitmaking activities of multinational corporations. "The market"—rather than law or citizenship—defines the very subjects of rights, assigning people a value and fixing them in place. These privatized rights are a counterpart of the armed repression of those who contest an economic model that condemns many to death.

The other major contribution of this book is to show why and how this is not the full story. Importantly, this is not the sort of "redemptive critique" that Ben Golder identifies in international legal scholars who offer criticism of human rights and yet end with a qualified retrieval of human rights all the same.[11] Rather, the crux of my argument is that there is a very different sort of appeal to human rights at play in struggles for less destructive and more ecologically sustainable ways of organizing and reproducing life. Critical theorists and philosophers have pointed out, in various ways, that appeals to rights can also unsettle oppressive logics of power and interrupt normative schemas that assign rights within the confines of the existing order of things. By thinking through engagement with actual struggles, the analysis in this book adds two important sets of insights to this overall line of argument. The first is a focus on the imbrication of law within the social relations of capitalism, and on the relations established with legality at moments when human rights are used in international litigation or in "alternative justice" mechanisms to make claims about forms of harm that cannot be fully recognized within the terms of dominant legal narratives. Strategic appeal to human rights in such contexts can advance what I call *counterlegalities* in ways that evince the violences enabled by the existing legal order through processes of critique that push the system beyond what it can contain.

The second set of insights concerns how struggles using human rights may also be sites at which alternative normative visions are forged in the wake of atrocity, as people have sought to reclaim land from which they were displaced and develop plans for less harmful ways of living. Ethics here is anything but an abstract exercise. The affirmation of human rights is inseparable from persistent critique of capitalist extraction and of the very conceptualization of the human that has long underpinned capitalism and "development." At the same time, however, these struggles reach beyond critique. By refusing to foreclose on human possibilities, they point the way to a human rights praxis that keeps open the question of the subject of rights and, indeed, of what it might mean to be human. I suggest, furthermore, that thinking through the lens of these struggles might provide us with the coordinates of a broader ethico-political orientation that I denote an "insurgent humanism." Whereas mainstream philosophical accounts of human rights have tended to invoke a transcendent human dignity rooted in an understanding of the human as sovereign individual, I point to a dialectic within these struggles between immanent critique of systemic violence and appeal to a transcendent sense of good that is elusive and beyond language, and that renders the normative coordinates shaped through these struggles far from merely "local." If law and the normative concepts that underpin it are constitutive of capitalist relations, then attention to the dynamics of an insurgent humanism has a lot to teach us about how we might think of our ethical obligations toward others.

The Human of Human Rights

Human rights advocates have come under fire from various directions for failing to address the power relations that shape prevailing understandings of humanity, legality, and justice. Mainstream political theory and doctrinal approaches to law view rights as claims, privileges, or "trump cards" held by individuals, increasing choices, advancing interests, or providing protection against abuse by the powerful.[12] From here, it is a short step to the argument that global justice requires the enforcement and diffusion of human rights norms.[13] The trouble with such approaches is that they fail to grasp how such norms are already power-laden, already the product of histories of violence. Human rights doctrine was formulated as a doctrine of what it means to be human by reference to various permutations of the figure of sovereign "Man," which, in Sylvia Wynter's words, "overrepresents itself as if it were the human itself."[14] Things start to look a good deal more complicated once we recognize "Man" not only as a parochial, cultural construct but also as one that has come to be taken for granted through the subjugation and enslavement of colonized peoples and, subsequently, the denigration and abandonment of populations deemed naturally lacking in the qualities required for success within the development of modern capitalism.[15]

One important line of critique has come from Latin American decolonial scholars, who have emphasized how modern understandings of what it is to be human were developed through skeptical interrogation of whether colonized peoples met the criteria to be classified as such. Enrique Dussel famously argued for the particular significance of the Spanish Conquest of the Americas, which, in his account, inaugurated modernity as an ostensibly innocent civilizing process. Modernity, Dussel argued, is based on a myth concocted to conceal its sacrificial violence toward colonized Others, who are presented as needing to be emancipated from their own faults.[16] While the atrocities perpetrated against the colonized were rationalized on the basis that Indigenous peoples were not fully human and thus did not count as subjects of natural rights, colonial brutality did not occur outside of moral discourse nor, contrary to what Achille Mbembe suggests in a well-known essay, did it reside at its core "in the exercise of a power outside of the law (ab legibus solutus)."[17] From the time of the Conquest, colonial violence was entangled with the ethics of war as "one of the characteristic features of European modernity."[18] In the Americas, theories of just war were elaborated to justify the forced subjugation of Indigenous peoples who did not accept the God of the Catholic Church or enter into commerce under the terms of the conquistadores.[19] Julia Suárez-Krabbe describes how the Nasa Indigenous people of Colombia speak of a colonial "death project," which persists in the present and is inseparable not only from "racism, capitalism, patriarchy and predatory behaviours against nature" but also from ethical discourse and the legal capacity to render people politically nonexistent.[20]

From this perspective, even apparently emancipatory extensions of rights have worked their own violence. A good example is the way in which the philosopher and theologian Francisco de Vitoria argued for the inalienable human dignity of Indigenous peoples following the Conquest. In so doing, de Vitoria intervened in the then hegemonic frames of the Spanish Empire, which failed to recognize Indigenous peoples as fully human. Yet de Vitoria's recognition of the shared humanity of Indigenous people occurred within specific conceptual parameters: those recognizable as subjects of rights were subjects with the capacity for "dominion" over themselves and their patrimony through the use of reason (in contrast to "wild beasts" and "irrational animals," which "have not dominion over themselves" and thus "can be killed with impunity, even for pleasure").[21] Indigenous peoples, he argued, did exercise dominion—because they had laws, a system of exchange, and so on, which required the use of reason. Only on this basis could they be recognized as subjects of natural rights and thus could not be deprived of their property or enslaved. Even de Vitoria's argument for the rights of Indigenous people was, simultaneously, a justification of colonialism: Indigenous peoples were now to be ruled, for their own good, by others with a stronger capacity for government.[22] More fundamentally, de Vitoria's very act of recognition of Indigenous peoples as subjects of rights was also an act of epistemic violence (violence at the level of knowledge itself). By affirming them as particular sorts of subjects that fit within a particular definition of the human and, only as such, worthy of recognition as subjects of rights, de Vitoria appropriated Indigenous peoples into colonial epistemic territory. As Walter Mignolo notes in the aptly titled essay "Who Speaks for the Human in Human Rights?'" de Vitoria "spoke for humanity and told half the story without realizing it," never stopping to ask whether the "Indians'" own relationship to land was one of property.[23] In fact, the idea of land as property is unintelligible within the metaphysics of Indigenous peoples of the Americas. Land is not something external to the human, an object that can be appropriated as a commodity or defended as property. It is a living being, to be respected and protected as part of life.[24]

The anthropological paradigm of the "rational" individual was entwined with the degradation, not only of colonized peoples, but also of European subaltern classes. For instance, in the context of enclosure of the commons and the rise of "commercial society" in Britain, elites consolidated a long-standing division between the "deserving" and "undeserving" poor by "blackening" the lower orders as inferior types of human through analogy to savages and slaves.[25] The paradigm of the rational individual was likewise inseparable from the degradation of women. The genocidal witch hunt that took off in Europe in the sixteenth and seventeenth centuries destroyed women's social power and enclosed them within the confines of an emergent capitalist regulation of the family and property. The witch hunts abated only in the eighteenth century when an ideology of rule of law became the preeminent means through which the ruling classes legitimized their property and status.[26] The ideology of rule of law was also central to the first Latin American constitutions of the early nineteenth century, which followed soon after the late eighteenth-century declarations of rights by the United States and France. By this point, the humanity of colonized peoples was no longer a topic of open debate. However, an epistemic shift was underway, with a more secularized understanding of the human defined increasingly as economic man—onto which Charles Darwin's understanding of natural selection would subsequently be projected. Instead of colonized peoples being defined in terms of degrees of subrationality—and, hence, subhumanity—civility was linked to economic success, as a rising European bourgeoisie sought to redescribe human activity in ways that would legitimate their own ascent to hegemony.[27] Thus, the new declarations of rights subtly bolstered colonialism, including internal colonialism in the case of the newly independent Latin American republics: in practice, to "fit into the category of citizen, a person had to fit into requirements concerning religion, blood, color, gender, knowledge, government, property etc. as defined by European male elites."[28] These observations resonate with Karl Marx's reflections on rights in the markedly different context of nineteenth-century Europe. The extension of political rights, Marx argued, created a dualism between the abstract figure of the citizen ("man as an allegorical and moral person") and "egotistical man" in the private sphere ("an individual withdrawn behind his private interests and whims and separated from the community.")[29] What is more, the (natural) human rights that the declarations of the "rights of man and citizen" considered political rights to defend (liberty, property, equality before the law, and security) were nothing other than the rights of this particular conception of isolated, egotistical, and self-sufficient "man."[30]

Socialists more widely have tended to be hesitant in regarding rights as a language of reform. In the early twentieth century, some states began to canonize social rights in their national constitutions in response to working-class struggle. (Notable examples are the constitution that followed the Mexican Revolution in 1917 and that of the Weimar Republic in Germany.) Social rights crept in piecemeal in Europe until their climax after World War II.[31] Meanwhile, in Latin America citizenship was increasingly defined in terms of social rights, even if the welfare state was to remain a distant aspiration. Nevertheless, socialists on both continents were skeptical as to whether rights could be rescued from their nineteenth-century libertarian associations, and Latin American socialists in particular argued that rights could not serve revolutionary ends or challenge the systematic inequality generated by capitalism. Even reformulations of rights as economic and social rights did not in themselves challenge inequality. After the adoption of the United Nations Universal Declaration of Human Rights (UDHR) in 1948, which enshrined social rights as international norms, the English historian and international relations theorist Edward Hallett Carr commented that without, at the very least, an equivalent emphasis on social obligations, rights were unlikely to change the equation.[32]

However, here too, the ambiguity around rights hinges on the question of the human. Decolonial critics are right to highlight the colonial origins of the concept of the human at the heart of human rights, but the problem extends beyond this. As Jacques Rancière puts it in his well-known essay "Who Is the Subject of the Rights of Man?," rights end up being allocated to categories of human symbolized as "functional parts" within the existing social order. Entitlements to speak and act are ascribed on the basis of the place and function people have within an unequal society. This includes postwar welfare states, in which politics was largely reduced to a "logic of consensus"—a process of negotiation or pursuit of technocratic fixes to ensure an optimal balance of interests within the terms of the existing order.[33] Thus, it is of little surprise that welfare states simultaneously reinforced hierarchies around race and gender, as well as class divisions, while the UDHR itself was, as Samuel Moyn notes, vague on the continuation of empire and had nothing to say about unequal distribution—within or among the sovereign states that now made up the United Nations.[34] New Third World states did seek to deepen international recognition of economic and social rights as part of a movement for a New International Economic Order that would enable greater equality among states, and that included proposals to subordinate multinational corporations to public authority on an international scale.[35] However, this movement largely placed questions of inequality within states to one side, relegating them to the pursuit of national "development." These proposals were, in any case, rapidly sidelined as neoliberal economic orthodoxy took hold. Meanwhile, a mode of international human rights activism flourished in which rights were, once again, detached from their loose, earlier twentieth-century connections with social welfare.[36]

Critics of the international human rights movement that emerged in the 1970s consider it a counterpart of the neoliberal reforms that devastated the lives of actually existing human beings, first in Augusto Pinochet's Chile and then more widely, with the stringent conditions placed on aid by the World Bank and International Monetary Fund from the 1980s.[37] For some, there are fundamental synergies between human rights and neoliberalism because human rights actively foster forms of selfhood compatible with the imperatives of capitalism. Stephen Hopgood, for instance, has suggested that human rights were the "small print" of the vision of "global civil society" that proliferated in the 1990s. By maintaining the kernel of the autonomous individual, human rights activism became a site at which supposedly "virtuous" identities are inculcated—in particular, that of "an autonomous and morally self-sufficient person able to pursue self-authored interests" who meets with other such individuals only to do this.[38] For Wendy Brown, human rights embody a false promise, a false capacity of the individual to pursue self-authored interests, because they carry conceptual baggage that disregards "the historical, political, and economic constraints in which this choice occurs." Human rights activism, for Brown, is "not merely a tactic but a particular form of political power carrying a particular image of justice." As such, it risks displacing the struggles and emancipatory political projects of its intended beneficiaries.[39]

The simultaneous rise of neoliberal economics and human rights activism does not, however, indicate an inherent compatibility between the two. It was, Moyn underscores, the fact that human rights advocates lost sight of the need to curb inequality that rendered the human rights movement a "powerless companion" to neoliberalism.[40] Things begin to look more complicated, however, when we consider the efforts made by neoliberal thinkers— starting in the 1940s—to promote a specific vision of human rights entirely at odds with the UDHR and with the commitment of many of its architects to curbing inequality. As Jessica Whyte has explored at length in a recent book, the Mont Pèlerin Society, founded at the instigation of the Austrian economist Friedrich Hayek in 1947 to oppose socialist planning, sought from its inception to defend a vision of "human dignity" in which humans are inherently unequal and in which those most in possession of the qualities required for economic success would—and should—benefit.[41] While the neoliberals rejected the Enlightenment belief in human equality, treating people equally (and so avoiding welfare and redistributive initiatives) was vital for (natural) inequalities to be perpetuated and for equilibrium to be generated through market mechanisms. This was the basis not only for opposition to socialist planning, but also for a broad-scale defense of colonialism and, from the 1970s, a rejection of Third Worldism and of demands for a New International Economic Order.[42] Moreover, as Quinn Slobodian highlights in his intellectual history of Geneva School neoliberalism, neoliberal thought emerged after the fall of the Habsburg Empire and during the final decline of the British Empire, and one of its key problems was to think about how to safeguard global order in the absence of imperial institutions.[43] In the 1970s, neoliberal thinkers began to mobilize the language of human rights in opposition to demands for postcolonial redistribution, arguing that Third World governments suppressed not only the civil and political rights of minorities but also the inflow of foreign capital, private firms, and licenses for economic activities.[44] As the international human rights movement gained traction, neoliberal ideologues developed a human rights discourse geared toward "securing the rights of investors and the wealthy in the face of challenges to their property and power."[45] Human rights were mobilized, not to establish colonized peoples' rights to self-determination or the rights of the poorest to basic welfare, but "to provide an institutional and moral foundation for a competitive market economy and to shape entrepreneurial subjects."[46]

It should now be clear that much of the existing critique of human rights centers on the question of the human taken to be the subject of rights. For some, the focus is on how human rights discourse takes for granted the figure of sovereign "Man" as representative of the human, with the effect that the holders of rights are presumed to conform to particular criteria of rationality; to pursue their own self-interest within a reasonable set of limits; and to exercise dominion over themselves, their property, and a natural world from which humans are presumed to be separate. For others, critique focuses on how rights are ascribed in practice to particular categories of people (e.g., workers in the context of capitalist social relations). For all the rhetorical commitment to equal rights, these categories take for granted in their very formulation a particular social order. When the rhetorical commitment to equality is removed—as it is with neoliberal thought—the subject of rights is reduced to just whoever is the right sort of human to adapt and flourish in a liberal market economy.

So far, however, these criticisms have turned on the discursive, cultural, symbolic dimension of social order. We must, however, not forget that rights are also legal categories—and that the law demands compliance rather than mere belief. The neoliberal reconceptualization of human rights did not just provide a moral foundation for neoliberal economics. It was also inseparable from proposals for legal reform, to put in place a global institutional structure privileging the rights of property and contract and the market freedom of private capital.

The centrality of law to social relations is often overlooked. It is, of course, widely acknowledged among critical thinkers that the law in liberal democracies protects private property and profit more than it does citizens. Meanwhile (as I discuss further in chapter 4), the punitive side of the legal system falls heavily on the poor. Yet at the same time, the law exercises its power in a manner quite distinct from brute force or arbitrary power: it claims to represent a series of universal rules, shaped through moral discourse and applied on the basis of a principle of equity. For instance, the commodification of the "free" worker's labor power under a system of wage labor relies on the "*fictio juris* of a contract" between workers and employers, formally grounded in principles of "liberty" and individual "right" (which, as Marx saw so clearly, masks the unfreedom of workers who are compelled to sell their labor power to survive).[47] Law is not just epiphenomenal to capitalist relations, superstructural to a separate material base, a means through which capitalism is regulated and violations of property rights are enforced. It is part of the fabric of social relations in a manner that makes it impossible to draw any neat distinction between material "base" and ideational "superstructure." Relations of production would be, as E. P. Thompson put it, "inoperable" without law.[48] For some—most notably, the Russian legal theorist Evgeny Pashukanis—the very form of law is capitalist. In Pashukanis's account, the legal form was the specific form of social regulation necessary to deal with the possibility of disputes among the formally equal, isolated, and egotistical individuals implied by commodity exchange, and it is no coincidence that the emergence of capitalism was coeval with the emergence of "Man" as a bearer of rights.[49] Pashukanis's view that law needed to "wither away" did not make him popular with the Soviet regime, which eventually had him executed. Nor would it find favor with many human rights advocates, for whom law—and, specifically, the prosecution of perpetrators of human rights abuse—is central. Nevertheless, Pashukanis's theory of law has underpinned a skepticism among Marxist legal scholars toward the idea that human rights can be the basis of any form of emancipatory struggle.[50]

Rights in Resistance

The arguments of those who reject human rights because of the tight relations between law and capitalism can be captured with the poet Audre Lorde's metaphor that "the Master's tools will never dismantle the Master's house. They may allow us temporarily to beat him at his own game, but they will never enable us to bring about genuine change."[51] Lorde, however, was referring to white feminists' using the tools of racist patriarchy against that same patriarchy as a result of white feminists' exclusion of Black and lesbian feminists from debates on feminist philosophy. Law might be better seen not merely as the "Master's tools," but as the fabric of "the Master's house," part of the very structure that is to be dismantled and reassembled into something able to accommodate those previously excluded, without (to stretch the metaphor horribly) the devastating ecological impact of the Master's way of living. After all, as Thompson emphasized in a critique of schematic Marxist accounts, law was as deeply imbricated within precapitalist agrarian political economy as it is within capitalism, and it is through conflict over law (e.g., indefinite agrarian use rights versus landowners' property rights) that class struggle has played out and a particular vision of "the law" has been consolidated.[52]

Such insights do not only caution us against a crude economism based on the idea that we can separate ideas from material structures. They also remind us that the legal categories constitutive of capitalist relations are cultural artifacts that rely on particular conceptions of what it is to be human—who can be included in that category and to what extent. While the subordination of wage labor to capital relied on a fiction of the "free" individual, chattel slavery (sidelined in Marx's account of capitalism but equally central to its rise) was justified and institutionalized through the legal codification of a category of person who was not a "free" worker but a commodity, stripped of any claim to legal personality.[53] Thus, as Gurminder Bhambra and John Holmwood emphasize, all of the complex forms of subordination of labor to capital (wage labor, slave labor, family labor, and so on) are "socially constructed (and resisted) and politically regulated."[54] What is more, legal categories—and the social relations to which they give form—have come about through struggle and conceptual innovation. From this perspective, there is nothing about the legal form that requires that the legal subject be defined in terms of the "free" rational individual. Indeed, as I show in chapter 4, a great deal of jurisprudential and philosophical argument was required to put the rational individual at the heart of law. By the same token, to reduce law to a mask for domination is to overlook how the idea of rule of law, as a guarantee against tyranny, and the idea of the free individual at the heart of modern law are also products of centuries of struggle against absolutism and arbitrary power.[55] Indeed, for Thompson it was precisely law's "logic of equity" that has made it a valuable tool of struggle: "The rulers were, in serious senses, prisoners of their own rhetoric: they played the game of power according to rules which suited them, but they could not break those rules or the whole game would be thrown away."[56] The law had to be seen to apply to everyone. Thus, writes Thompson, law, "in certain limited areas," was "a genuine forum within which certain kinds of class conflict were fought out."[57] Likewise, as José-Manuel Barreto reminds us, the foundations of human rights law and theory "are to be found not only in the Enlightenment, but even before that, in resistance to the display of the capacity for destruction of imperialism—the dark side or the other constitutive pillar of modernity."[58]

These histories of struggle over both the form and the content of law need to be borne in mind when we consider that human rights—including legal struggles that invoke human rights—have been a visible thread binding the struggles of the dispossessed. What is more, the impetus here has not come merely from the world of international NGOs and "cause lawyers" but from within struggles of anticapitalist, anti-imperialist, and decolonial social movements that are keenly aware of the contradictory politics of rights.[59] In his assessment of the "endtimes of human rights," Hopgood presents the demise of the human rights sanctioned by the institutions of liberal global governance as freeing space for human rights as weapons of the weak against violence and deprivation. For the oppressed, he suggests, any language is useful that helps to raise awareness, generate transnational activism, put pressure on governments, facilitate legal redress, and attract funds for campaigning (human rights, solidarity, love, or whatever).[60] The question arises, however, as to what it means for a language of resistance to be "useful." What formulations such as Hopgood's miss is the capacity for abstract ideals to be taken up in ways that bolster the very forms of power that those in struggle seek to contest. This may be the case even when these interventions involve an apparently progressive recognition of those previously not recognized, as we saw with the extension of rights of Indigenous peoples in the decades after the Conquest. In *Red Skin, White Masks*, Glen Coulthard underscores not only that recognition was part of colonial politics but that "the politics of recognition in its contemporary liberal form promises to reproduce the very configurations of colonial, racist, patriarchal state power that Indigenous peoples' demands for recognition have historically sought to transcend."[61]

Another set of arguments, more nuanced than Hopgood's regarding the potential of human rights as a weapon of the weak, has focused on how rights might be used innovatively or disruptively "from below." Boaventura de Sousa Santos has proposed that human rights should be reconceptualized as multicultural via mutual critique of different cultures' conceptualizations of human dignity. This, he suggests, should mobilize the version of each culture that represents its "widest circle of reciprocity," reappropriating and subverting cultural formulations that legitimate oppression.[62] In a recent book, Sumi Madhok draws on engagement with mobilizations in India and Pakistan to show how subaltern struggles use human rights to enact radically different ideas of justice, politics, and citizenship in struggles for rights to food, to gender and caste equality, to ancestral forests, and in working-class struggle against the military. Madhok combines ethnographic investigations with political philosophy not merely to insist—as Santos does—that human rights *can* be conceptualized as multicultural, but also to argue that decolonization of human rights demands a reckoning with the multiple forms of world making at play within actual struggles for rights.[63] Robin Dunford has likewise shown in relation to transnational peasant struggles how subaltern struggles can be sites at which human rights discourses are created, and that these alternative understandings of rights can "travel" to shape global norms—albeit always with the risk of co-optation by global institutions.[64]

Struggles for the Human also combines ethnographic engagement with political philosophy to consider how possibilities for human rights might be expanded by attention to social movement struggles outside the "West." At the same time, however, I want to consider how human rights struggles "from below" pose a challenge not only to Eurocentric histories and theories of rights, but also to the ways in which prevailing legal and policy narratives draw lines between worthy and unworthy lives. It is a well-worn claim that demands for rights can challenge and disrupt prevailing normative schemas (rather than just demanding that more be included within existing norms).[65] However, while much of the second part of this book focuses on the disruptive potential of rights, there are two aspects that come into the foreground as a result of thinking through actual struggles. First, not all such forms of disruption are equivalent. "What are we up against?" and "What are the broader dynamics that have necessitated this struggle at this juncture?" are unavoidable questions for actual human beings resisting the depredations of capital on the ground. On the one hand, if law—and the moral economies of representation shaping law—are constitutive of capitalist relations, then struggle over law and legal categories is arguably necessary (though not sufficient) to struggles for alternative political economies. On the other hand, however, to grasp what is at stake in struggles over rights, we also need a sense of the material relations of power and violence that are both constituted and concealed through the law. What is missed by an overemphasis on shifts and dislocations within the field of representation is the continuity in the wider terrain of capitalist extraction, as well as the capacity of capital to integrate what once appeared as transgressive. The "privatized" human rights that I discuss in this book can be considered an extreme example of capitalism's absorption of an apparently disruptive articulation of rights. Yet the problem runs deeper. Whether an emancipatory logic can be attributed to the disruptive or transgressive depends, as Emilios Christodoulidis emphasizes, on whether this has "the capacity to transform the power structure as a whole."[66] In other words, what matters is immanent critique in the Marxist sense: pushing the system beyond what can be contained within the order of capital and its economy of representation. Undermining the selective recognition of "the human" may be an important part of this, but we must consider how such disruptive appeals to rights are bound up with wider social movement struggles and pedagogical practice.

The second aspect that comes to the fore as a result of attention to struggle is the question of ethics, of the relation between politics and its outside, between the immanent and the transcendent. Traditionally, philosophical accounts of human rights have tended to rely on a humanist position, justifying the universalism of rights by grounding them in the inherent dignity of the sovereign, rational individual. For some, following Wynter's insistence that liberatory praxis must involve resignifying what it is to be human, the question of grounds is superseded by the task of decolonizing the praxis of being human by breaking with the "master code of symbolic life and death" that justifies expropriation and exploitation.[67] For others, the response has been to rethink the normative underpinnings of human rights as immanent to the practices through which those rights are asserted, or—in Judith Butler's influential formulation—as a response to a constitutive vulnerability of all of us *qua human* that demands a "more robust universalization of rights" at the same time that is requires a resignification of the norms through which humanness is recognized.[68] The ethnographic lens of this book leads me to a slightly different approach. Instead of trying to theorize ethics in advance, I begin from reflection on how ethical coordinates are shaped in struggles that seek to unsettle the concept of "the human" that has underpinned capitalist and colonial relations. From there, I consider how we might approach human rights as an expression of a deeper ethical call that implies the construction of alternative political economies, as well as contestation of renderings of "the human" that mask and underpin systemic violence.

Thinking Through Struggle

This book, as I have said, develops its concepts through many years of involvement with the struggles of grassroots organizations, both at their sites of emergence in Colombia and through associated transnational campaigns. The primary vehicle of my involvement since about 2005 has been la Red de Hermandad (Network of Brotherhood/Sisterhood, known as la Red), a loose grouping of peasant, Indigenous, Black, labor union, and human rights organizations established in 1994, at a juncture at which massacres and selective killings by state-backed paramilitaries were proliferating in the context of neoliberal reforms. These organizations came together, in part, to better coordinate their activities, which included projects documenting the atrocities; an "observatory" to monitor the involvement of multinational corporations in abuses; and numerous struggles over land, livelihood, and labor conditions across the country. However, a core aim of the network was also to give international visibility to what was happening. Thus, la Red also incorporated solidarity collectives from various European countries on the principle of "horizontal relations among peoples." From the outset, la Red's internationalism was conceived as an alternative to mainstream humanitarian and developmentalist assistance. There is a word for the latter in Spanish—*asistencialismo* (lit., assistance-ism, which connotes helping but not standing alongside and being part of the struggles of others). European groups in la Red mobilize contacts when someone is killed or threatened and promote international campaigns such as the boycott of Coca-Cola that was launched by the Colombian Food Workers Union after the murder of several of its members. However, central to the network are the activities of *internacionalistas* (internationalists) across Colombia, who provide protective accompaniment for human rights defenders, labor unionists, and rural communities in areas with particularly high levels of armed repression. Accompaniment implies a tactical mobilization of the divisions between lives that are protected and those that are not within the racialized matrices of global capitalism (sometimes described as being a sort of "unarmed bodyguard").[69] Yet unlike some international NGOs, which offer accompaniment on strict principles of political neutrality, accompaniment within la Red is provided on the basis of political affinity, with emphasis placed on *internacionalistas* working as part of the social movement and sharing relevant skills (anything from research to installing electrical wiring) while learning from Colombian organizations. In my case, this involved contributing to research and writing—for instance, by writing human rights reports, helping prepare legal cases, and cowriting a book on the oilfields of BP (formerly British Petroleum) with an organization set up by peasant leaders who had been forcibly displaced from the region. In la Red's lexicon, this day-to-day work alongside Colombian organizations is also sometimes referred to as accompaniment: part of a practice of walking alongside others in struggle.

The rejection of *asistencialismo* and commitment to horizontal relations of solidarity is central to what I will characterize as la Red's decolonial ethos. Organizations in la Red rarely describe themselves as involved in a decolonial struggle, but the concept pervades their activities, even if the word does not. While human rights and law-based struggle are central to la Red's activities, the network is a site of persistent critique of legacies of colonialism that shape contemporary capitalist relations, as well as of the associated epistemic frameworks that characterize dominant narratives of development, law, and human rights. That said, by referring to decoloniality as an ethos, I also want to highlight the complexity and plurality of these struggles rather than imply that they can be neatly contained within a framework derived from decolonial thought. I started reading decolonial scholarship when I was already involved with la Red in Colombia and remember recognizing much in what I read that was already part of day-to-day conversation on the ground. Peasant, Indigenous, and Afro-Colombian critiques of the violence of development, for instance, found resonance in the analyses of Arturo Escobar (who acknowledges the influence of Afro-Colombian thought and whose earlier genealogy of "development" has, in turn, influenced Colombian social organizations).[70] Mignolo's "border-thinking" captured the sort of dialogue or threshold between ways of knowing in meetings where, for example, one person would invoke the concept of popular sovereignty over natural resources, while another would highlight the colonial origins of the term and argue in favor of self-determination based on equilibrium between humans and nature.[71] Yet all this is lived, often implicit, permeating conversation and praxis without any of the neologisms (*coloniality*, *pluriversality*, and so on) that pervade the appropriation of Indigenous and social movement thought within the academy. By the same token, the network has a distinctively modern intellectual heritage. There is a strong Marxist current of analysis running through the heart of the network's activities. Likewise, anarchist and feminist concepts, and even tropes of liberal political theory, are combined within a plural intellectual constellation that shapes—and is shaped by—struggle. It is worth underscoring, too, that this plurality and intersection of intellectual traditions is not a specifically Colombian phenomenon but something reflected in the struggles of grassroots movements more widely in Latin America.[72] The Aymara/Bolivian sociologist Silvia Rivera Cusicanqui condemns lauded "decolonial" scholars in the North American academy for neglecting these dynamics in favor of extractivist intellectual production that has commodified the thought of social movement intellectuals, offering it up for consumption in romanticized and reified terms that occlude the counterhegemonic strategies and often characteristically modern aspects of Indigenous struggles.[73]

Rivera Cusicanqui's attack on "decolonial" intellectuals is part of a wider critique of a "political economy of knowledge" in which I have one foot firmly planted simply by virtue of receiving a salary from a British university and publishing in English with Duke University Press.[74] *Struggles for the Human* began as a contribution to a conversation that is ongoing—in Colombia and within movements resisting capitalist extraction in many other parts of the world—about the place of human rights and legal strategy in struggles against the depredations of what we might (to go with a now well-established neologism) call capitalist coloniality. I have had an odd positionality in these encounters, being fully part of la Red during the early years of this project as an *internacionalista*—a role that la Red was set up to incorporate—while also, by virtue of that role, being an *extranjera* (foreigner), *europea*, someone from outside whose involvement was enabled at that time only by funding for a doctorate. I was engaged in research and writing directly for and with Colombian organizations. At the same time, however, I was also doing my own research and writing in a political environment that is itself rich in public intellectuals and popular educators who provided an intellectual community as well as being *compañerxs* ("friend-comrades," expressed in gender-neutral form). From time to time, I came close to interviewing people I was working with, but even then what might have been planned as an informal interview became, in reality, a conversation fueled by beer, wine, or *aguardiente* (cane liquor), recorded (by consent) so that I could remember what we talked about in the morning without having to rely on sparse or illegible notes. Most of these more focused discussions involved going more deeply into the history or experiences of a particular struggle or organization than was possible in the context of day-to-day working relationships. While drinking in the presence of a voice recorder might better be described as a social activity than a research "method," there is value in sociability (in Deepak Nair's terms "playful social interaction pursued *as if* for its own sake") for creating shared understandings and relationships as comrades and interlocutors.[75] Indeed, my thinking was shaped even more profoundly by the far greater number of conversations (during drinks, meals, long car journeys through the mountains) that took place spontaneously, intermittently, picking up on threads of earlier conversations, after meetings, or because one of us had been reflecting on something the other had said previously. From other interactions, I have learned more about courage, endurance, and political imagination in a way that is hard to convey within the conventions of academic writing. Certainly, the process of thinking behind this book has been inseparable from relationships with people with whom I have worked over the years, from a desire to listen, to think in conversation, which, as Sara Motta points out, also requires self-critical "listening" to one's own internal narratives.[76] It has also been inseparable from anger, grief, fear. All of the analysis here has been shaped, in ways that are difficult to express, by the first student protest I attended in

Colombia, when police fired tear gas and rubber bullets at students at the Universidad del Valle and later stormed the campus, shooting dead twenty-two-year-old Jhonny Silva, who could not run away with the others because of his disability. The few days after that, working with human rights defenders, was when I think both the limits and the necessity of human rights really hit home.

Thus, the starting point of this book is a relational and embodied approach to knowledge production akin to what Diana Taylor calls *acuerpamiento*—"learning of a situation by living it in the flesh," connecting knowing to sustained and reflective action in the company of others; to relationships of care, of listening, of *hermandad* (brotherhood/sisterhood).[77] Yet the book itself has been written in an uncomfortable in-between space, on the borders between lifeworlds and knowledges—mostly in Britain while continuing my involvement in solidarity work, visiting Colombia for shorter periods and maintaining online relationships with *compañerxs* there. My position within the political economy of knowledge has given me paid time to write, reflect, and read, but it also comes with limitations. The aim of this book was never to simply describe how social movements approach human rights; nor do I seek to speak for or replicate the ideas of those at the heart of these struggles. Still, much of this book has been written at a distance, back in Britain, where the day-to-day conversations I had with people when I was living in Colombia were not possible as my ideas developed. I do not think that this is entirely a bad thing. Gaining distance can be vital to reflection. Michel Foucault once referred to critique in terms of a "distant view," and this book, as a political and ethical inquiry, has demanded a step back from the immediate concerns of struggle to reflect on deeper questions.[78] The challenge that accompanies this, however, is how to step back in this sense without betraying knowledges shaped in struggle and without losing sight of the "big picture" or of what is at stake.[79]

Distance in this case, however, has been physical, as well as intellectual, which means no longer having the immediate sense of things that comes from being with people and working directly together. Thus, there has been an increasing temporal distance that inevitably further dislodges my account from the time when some events and encounters that I narrate took place. This has been exacerbated by other aspects of my position within the political economy of knowledge: being in a British university, where constant funding squeezes limit the possibility of travel, as well as being a full-time solo parent, both unable to fund the costs of my daughter traveling with me to Colombia and unwilling to subject her to a context where my own political involvement had even the slightest possibility of generating risk for her (a freedom that I recognize does not exist for *compañerxs* in Colombia who have had their own children targeted as a result of their political activity). This is not to say that I have been entirely disconnected during this period of writing, or that I have been unable to discuss many of the ideas here with people in Colombia. A fellowship and other smaller research grants have made it possible to visit Colombia, catch up with *compañerxs*, and discuss ideas and solidarity initiatives on several occasions since 2014. In addition, my discussion of strategic appeal to human rights owes much to my involvement in work surrounding Gilberto Torres's case in the London High Court against BP for his kidnapping and torture as a result of his trade union activities. Conversations with Torres while I accompanied him on a speaking tour in Britain in 2015 led to a shared project on the politics of strategic litigation, in which much of the content of the first five chapters of this book was discussed in workshops with social movement leaders and lawyers during 2017–19—a process that Torres described as "building collective critical thought."[80]

It is important to emphasize that the in-between space from which I have written this book has also meant that I am writing for another set of interlocutors: an academic community, publishing mostly (albeit not exclusively) in English. In addition to drawing inspiration from the lived thought at play within Colombian social movements, *Struggles for the Human* has been informed by close engagement with texts from across the array of disciplines referred to earlier. When I write in the first-person plural, I do not write for a pre-formed "we." That is to say, I do not appeal to a scholarly "we" whose frameworks and questions define the conditions in which thought can be validated.[81] Nor do I write for a "we" in resistance, whose field of action is already neatly delineated.[82] I approach writing as an attempt to enlist the reader into a narrative and thus construct a "we"—at least momentarily. The decision to publish this book in English in the first instance reflects my own position within a global political economy of knowledge that demands publications and citations to such an extent that even my Colombian academic interlocutors publish mostly in English. I also think and write better in English, and the Colombian poet and author Álvaro Marín, a dear friend who had offered to help me finesse a simultaneous Spanish version, was found dead shortly before I submitted the book proposal. It thus seemed better to rely on an Anglophone-weighted political economy of knowledge to facilitate a Spanish translation. Nevertheless, this book can be read as an attempt to bring together two sets of interlocutors and to insert insights shaped through struggle into traditions of scholarly writing that so often fix and reify ideas or legislate for resistance on the basis of theoretical reflections about the nature of capitalism, law, the coloniality of power, or even the inexorable fluidity of power-knowledge relations.

Thinking through engagement with specific struggles, rooted in specific historical and material conditions, makes it difficult to read the politics of rights off a fixed framework at the same time that it demands attention to the big picture of an extractive and exploitative political economy whose violence is underwritten by a global configuration of legality. Attention to how struggles have been neutralized or contained casts light on how what might look humanistic or emancipatory in fact is not (Marín, in his book with Cárdenas, wrote about the propensity of global institutions and compliant NGOs to *defender la vida diseminando la muerte* [defend life by spreading/ sowing death]).[83] Attention to struggle can also counter tendencies to confine our understandings of the potential of human rights or strategic appeals to law within the parameters of pre-given theoretical commitments. It is also, sometimes, within attempts to articulate alternative social relations that deeper human possibilities are revealed.

Outline of the Book

Chapter 1, "Necroeconomics: Violence, Law and Twenty-First-Century Plunder," builds on the insight that law and its underlying moral economy are constitutive of economic relations. It sets the context for the discussion of human rights in the next chapters via a recalibration of how we understand violence in relation to law. Colombia is an extreme example of how the violence of armed repression intersects with less visible violence inherent in the ordinary operation of capitalism, a point that I seek to bring home via a juxtaposition of the situation in Colombia with neoliberal reforms in Britain. The myth of a neutral, natural legal order conceals these deeper dynamics of violence, with liberal legal narratives of freedom and equality embodying moral reference points that are at odds with the political economy within which they are asserted. Yet while classical liberal thinkers attempted to resolve these contradictions by separating the principles for moral and economic action, neoliberalism was, from its inception, both a moral and a legal doctrine. With the globalization of neoliberal legality, the very meanings of democracy and ethics have been transformed. Deadly economic policies are often rationalized in terms of law and ethical discourse, a fact that should incite caution about how human rights might be taken up within this Orwellian scenario.

Chapter 2, "Deadly Colonial Ethics: Development Policy-Speak and Corporate Responsibility," identifies these dynamics within the emergence of the corporate code of conduct for human rights in the late 1990s. Voluntary corporate responsibility for human rights, I maintain, represents a privatization of human rights unanticipated by the UDHR or by Third Worldist efforts to harness human rights to the taming of corporate power in the 1970s. To arrive at this position, I trace the trajectory of peasant struggles at what might be considered the birthplace of the contemporary configuration of voluntary corporate responsibility for human rights: BP's Colombian oilfields. Drawing on my own involvement in a project seeking to recover historical memory of what took place, I make the case that voluntary corporate responsibility sustains a moral discourse that equates resistance with irrationality or subversion, thus rationalizing death in the name of "development."

Chapter 3, "Privatizing Workers' Rights: Social Partnership in a Neoliberal World," picks up on the story of the privatization of rights almost a decade later, in the mid- to late 2000s. Once again, I trace the trajectory of a specific struggle—in this case, the international campaign against Coca-Cola launched by the Colombian Food Workers Union following murders of union leaders and other grave abuses of human rights. The puzzle that motivates my inquiry is how it was possible that the global union for the food sector campaigned *against* the Colombian Food Workers. Reluctant to allow companies to set their own codes of conduct, global unions had begun to promote "global framework agreements," negotiated with multinational corporations on behalf of unions worldwide. While these agreements are said to embody a global version of postwar "social partnership" between labor and capital, the rationale for protecting rights within so-called global social partnership is "market"-based, separated from the social-democratic legal frameworks that defined postwar social partnership. Through attention to the trade union–led campaign against the Colombian Food Workers, I explore how this prevailing mode of protecting workers' rights is part of a scenario in which managerial logics of audit prevail over concerns about past abuses, while violations of workers' human rights cease to feature as justiciable wrongs.

Chapter 4, "Elusive Justice: Capital, Impunity, and Counterlegality," moves on another decade to consider current renewed efforts to use law to combat the problem now frequently referred to as "corporate impunity." Although such efforts risk legitimating the legal fiction of the "corporate person" while turning compensation payments into externalities to be brought into companies' cost-benefit analyses, it is important to consider how social movements that are fully cognizant of these problems nevertheless make strategic use of law. I draw here on my ongoing involvement with the struggles of Colombian social organizations to show how law can be an important site of immanent critique of both law and capital via the articulation of "counter-legalities" that draw attention to violence that constitutes the existing legal order. Impunity appears here as a different sort of problem from that given shape within mainstream human rights narratives. Human rights abuses are neither conceptualized as individual acts nor narrated as past events. They are exposed as an ever present possibility with roots in the (mostly legal) operation of capitalism. In this light, struggles over corporate impunity demand that we address the relationship between violence and legality, between past atrocities and a present order of things in which corporations are declared ethical actors who can show "due diligence" for human rights.

Chapter 5, "From Pernicious Optimism to Radical Hope: Human Rights beyond Abstract Values," draws together the threads of the analysis so far, returning to the question of human rights as an ethical and political vocabulary. I suggest that the privatization of human rights, as add-ons to a political economy bringing widespread premature death to actually existing human beings, reflects an approach to ethics now predominant among the self-proclaimed representatives of global civil society, which I denote "pernicious optimism." In this prevailing ethical orientation, the fetishism of abstract values facilitates disavowal of the consequences of capitalism, of the ways in which ordinary law and economic policy condemn many to untimely death. I contrast this to how human rights are mobilized to expose the violence of capital and law within a wider series of struggles where rural populations have sought to reclaim land and build ways of sustaining and reproducing life that are less harmful, less predatory on people and planet. These struggles, I suggest, embody a radical hope that is antithetical to the pernicious optimism of much cosmopolitan ethics. The life toward which these struggles strive is an indistinct, perhaps ever-receding horizon, but it is embodied in an ethical and spiritual disposition toward others and the natural world that implies the transformation of the human. There is nothing programmatic or triumphalist about these initiatives, no expectation that their struggles will eventually prevail. There is, however, a commitment to continuing to try and transform the world in the face of devastation, embodied in the refusal of an intolerable reality, reaching toward a sense of the good that remains yet to be defined.

It should be clear by now that it makes little sense to assess the politics of human rights in the abstract. The issue is not to decide "for" or "against" human rights but to consider how "the human" is configured as the subject of rights and how harm and violence are understood in relation to this. In chapter 6, I sketch the contours of an "insurgent humanism," in which the human is redefined in tension with persistent critique of the relations of violence that destroy and negate life. The sense of the good to which the struggles discussed here appeal is not rooted in an inherent human dignity or in qualities of "the human" deemed morally valuable within a modern/colonial economy of knowledge. Yet this does not mean that the question of the basis of ethics is superseded. Rather, it invites a reconsideration of the relations between the immanent and the transcendent, between politics and its outside. In conversation with the moral philosophy of Iris Murdoch, I suggest that the sense of good inspiring a radical hope has no vocation to be caught directly within the categories of language. It is known, not only through critical sensitivity to the effects of power and violence, but also through a loving attention to the world and to the struggles of others.

necroeconomics

Violence, Law, and
Twenty-First-Century Plunder
CHAPTER ONE

Before we can begin any assessment of the politics of human rights, it is necessary to tackle two myths that pervade much mainstream discussion. The first myth is that large-scale human rights abuses are best understood in terms of an absence of "rule of law." Take, for example the opening sentence of an article by Amnesty International: "In Colombia, nominally Latin America's oldest democracy, the rule of law continues to be weak and impunity reigns."[1] If you were to ask a human rights advocate what they meant by "rule of law," the chances are that they would be referring to features such as an independent judiciary; the separation of the executive, legislative, and judicial powers of the state; and independent and effective law enforcement. The rule of law, understood in this sense, is perceived as neutral and benign. Violence, meanwhile, is spectacular and interpersonal, taking place predominantly outside of the law. If we look more closely, however, we find that the ordinary operation of the law is deeply imbricated in the dynamics of unlawful killing. This, as I show, has long been the case historically, although with the globalization of neoliberal political economy, a particular conceptualization of rule of law has been constitutionalized at a global level, underwriting plunder and dispossession.

Limited recognition of this fact is tied to another myth, heavily criticized by intellectual historians but still commonplace in everyday discourse—that is, that neoliberalism should be understood as an amoral doctrine of "market rule," involving the "rollback" of the state. In reality, as I show later in this chapter, neoliberalism is both a moral and a legal doctrine, premised on an understanding of human beings as of profoundly unequal worth and advocating a vision of rule of law that elevates private property, contract, and investment rights above all else. If we want to understand the context in which human rights abuses have proliferated amid neoliberal reforms around the world, it is crucial that we delve more deeply into the links among law, violence, and twenty-first-century plunder. What is more, to make sense of appeal to human rights in opposition to these dynamics, it is necessary to grasp the extent to which this vision of rule of law has been entrenched, not merely through appeal to the demands of "the market," but also through humanistic, "social," and ethical discourse: the scenario that Humberto Cárdenas and Álvaro Marín refer to as "defending life by sowing death."[2]

Visible and Invisible Violence

As a way into considering the entanglements between violence and legality, let us begin with the immediate origins of the struggles that I discuss in subsequent chapters. Neoliberalism came later to Colombia than to much of Latin America, but from the early 1990s Colombia's "economic opening" set the scene for an upsurge of state-backed armed violence. As successive governments adopted and entrenched neoliberal economic policies (geared toward the pursuit of foreign direct investment in natural resource extraction, alongside "flexible" and "competitive" labor markets), massacres and selective killings proliferated at the hands of paramilitary death squads working closely with state security forces. While workers were stripped of hard-won rights, trade unionists were subject to repression so widespread and brutal that the historian Renan Vega coined the term *sindicalicidio*—or trade union genocide—to make sense of it.[3] From the mid-1990s, paramilitaries began to take over entire regions, chainsaws in hand. Those deemed subversive or surplus to requirements were massacred, displaced, or "disappeared." Landholdings were concentrated, and an authoritarian social order was imposed. Afterward, state institutions would add a veneer of legality to the process.[4] In this way, vast swathes of Colombian territory were handed over to the operations of multinational corporations.

The involvement of many of those corporations in atrocities has been pains-takingly documented by human rights organizations. Chiquita Brands even admitted to having paid US$1.7 million to state-linked paramilitaries between 1997 and 2004, as well as to supplying paramilitaries with weapons. Accord-ing to Colombia's attorney general, these payments led to the murder of four thousand civilians in the banana regions of Colombia and aided the expansion of paramilitary groups throughout the country.[5] In 1999, seven-teen civilians were killed when the village of Santo Domingo, in the oil-rich Department of Arauca, was bombed. There is compelling evidence not only that the bombing was planned by Occidental Petroleum and the Colombian Air Force in the company's offices, but also that aerial surveillance for the mis-sion was carried out by the US security contractor Airscan using a Skymaster plane supplied by the oil company. Witnesses were later killed by paramilitar-ies.[6] The Corporación Social para la Asesoría y Capacitación Comunitaria (Social Corporation for Community Advice and Training), the organization that I worked with while investigating the impact of BP's oilfields, was set up by peasant leaders forcibly displaced from the region in the late 1990s, when the murders of numerous peasant activists generated an international media outcry over BP's links to the Colombian Army and the private security con-tractor Defence Systems Limited.[7] By 2002, when Gilberto Torres was kid-napped in a van that belonged to BP's oil pipeline company, BP was vocal on the international stage promoting the idea that human rights were a matter of concern for corporations. Nevertheless, in a trial in Colombia, Torres's kid-nappers said they took direct orders from pipeline company Ocensa and that the company had paid them an extra US$40,000 to "disappear" him.[8] While I was working in the region between 2006 and 2008, peasant leaders continued to be killed. Indeed, as I discuss in the next chapter, almost 2,500 people had been "disappeared" by the time BP departed from the region in 2011.[9]

In chapter 3, I talk about the Colombian Food Workers Union and its international campaign against Coca-Cola. Between 1994 and 2002, eight unionized Coca-Cola workers were killed by paramilitaries.[10] Four of them were workers at the same bottling plant, in the northwestern city of Carepa. After three leaders of the union were killed in the run-up to negotiations with plant management, paramilitaries killed the local branch's general-secretary, set fire to the union's offices, and then assembled workers to tell them that they would be killed if they did not resign from the union. Witnesses said the resignation letters were prepared on company computers and collected by management.[11] In 2002, Adolfo Múnera, a leader of the union, was shot dead upon his return to Barranquilla on the Caribbean coast, after having spent some time in exile following his role in a successful strike. There was abundant evidence of collusion among bottling plant management, state forces, and paramilitaries in Múnera's murder. Months later, paramilitaries publicly announced plans to kill more members of the union because they were interfering with Coca-Cola's business.[12] Fourteen members of the Colombian Food Workers Union working at Nestlé have also been killed.[13] I accompanied the union during negotiations with Nestlé in southwestern Colombia in April 2006. Before talks had even begun, members of the negotiating committee reported being followed by cars with blacked-out windows. One of the union members I got to know during that visit was Oscar López. In 2013, López was shot dead during a hunger strike. The day before his murder, several union activists had received text messages from a paramilitary group threatening them with death for "bothering Nestlé."[14]

In the wake of horrors such as these, our gaze is automatically directed to acts most clearly recognizable as violence: those direct acts carried out by identifiable agents. Yet it is clear to the victims themselves that the violence penetrates far more deeply. On its list of twenty-nine members killed since the union was founded, the Colombian Food Workers Union includes Guillermo Gómez, whose desperation at the closure of the Coca-Cola bottling plant where he worked led him to take his own life. Also listed is Walter Rengifo, who died from a brain aneurism "caused by the constant repression, persecution and permanent labour conflicts" with Nestlé.[15] Selective assassinations are part of a continuum of ways in which capitalism generates death—through hunger or the precarity that creates the state of "total crisis" that Gómez described in his suicide note. When I was accompanying union leaders in various parts of the country during the time I was living in Colombia, a recurrent topic of conversation was labor conditions at Coca-Cola bottling plants as a result of casualization, which leaders often described as "inhuman." Workers were laboring from five in the morning until eleven or twelve at night for wages that barely covered the cost of food and rent. They were undertaking long and exhausting treks to the workplace because deregulated housing markets had pushed the cost of local accommodation beyond their reach. Extensive subcontracting meant that most had to cover the costs of their own tools and uniforms, health care, and social security.[16] In the union's discourse, these violences, too, constitute crimes against humanity. As does the widespread hunger generated by a food and agriculture industry designed for corporate profit rather than the well-being of the population.[17]

Reading Marx through a lens of violence and visibility, Amedeo Policante suggests that, from the preface to the first German edition of *Capital*, Marx framed his endeavor as an effort to uncover the systemic violence at work beneath the "civil peace" of nineteenth-century liberal society.[18] For all the horror of land dispossession, for all the brutality of laws that criminalized the dispossessed, for all the "extirpation, enslavement, and entombment in mines" of colonized peoples, there is another, less spectacular form of horror inherent in capitalism: the constant extraction of life from those without capital, "the vampire thirst for the living blood of labour."[19] Other violent modes of extraction are also a major focus of movements that are the recipients of corporate-backed acts of direct violence—for instance, the overwhelmingly racialized public-health impact of extractive industries alongside what some Indigenous peoples would describe as a thirst for the blood of nature itself. In 2016, I shared a platform at a conference in London with Luz Angela Uriana, a Wayuú Indigenous campaigner who lives near the Cerrejón open cast coal mine in La Guajira, a department in northeastern Colombia. Over the previous eight years, almost five thousand Wayuú children had died because of a lack of water and food caused by the ecological impact of the mine, while the London-listed companies that own the mine—Anglo American, BHP, and Glencore—made skyrocketing profits.[20] Many more children, including Uriana's then four-year-old son, Moíses, were suffering respiratory illness. Uriana had come to London to denounce the multinationals on their home territory as company representatives continued to deny responsibility by insisting that they operate within the parameters of the law.[21]

Furthermore, as Uriana also emphasized, adequate medical care is unattainable for most of those affected. The cost of comprehensive health insurance is prohibitive, as it is for precarious workers, the unemployed, and those participating in the informal economy, while public hospitals are drastically under-resourced and any form of medical care is beyond the reach of many rural populations. In September 2006, while I was accompanying representatives of the Colombian Food Workers Union in Barranquilla, I was introduced to members of the National Association of Hospital and Clinic Workers who talked about further violence visited on the population by the denial of treatment and the transformation of health care from a right into a business.[22] One union leader invited me to visit a public hospital, where patients in many wards were two to a bed. This union, too, had experienced high levels of armed repression for its defense of public health care. Yet it was the privatization of public services that my companion wanted to talk about. He took me to the hospital morgue and explained that the young man whose body was lying there would have been saved had the hospital had the basic resuscitation equipment available in the private sector.

I was reminded of that visit to the morgue a few years later when I read that researchers had attributed thirty thousand "excess deaths" to health-care cuts in England over the course of 2015 alone.[23] That, of course, was before the COVID-19 pandemic, when tens of thousands of further avoidable deaths occurred as a result of the cuts and privatization that left the country exposed to the virus.[24] Britain was in the grip of "austerity," a euphemism for drastic cuts to public expenditure on the basis of the same neoliberal policy prescriptions that have long assailed populations at the peripheries of global capitalism. Neoliberalism took off in Britain in the 1980s with Prime Minister Margaret Thatcher's mantra "There is no alternative," but attacks on the social safety nets once designed to protect people were accelerated in the wake of the financial crisis of 2008. In the years before the pandemic, auster-ity had already had—as Vickie Cooper and David Whyte put it—"profoundly violent effects."[25] Corporate and political elites had vastly increased their wealth, benefiting from generous tax cuts alongside the transfer of lucra-tive contracts for once public services to private providers.[26] In 2012, legisla-tion crafted by the international management consulting firm McKinsey and Company had abolished the state's responsibility to provide comprehensive health care.[27] By the start of 2017, the Red Cross had declared Britain's Na-tional Health Service (NHS) to be in a state of "humanitarian crisis," while more than ten thousand disabled people had died after being assessed "fit to work" following welfare reforms, and more than a million people lacked food, toiletries, and even beds.[28] The working conditions that the Food Workers Union described in Colombia would sound familiar to the approximately one million workers by then on zero-hours contracts. In 2016, as homeless-ness proliferated, legislation written with extensive input from the global real estate firm Savills had devastated remaining public housing stock to the benefit of corporate landlords, while the government voted against legislation demanding that landlords make properties "fit for human habitation."[29] The Grenfell Tower fire, which killed seventy-two residents of a high-rise hous-ing block in June 2017, soon came to stand in for the wider implications of austerity. The catastrophe had long been foreseen by campaigners. The tower had been covered in cheap, flammable cladding to prevent it from being an eyesore to wealthier area inhabitants. Residents had been complaining for years about the absence of fire extinguishers and had repeatedly raised con-cerns about the use of hazardous materials.[30] Cuts to legal aid had meant that they were unable to afford advice from lawyers. Instead, the building's tenant management organization had threatened campaigners with legal action for questioning fire safety.[31] It was reported that, across Britain, thirty thousand other buildings were covered in the same illegal cladding.[32]

Shortly after the Grenfell fire, Britain's shadow chancellor sparked outrage by referring to the deaths as "social murder."[33] Friedrich Engels had coined that term in *The Condition of the Working Class in England in 1844* to describe the early and unnatural deaths in factories, slums, and poorhouses that were a normal feature of working-class existence.[34] Commentators spouted disbelief that events such as Grenfell could happen in Britain, in 2017, voicing sentiments such as *Surely not here, not now*; *These things only happen elsewhere, or at another time*; and *Are we returning to the levels of inequality characteristic of Victorian England?*[35] These expressions of disbelief indicate something that is common to much mainstream human rights activism: a refusal to recognize that, outside of the selective amelioration of exploitation within postwar welfare states, capitalism kills as a matter of routine—especially if you are situated on the wrong side of the color line or if you are undocumented, a noncitizen, or not quite a citizen; especially if you are female; especially if you are sick or disabled and thus unable to work to sustain your existence.[36] The placards and signs near the ruins of Grenfell Tower grasped this reality: "Corporate Murder" and "People's Lives Don't Matter under Capitalism."[37] From the slow deaths of workers from sickness and exhaustion, deaths from hunger, or the public-health impact of ecological harm, to the tragedy of Grenfell Tower, premature death is a normal, predictable, and often entirely legal outcome of capitalist extraction.

I juxtapose the two countries in which I have been based while writing this book, not to downplay the profound differences between Colombia and Britain, and still less to attempt a historical sociology of their uneven and combined development, but with the more modest aim of situating Colombia in a global conjuncture marked by ever increasing penetration of corporate power. Colonial-style relations of extraction and expropriation have now boomeranged back into the former heartlands of empire.[38] The human rights movement that emerged in the 1970s was the product of a different era, of the activities of citizens enjoying the benefits of inclusion within Western liberal democracies. As such, it was shaped from its inception by a focus on egregious violations of civil and political rights by Third World states.[39] The fact that prominent neoliberals of the time used human rights to oppose demands for postcolonial redistribution and to link Third World governments' restrictions of the rights of foreign investors to violation of civil and political rights has shaped the mainstream discourse of human rights ever since.[40] Yet, as becomes clear in subsequent chapters, a deep understanding of the systemic violence of capitalism is central to how many social movements make appeal to human rights. Thus, to grasp the politics of human rights in these struggles, we must, as Slavoj Žižek insists, "learn to step back, to disentangle ourselves from the fascinating lure" of the immediately visible sort of violence carried out by identifiable agents—crime and terror, civil unrest and war. "We need to perceive the contours of the background which generates such outbursts": the real but unseen violence that is "the spontaneously accepted background" against which we register more visible acts of violence.[41] The everyday workings of the law are enmeshed within this background, though they are often hidden from view by the ambivalent concept of rule of law.

Rule of Law

The rule of law is one of the most powerful myths of Western political thought. The connotations are usually positive: the term *rule of law* is presumed to imply a just and ordered society where law applies equally to everyone, whatever their rank or status. Nevertheless, as Ugo Mattei and Laura Nader point out, few people seem to have a clear idea of what, exactly, they mean when they refer to the rule of law.[42] When the former English judge Tom Bingham was invited to give a public lecture at the University of Cambridge in 2006, he chose *rule of law* precisely because he was neither sure what the term meant nor convinced that others knew what they meant when they used it. Bingham's subsequent book-length discussion sets out the purposeful function of law as the foundation of a fair and just society, a guarantee of responsible government, and an important contributor to economic growth.[43] The starting point of Bingham's discussion is the English Magna Carta of 1215, which reflects the sense of rule of law to which human rights advocates tend to appeal: "No free man shall be seized or imprisoned or stripped of his rights or possessions ... except by the lawful judgement of his equals or by the law of the land."[44]

Nevertheless, Magna Carta established not democracy but the constitutional nature of English monarchy. When we consider the earliest uses of the term *rule of law*, at the start of the seventeenth century, we find it referring to the specialist status of lawyers as "guardians of a government of laws," a role that was "in fact born out of their role as guardians of a given, highly unequal, and certainly non-democratic distribution of property."[45] It was not, however, until the following century that an ideology of rule of law began to be consolidated. When the European witch hunts subsided in the late seventeenth and early eighteenth centuries, arrests for damage to property and assaults proliferated, while new crimes entered the statute books.[46] England's Black Act of 1723 created "at a blow some fifty new capital offences" against property and the person, bringing into force a new and particularly severe criminal code that then became "a spawning ground for ever-extending legal judgements."[47] As E. P. Thompson underscores in opening his book on the origins of the act, legislators were already clear at the start of the eighteenth century that the British state "existed to preserve the property and, incidentally, the lives and liberties of the propertied."[48] It was only during the course of that century, however, that rule of law gained preeminence as the "central legitimising authority" for the power of the ruling class, giving way in the nineteenth century to political liberalism, free-market ideology, and intensified imperial plunder.[49] Indeed, as Brenna Bhandar has explored, the English common law of property became "the *sine qua non* of civilized life and society" in the legal narratives that shaped the practice of colonial rule, "an axiom sharpened at the expense of indigenous peoples throughout the colonial world."[50]

An ideology of rule of law was also central to the construction of legitimate authority in Latin American republics after their wars of independence. Nevertheless, as Ignacio Abello notes, law was largely an abstract phenomenon, and the oligarchy "never seriously thought of a . . . society in which the principles and rights for which they had fought in Congress and on the battlefields would really include indians, blacks, *mestizos, mulatos, zambos* and all the other groups that they . . . dedicated themselves to classifying as objects of scientific observation."[51] Colonial rule in what is now called Latin America—as elsewhere—split its subject populations into a minority whose humanity was legally and socially recognized and a majority excluded from the protection of law. The boundaries between legitimate and illegitimate violence remained in constant flux after independence, as rival leaders seized power.[52] Colonial and postcolonial discipline often involved armed groups funded by corporations—as the British diplomat and later Irish revolutionary Roger Casement documented in the Congo of the late 1800s and the Amazon of the early 1900s—despite the latter falling within the jurisdiction of Colombia and Peru. In what is now the Putumayo region of Colombia, the extraction of rubber was accompanied by the shooting and mutilation of enslaved Indigenous rubber collectors under the control of the London-registered Peruvian Amazon Company. "The diabolical maxim, 'the Indian has no right' was," Casement reported, "stronger than remote laws that were rarely implemented."[53]

Even this, however, does not mean that those laws were worth nothing. Thompson's comments on the consolidation of an ideology of rule of law in England are also pertinent to the republicanism of nineteenth-century Latin America. Elites in postindependence Colombia espoused republican ideology as a minority project, with citizenship afforded only to those males who met certain criteria of property or income.[54] Nevertheless, the fact that they grounded the legitimacy of the state in a discourse of rights and the universality of law also made members of the Colombian ruling class "prisoners of their own rhetoric" in the sense that Thompson describes.[55] Elites required the support of subaltern groups in the seizures of power by rival Liberal and Conservative factions that marked the decades after independence. While this gave rise to dense structures of patronage, this does not mean that peasants, Indigenous groups, and Afro-Colombians were mere clients of a corrupt oligarchy. As James E. Sanders has explored in relation to the southern region of the Cauca in the nineteenth century, "Republicanism offered new and powerful ways of talking about and engaging in politics that Plebians appropriated," and Colombia's political culture was, as a result, "as innovative and democratic as any in the republican world."[56] Both elites and subaltern groups "had to play by the rules... of republican politics," and Afro-Colombians, peasants, and Indigenous peoples fought continuously within the parameters of republican discourse to make society more democratic.[57]

The clashes between legal principles of freedom, equality, and natural right and the legal architecture of conquest, plunder, and enslavement are reflected in two distinct constellations of meaning around the rule of law.[58] Principles of equality and human rights emerge—broadly speaking—from a liberal political tradition rooted in ideas of "natural law," developed (originally from the Ancient Greek Stoic tradition) by fifteenth- and sixteenth-century Spanish Jesuits and "later becoming a dominant jurisprudence through Europe (including Great Britain), in the more secular form of 'rational law.'"[59] "According to this tradition," Mattei and Nader explain, "society should be governed by the law and not by a human being acting as a ruler (*sub lege, non sub homine*). The law is impersonal, abstract and fair, because it is applied blindly to anyone in society."[60] As such, the rule of law is a defense against the tyranny of rulers because they, too, must be bound by the law. It is this conception of rule of law that human rights advocates invoke when denouncing the actions of ruthless governments. In a different direction, this broad conception of law also underpins the "social" theories of law developed by nineteenth-century reformers and taken up by postwar welfare and developmental states, according to which property rights can be limited or curtailed in the name of justice and social solidarity.[61]

We should not romanticize any of this. "Social" theories of law, for instance, have also underpinned authoritarian and deeply racist forms of populism. Nevertheless, the tradition of natural law and natural rights has been marked since antiquity by what Tarik Kochi describes as "a tension between an ethic of human sociability and fellowship, and, a theory of the utility of unsocial and self-interested private property and commercial relations."[62] The latter has fed a rather different conception of rule of law in liberal jurisprudence, referring not to human equity or social solidarity but to institutions that secure property rights and rights to accumulation.[63] This is the vision of rule of law that prevailed within colonial rule and that continues to shape what Bhandar denotes "racial regimes of ownership."[64] It also informed the legal vision of neoliberal thinkers, according to which state regulation to protect socioeconomic rights (e.g., through wealth redistribution or welfare provision) is said to undermine a "natural," merely technical legal order, protected by courts as "neutral" solvers of private conflicts arising in a free market.[65] Efforts to fix the meaning of *rule of law* in these terms at a global level have been fundamental to the rise of neoliberalism and—by the same token—to the defeat of the Third Worldism, which, in the 1960s and '70s, represented to neoliberals "the scandalous prospect of a decolonization of international law."[66] This, as I show, is central to understanding the intersecting forms of violence faced by populations around the world as neoliberalism has prevailed on a global scale.

Necroeconomics

The myth of a neutral, natural civil order has long generated a sort of cognitive dissonance on the part of liberal thinkers. Indeed, the slippage in meaning around *rule of law* is reflected in Marx's observation, more than twenty years before he published *Capital*, that liberal principles of freedom and equality embody a completely different vision of humanity and completely different moral reference points from the capitalist order within which they are asserted.[67] Liberal philosophers have—in different ways and to different degrees—tried to get around the problem by drawing distinctions between the criteria for moral action and the criteria for economic action.[68] Adam Smith's moral philosophy, for example, was worked out in perpetual tension with his political economy. In *The Wealth of Nations*, Smith made clear not only that societies must exercise the right to kill to generate terror of punishment for crimes against property, but also—as Warren Montag puts it—that the "the market . . . must necessarily at certain precise moments, 'let die.'" Montag coined the term *necro-economics* in relation to this aspect of Smith's thought. Smith's metaphor of the market's "invisible hand," which steers the natural order of things in accordance with providence, was an attempt to reconcile morality with a commercial society based on selfishness and greed. That some must be abandoned, even to death, is covertly set out by Smith as the basis of social harmony.[69] Smith could oppose slavery only because his moral sentiments coincided with his economic reasoning on the matter: slavery was not only inhumane but also inefficient.[70]

The extension of citizenship rights that marked twentieth-century social-democratic thought sought to alleviate the tension not by separating the criteria for economic and moral action, but by establishing rights as limits to what can be authorized on economic grounds. That said, these were limited limits. The discourse of social rights that accompanied this provided little more than what Wendy Brown has referred to as a "modest ethical gap" between economy and polity.[71] Moral arguments for the welfare state, found most notably in the insistence in the United Nations Universal Declaration of Human Rights (UDHR) on "the inherent dignity and of the equal and inalienable rights of all members of the human family," coexisted with more explicit economic arguments for the stabilization of capitalism by preventing "the economy" from becoming "disembedded" from the social conditions that sustain its reproduction.[72] What is more, the application of social rights was deeply marked by racialized divisions between those whose rights were and were not recognized in practice. Although the UDHR was a manifesto for the welfare state, actually existing welfare states in the West served largely to redistribute the spoils of colonialism to white working classes.[73] In Britain, proposals for state welfare were fueled by eugenicist desires to maintain "good racial stock" and preserve the British Empire.[74] The direct state provision of national welfare in the twentieth century followed the same path as the more limited provision of the previous two centuries (through voluntary organizations, friendly societies, and private charity, alongside limited state interventions), which had been made possible only through imperial relations of extraction and aggressive taxation.[75] Although the consolidation of the welfare state coincided with the formal dismantling of the British Empire, "the imperial dividend continued after empire and was integral to the construction of the post-war welfare state."[76]

Neoliberal thought was, from its inception, a rejection of social welfare and of the liberal belief in inalienable rights at the same time that it sought to maintain the colonial division of labor. Yet what really marks out the neoliberal project is that, rather than separating the principles for moral and economic action, it recast classical necroeconomics with an explicitly moral hue. The neoliberal argument for the competitive market was, Jessica Whyte emphasizes, "moral and political, rather than strictly economic."[77] Jettisoning the optimism of classical political economists' free-market laissez-faire, the thinkers who came together in the Mont Pèlerin Society of the 1940s were explicitly concerned with creating the social and institutional foundations of a competitive market order, including the "moral values and subjective qualities" that such an order required.[78] The basic error of classical political economy, for neoliberal thinkers, was "to confine the role of the state to the maintenance of order and the enforcement of contracts" when what was required was an appropriate *legal* structure and means of inculcating the appropriate moral values to ensure the institutional conditions in which wealth could remain in the hands of those deemed most capable of using it.[79]

With human dignity redefined in terms of successful self-reliance, the dissonant conceptualizations of humanity to which Marx drew attention in classical liberal thought were jettisoned in favor of an explicit commitment to an inequality of worth among human beings.[80] Equality was reduced to equality before the law, with the rule of law itself redefined to privilege the rights of property and private investment above all else. So, too, what Friedrich Hayek referred to as "the morals of the market" involved "a set of individualistic, commercial values that prioritized the pursuit of self-interest above the development of common purposes."[81] Notions of social justice, and the economic and social rights of the UDHR, threatened civilization itself.[82] In the wake of the Great Depression, some neoliberals were willing to countenance a minimal level of assistance, targeted to the most destitute, so long as this did not interfere with economic incentives. However, what was universally rejected was a "cradle-to-grave" welfare state, any move toward greater equality, and—crucially—the idea that even the most minimal level of assistance could be claimed as a "right."[83]

Montag has explored the necroeconomic aspect of neoliberal thought with particular reference to Ludwig von Mises, who stood out among his colleagues by arguing at the first meeting of the Mont Pèlerin Society that all public assistance should be abolished and who insisted that there could be no such thing as "an enforceable human right to subsistence," or even a right to existence.[84] "While Adam Smith might in all sincerity argue that famine could only arise from government interference in market rationality," Montag writes, von Mises was clear that famine at times would be the consequence of the competitive market order and that this required that states refrain from intervening through price controls or mass distribution of food to the hungry.[85] Whereas, for Marx, "the capitalist class was unfit to rule because it could not assure the existence of its own labourers; for Mises it is fit to rule only if it knows enough to refuse any such assurance on principle."[86] And while neoliberal ideology does not consider it legitimate for the state to actively kill those who lack access to food, housing, or medicine, it demands a willingness to use armed force to repress those who demand that things be otherwise.[87] As early as the 1927 uprising in his home city of Vienna, Quinn Slobodian notes, the "right to kill with impunity under emergency powers . . . met with Mises's approval."[88]

Von Mises was also explicit that the same armed force of the state must be applied in the Global South where governments or populations "resist the freeing up and development of the natural wealth with which they merely co-exist and therefore the natural necessity of the market out of fear of the destitution that such development brings."[89] Ideas of inviolable national sovereignty and the rights of Indigenous peoples to collective territories are "utterly without force or effect."[90] Indeed, as Slobodian explores in his exposition of twentieth-century European neoliberal thought, the core of the neoliberal project was a quest to find the institutional framework to safeguard capitalism on a global scale in the absence of formal colonialism.[91] Von Mises developed his own "just war" argument against postcolonial states' sovereignty over natural resources on the basis that it was an injury to all humanity for a country to deprive others of access to its resources.[92] He also sought explicitly to rescue the "germ" of biological racism for "a 'modern' race theory that ascribed racial hierarchies to an evolutionary process that had given certain races so long a lead that members of other races could not overtake them within a limited time."[93] Likewise, in the postwar period, as decolonization accelerated and Third Worldist demands for a New International Economic Order took shape, "neoliberals commonly resorted to one particular argumentative strategy," Lars Cornelissen notes: one of casting the colonial population in racialized terms as "culturally underdeveloped" or "immature." Thus, neoliberals "could assert that [the colonial population] was not yet ready for self-determination, that if left to self-govern it would fall victim to anticapitalist propaganda, thus destroying its prospects for economic (and therewith civilizational) growth."[94] Followers of Hayek within the legal office of the General Agreement on Tariffs and Trade (GATT) were major drivers of a counteroffensive to Third Worldism and to the social understandings of law that shaped welfare states. This counteroffensive sought "to reclaim law as an enforcer of private property and competition" and was central to the GATT's transformation into the World Trade Organization in the 1990s.[95]

This is not to say that political articulations of neoliberalism have followed smoothly on the prescriptions of intellectuals like Hayek and von Mises. In Britain, for instance, one of the first neoliberal politicians was arguably the notorious Conservative Enoch Powell, who, in the 1960s, made the moral case for neoliberal "free enterprise" in the context of a racist nationalism that rejected dependency on the riches of empire in favor of a white English heredity "founded on the principle of orderly independence."[96] A different sort of racist nationalism has been tightly entwined with neoliberalization in Colombia. Not only has a neoliberal vision of development been tightly articulated with a nationalist narrative of defense of "the nation" against those who would undermine progress, but this has drawn on a heavily racialized moral discourse through which the state's developmentalist intervention is legitimated. As Margarita Serje has explored in depth, the discursive artifact of the Colombian nation—since the nineteenth century—has drawn on colonial imaginative geographies that are reproduced within the national territory. Areas rich in natural resources have persistently been represented as savage lands, inhabited by immature, barbarous, surplus populations.[97] National development discourse since Colombia's "economic opening" has drawn heavily on this imagery. Rural areas with high levels of poverty and armed conflict are charted as terrain scarred by the pathology of rebellion and occupied by childlike populations who must be "developed" and "protected." "Protection" implies targeting these populations with brutal counterinsurgency techniques, while "development" involves dispossession, displacement, or subjection to the slow violence of environmental degradation.[98]

From another direction, despite the insistence of von Mises and his colleagues that economic laws were "indifferent to human conceptions of justice," political articulations of neoliberalism in practice often have been accompanied by formal recognition of economic and social rights enshrined in the UDHR and subsequent international covenants.[99] Of course, even when these rights are formally recognized, enforcing them depends on the capacity to resolve the contradictions between formal rights and the laws and policy decisions that undermine those rights. David Whyte has highlighted this in relation to deaths at work. At a basic level, the law undermines workers' rights via legal fictions such as workers' "freedom" of contract with employers or the corporate "person" and associated ideas of employers' limited liability for deaths and injury of employees. Economic power is also persistently redefining the boundaries of law, creating a sort of state of exception in which formal rights can be lawfully violated. In the fast-disappearing social democracies of the West, regulatory agencies have tended to intervene more consistently in the face of these contradictions, rendering those who lack access to the means to secure their subsistence less exposed to the brutality of economic force than they are in the Global South. Yet the neoliberal assault on the welfare state has eroded much of this regulation, as well as other forms of social protection, such as welfare benefits and comprehensive health care. In Britain, for example, the Health and Safety Executive (the British government regulator for workplace health and safety) has made such drastic cuts that some local authorities no longer have any protection or inspection of workplaces. As a result, workers are completely exposed in the face of economic force. They are excluded from the protection of law despite the existence of formal rights.[100]

These contradictions are not unique to the erstwhile social democracies of the West. In much of Latin America, neoliberal policies have been accompanied by an emphasis on economic and social rights. Colombia is a pertinent case in point. The country's so-called economic opening was marked, in 1991, by a new National Constitution, said to include more citizenship rights than any in the world, including an array of labor rights and the territorial rights of Indigenous and Afro-Colombian populations. Enshrined within the constitution was the principle of the Social Rule of Law (Estado Social de Derecho), a legal order "with the citizen at the center, and in which the social is the reason for the existence of political powers."[101] This was, however, accompanied by a series of legislative reforms that served to block access to the rights formally recognized in the constitution. Take labor law. The 1991 constitution recognized a series of rights that, if actualized, would have made precarious labor impossible. It incorporated International Labour Organization (ILO) conventions on freedom of association and the rights to organize and bargain collectively.[102] It also committed the Congress of Colombia to producing a labor statute that would protect minimum fundamental principles, such as stability of employment, social security, and adequate rest for workers.[103] Yet the constitution came into force almost simultaneously with an array of laws designed to generate "flexible labor markets" and attract foreign investment. For example, Law 10 of 1989 created "associated work cooperatives," through which workers are forced to bid for contracts, covering the costs of their own materials and social security. This was a policy promoted with the support of the World Bank, as well as that of paramilitary organizations, and has become central to corporations' strategies of cost reduction.[104] Subsequent laws have lengthened the working day, cut payments for overtime, facilitated mass layoffs of employees, and generated extensive subcontracting of labor that obliterates the possibility of stable employment and social security.[105] The result has been working conditions such as those the Colombian Food Workers Union has attempted to resist on Coca-Cola bottling plants. Permanent, generally unionized employees were replaced by temps subcontracted through agencies, and by ad hoc employment of the reserve army of former workers that I chatted to with union leaders in Barranquilla while they waited outside bottling plant gates in the hope of getting a few hours' employment. Delivery trucks were handed over to "cooperatives" composed primarily of former employees who became responsible for the maintenance of the vehicles and their own salaries. Those who were reemployed and new casual workers received wages that were approximately 35 percent lower than those of workers on direct contracts, while the wages of those contracted through cooperatives were reduced in real terms by three-quarters.[106]

This dispossession of workers has likewise been accompanied by actions that illustrate the capacity of economic force not only to shape unconstitutional—and so, effectively, illegal—reforms of labor law but also to act outside the law in the name of economic necessity. For example, the Ministry of Social Protection has repeatedly complied with requests from bottling companies to refuse recognition of local union committees. This is so despite the ministry's lack of jurisdiction over the internal affairs of trade unions, and despite Colombia's ratification of international labor conventions that grant trade unions the autonomy to define their own statutes and elect their own representatives.[107] In 2003, when Coca-Cola–Fomento Económico Mexicano closed eleven out of sixteen Colombian bottling plants as part of the Coca-Cola Company's drive to achieve a more "efficient" global system, it simply ignored legislation prohibiting closure of factories or branches without authorization from the Ministry of Social Protection. More than three thousand workers were laid off, with mass resignations achieved by forcibly detaining workers in the presence of armed security guards. The workers were blackmailed into resigning their contracts for financial compensation, under threat of otherwise being fired, and they were not allowed to leave until they had done so.[108] The ministry, for its part, went on to authorize the closures retrospectively alongside the laying off of those workers who had refused to resign. Most of those laid off were forced into destitution. Many had worked for the company for more than twenty years, in a context in which finding new work beyond thirty-five is almost impossible (even more so when a person has a history of being a union member).

The territorial rights recognized by the National Constitution are also undermined by a combination of law and action outside of the law. For example, Transitory Article 55 gave rise to Law 70 of 1993, intended to protect the cultural and territorial rights of Afro-Colombian communities. Yet other legislation—such as that granting concessions to mining companies—undermines the territorial rights that have been recognized. In most cases, the right to prior consultation in accordance with ILO Convention 169 on Indigenous and Tribal Peoples has been, as von Mises might have put it, "without force or effect" in practice.[109] What is more, while Afro-Colombian communities were given land on the Pacific coast, their attempts to return to lands from which they had been displaced in the Inter-Andean Valleys were rejected. These lands were in the hands of Colombia's oligarchic families, who, like multinational corporations, have long benefited from the capacity to act outside the law when it suits them. This, too, corresponds with wider patterns across the world. For instance, as Charles Hale has discussed in relation to Indigenous struggles in Guatemala, territorial rights have been recognized selectively, only in the "empty spaces" not of use to capital.[110]

This is not to say that the formal recognition of rights is a mere sham. Even in Colombia, the constitutional rights of Indigenous and Black populations to prior consultation over the use of their collective territories have been vital tools to social movements and lawyers opposing extractive projects. The right to appeal the violation of a "fundamental right" before a judge, meanwhile, has enabled trade unionists to be reinstated following unfair dismissal.[111] Adolfo Múnera, the Coca-Cola worker shot dead in Barranquilla, had returned to the city following a successful appeal of his dismissal, which was deemed unlawful, given that death threats resulting from his trade union work had forced him to flee his employment. However, here, too, court rulings clash with the power to act outside of the law. Múnera was shot dead when he returned to resume his employment. When Luz Ángela Uriana traveled to London to address BHP Billiton shareholders in 2016, the Cerrejon mine had already failed to comply with a ruling by the Colombian Constitutional Court that it must guarantee a healthy atmosphere for her son (and, by extension, other children).[112]

States of Exception

It is important to emphasize, however, that not even trade union genocide and massacres of populations occupying territories destined for resource exploitation have taken place within a legal vacuum. Giorgio Agamben famously highlighted the hypocrisy of knee-jerk bewilderment in the face of atrocity. "It would be more honest and, above all, more useful," he says, "to investigate carefully the juridical procedures and deployments of power by which human beings could be completely deprived of their rights and prerogatives that no act committed against them could appear any longer as a crime."[113] The atrocities in Colombia must be understood in direct relationship to law—not as indicative of state absence or weakness, but as taking place in the context of a normalized state of exception, the active suspension of ordinary legality in the name of "necessity," which is an "illegal" but nevertheless "perfectly juridical and constitutional measure" central to the operation of state power.[114] Agamben himself was hasty in claiming the concentration camp as both unique and archetypical of modernity. He overlooked how colonized peoples have been systematically excluded from the protection of law, and how extermination and genocide have been routinely justified by a mythology of progress that is inseparable from the degradation of the natures of populations racialized as Other. These legacies of colonialism have been central to security apparatuses, authoritarian rule, and the repression of resistance that have accompanied neoliberal reforms in contexts such as Colombia and Pinochet's Chile (praised by the World Bank as the forerunner of the structural adjustment programs subsequently imposed across the Global South).[115] Across what is now Latin America, the racism instilled by the Conquest "left an inheritance of guilt and a fear that the old gods would return." Subsequent anxieties over modernization "transposed racism into a different key and turned the indigenous from an exploited labour force into a negative and undesirable mass."[116] In this context, the idea of an "enemy within" has long underpinned a culture of exception in which rights and liberties can be suspended when required.[117]

The "massacre of the banana workers," commemorated in Gabriel García Márquez's *One Hundred Years of Solitude*, is an infamous case in point. In 1928, long before left-wing guerrilla groups were formed and counterinsurgency became the rationale for repressing protest, the Colombian Army killed about one thousand striking banana workers. The United States had threatened to invade with the Marine Corps if action was not taken to protect the interests of the United Fruit Company (a previous incarnation of Chiquita Brands). By the mid-twentieth century, anticommunism in Colombia had reached a "genocidal pitch."[118] The formal use of exceptional measures became predominant during a twelve-year period of civil war that began in 1948. Armed conflict among factions of the oligarchy subsided in the 1960s in the wake of a power-sharing deal. However, the consolidation of insurgencies representing subaltern forces had reconfigured the terrain of struggle. So, too, had development entered the scene. In his inaugural speech of January 20, 1949, US president Harry Truman set out his vision of a "fair deal" for "freedom-loving peoples," an essential component of which was solving the problems of "underdeveloped areas." Later that year, Colombia was the site of the first ever mission of the International Bank for Reconstruction and Development aimed at formulating a general development program for a country. This resulted in proposals for a "multitude of improvements and reforms" through careful planning and administration of resources that would make Colombia an "inspiring example" for the underdeveloped world.[119] Although leaders framed industrialization as necessary for the consolidation of democracy, development in practice was inseparable from the growing international anticommunist crusade that authorized extreme terror against dissidents and their possible supporters.[120]

The left-wing insurgencies of the Fuerzas Armadas Revolucionarias de Colombia (Revolutionary Armed Forces of Colombia [FARC]) and Ejército de Liberación Nacional (National Liberation Army) were formed in 1964 amid this repression.[121] From the 1960s, enthusiastic adoption of US counterinsurgency recommendations saw armed civilians routinely incorporated into military strategy. In 1965, during a state of siege, Decree 3398 provided a legal basis for the formation of paramilitary groups (on the grounds that the "defense of the nation" was a task for everyone).[122] By the second half of the 1970s, a "dirty war" was being waged against rural populations by state forces and paramilitaries, with the aim of eliminating insurgents' potential supporters.[123] Larger paramilitary groups were subsequently trained by the Colombian armed forces, with the support of US military aid, businesspeople, and drug traffickers. These paramilitaries went on to perpetrate more than 12,800 political killings over the course of the 1980s.[124] By the time unsuccessful peace negotiations with the guerrillas began in the early 1980s, a culture of juridical exception had become normalized. The provisions of once exceptional decrees had been incorporated into ordinary law.[125] Decree 3398, for example, was absorbed into Law 48 of 1968.[126] Systematic impunity had likewise become institutionalized as the result of refusal to investigate abuses by state and parastatal forces. This generated a state of de facto exception, facilitating the dirty war in defense of society and nation.[127]

The 1991 constitution entered into force the same year that a military intelligence reorganization plan placed paramilitary death squads directly under the orders of the military high command, with the support of ongoing US military aid.[128] Although, with the new constitution, means were introduced to limit the duration of states of siege, and the suspension of fundamental rights and liberties was prohibited, the constitution was it-self enabled by recourse to exceptional measures.[129] Exceptional decrees of previous years were once again converted into permanent legislation, while impunity was further entrenched in the justice system.[130] A "faceless system of justice" was also established, allowing the accused to be tried while the identity of witnesses and judges remained secret.[131] Law here is itself the ve-hicle of exceptional tactics: criminal law is a "tool of war" that "invokes not the figure of the delinquent but that of the enemy."[132] Numerous features of states of exception were thus to be found, with their origins disguised, within the new "Social Rule of Law."

In Britain, too, there is a long historical lineage of recourse to exceptional tactics in the context of the ideology of rule of law that came to prevail from the eighteenth century. That ideology was consolidated in the context of the invention of new capital crimes that gave the impression of a national emergency in the absence of any new threat to order.[133] Less than a decade before the Black Act passed, the Riot Act of 1714 had made it possible for a justice of the peace or other specified authority to deliver an oral warning to any group of more than twelve "unlawfully, riotously, and tumultuously assembled together" that suspended ordinary protections and enabled the group to be forcibly dispersed, on pain of death.[134] Thus, the English common law that became the standard of civilization in the nineteenth century was sharpened not only at the expense of Indigenous peoples, but also through systematic repression in Britain, where the democratic demands of the lower orders met with massacres on several occasions over the following century and a half.[135]

Yet there are aspects of the exceptional tactics that have accompanied neo-liberalism in Britain that also resonate with those in Colombia. Such tactics were already evident in Margaret Thatcher's and Ronald Reagan's deliberate exaggeration of the Soviet threat during the early days of neoliberal reforms in the United States and United Kingdom, which facilitated the transfer of resources from welfare to the repressive apparatuses of the state.[136] The in-tensification of neoliberal reforms over recent years has been accompanied by an escalating use of state and institutional power to undermine formal democratic rights through the criminalization of resistance, and an array of illegal or quasi-legal provisions and restrictions on freedom of assembly and protest. Protests and mobilizations that once would have been considered an essential part of democracy have been framed as "extremist" attacks on "democracy" that demand a repressive response.

The repression of student mobilizations is a good example of the continuities between present-day Colombia and Britain. In 2005, I was present at a protest at the University of Valle, in Cali, where police killed the twenty-one-year-old chemistry student Jhonny Silva. Protests had erupted across the country in opposition to a free-trade agreement being negotiated between Colombia and the United States that week. Earlier that day, residents of a poor neighborhood had taken to the streets to protest privatization and ongoing cuts to water and electricity. Riot police had been indiscriminate in their use of tear gas, resulting in the death of a young child. When the students went out to protest, the police drove them back inside the campus and spent the afternoon illegally firing stun grenades and tear gas directly at the bodies of protesters. Later, as the protest drew to a close, the police illegally entered the campus and began firing tear gas and live ammunition. Silva could not run as fast as the other students, having suffered polio as a child. He was shot at point-blank range and died on the way to hospital. Another student was seriously injured by a tear-gas canister. Two more were detained overnight, threatened with being "disappeared" and dismembered, then released the next morning without charge.[137] The day after Silva was killed, the British university delegation I was with met the secretary of the governor of the Administrative Department of Valle del Cauca, Gladys Hernández, who justified the actions of the police on the basis of their duty to "protect public order." The same day, far-right president Álvaro Uribe Vélez visited the city and proclaimed that the police and public authorities could count on his "instant authorization to go in, finish off and capture the violent people" on campus.[138] These events reflect a systematic criminalization of protest in Colombia, which has been further intensified over recent years.[139] In the context of the ongoing dirty war, members of the university community were already recipients of frequent death threats. A year later, twenty-nine-year-old Julian Hurtado, a member of the Truth Commission investigating the murder, was shot dead by *sicarios* (hired assassins) upon his return home from an event commemorating the first anniversary of Silva's death.[140]

There were echoes of this logic of repression five years later in Britain, during the 2010 protests against spending cuts and university fees. I thought of Jhonny Silva when the protester Jody MacIntyre was dragged from his wheelchair by police. The media even implied this was an appropriate response, given McIntyre's thought crime of holding "revolutionary" views.[141] The parallels were perhaps even more pronounced in the case of Alfie Meadows, who suffered life-threatening injuries after receiving a blow to his head from a police baton the same year. The Metropolitan Police subsequently charged

Meadows and a fellow student, Zak King, with violent disorder. Meadows and King were acquitted in 2013 after a jury accepted that they had been attempting to defend themselves and fellow protesters. Their acquittal highlighted the extent to which police had begun to make unlawful use of Section 2 of the 1986 Public Order Act, which defines the crime of violent disorder, to repress protesters. Eighteen out of nineteen students charged with violent disorder during the tuition fees protests were likewise acquitted. Counsel for Zak King described the use of the Public Order Act as a "sledgehammer" against peaceful protestors that "failed to differentiate between the actions of a crowd and individuals within it."[142]

Illegal Rule of Law

It is important to emphasize, however, that authoritarianism and coercive repression are not just means to impose unpopular neoliberal policies.[143] Rather, authoritarianism is, as Ian Bruff writes, "a *permanent* and *necessary* part of neoliberal ideology, institutionalization and practice." We find it not only in the exceptional measures of repressive legality but also, Bruff continues, "in the reconfiguring of state and institutional power in an attempt to insulate certain policies and institutional practices from social and political dissent."[144] Indeed, if the state of exception is a useful concept, it needs to be extended beyond the active operation of state power to cast certain populations and individuals outside of the protection of law. As José Atiles-Osoria and David Whyte point out, it also opens up a way to understand the legal ordering of contemporary capitalism.[145] We saw in the previous section how social and economic rights are cast aside not merely by action outside of the law, but also by legislative measures that block access to those rights. So too have we seen how corporations have become quasi-sovereign authorities, because the idea of rule of law as a neutral means to economic competitiveness has made them into natural counterparts of government in drafting legislation. Yet the backbone of the specifically neoliberal assault on democracy is the transformation of a Hayekian vision of rule of law into a global constitutional structure. It is this, I now show, that has fomented an unprecedented capacity for legal intervention into politics that has served, in effect, to outlaw democratic demands for an alternative.

It is, Mattei and Nader write, no coincidence that neoliberal globalization took off at the time that the rule of law began to be understood as a universal minimal legal system, conceived as a neutral, merely "technical" means of ensuring growth but in fact generating "harsh control of any individual threatening the bottom line of property rights and incapable of limiting corporate actors."[146] In relation to Pinochet's Chile, both Hayek and Milton Friedman insisted that "freedom" required a legal structure that would protect private property, individual enterprise, and investment rights (as well as insisting that normal political freedoms may have to be temporarily suspended as a matter of necessity to preserve the institutions required for a competitive market order).[147] In Colombia, too, the transformation of a neoliberal vision of legality into a global constitutional structure has set the parameters not just for reforms of specific laws that undermine constitutional rights, but also for constitutional reforms that undermine those rights. In 2011, the Colombian Constitution itself was modified by Legislative Act 3, which "gave constitutional recognition to fiscal sustainability, as a right of citizenship," endowing the authorities with the duty to control public spending and public debt.[148] This gave rise to new fiscal rules prohibiting any public spending that exceeds public income.[149] These reforms represent not simply the bypassing of constitutional rights but a paradoxical constitutionalization of austerity in the name of citizens' rights. This constitutionalization of neoliberal policy prescriptions is now a worldwide phenomenon. In the international order that was consolidated after World War II, the World Bank and International Monetary Fund (IMF) were prevented from intervening in countries' legal systems by their own bylaws, which prohibited political intervention. Lawmaking was still seen, at least officially, as the prerogative of sovereign states (notwithstanding the covert interference in independent states that took place in the context of the Cold War and decolonization). Redefining law as nonpolitical and merely technical allowed the IMF and World Bank to sidestep these bylaws and make domestic law reform a condition of aid. The contractual power of international financial institutions to condition aid to domestic law reform has helped shape this particular vision of rule of law into a global constitutional structure.[150]

Once again, none of this is peculiar to the postcolonial world. Indeed, Bruff suggests that Europe is a particularly useful place to begin to explore the authoritarian nature of neoliberalism precisely because "more than anywhere else in the world, Europe's self-image is that of a socially-aware, more generous and more inclusive form of capitalism than in other world regions."[151] Europe's self-image notwithstanding, the same reconceptualization of rule of law that has shaped international economic law and enabled international financial institutions to condition aid on domestic law reform has also underpinned an increasingly undemocratic shift within European states. The intensification of neoliberal reforms since the 2008 global financial crisis involved increasing legal intervention into politics with the aim of eliminating democratic control over "the economy." Resistant governments were forced to implement austerity measures by (often supranational) constitutional and legal rules, portrayed as "necessary" and beyond question.[152] There were precursors to this long before the crisis. The treaties of the 1970s and '80s that anticipated the creation of a single market extended the power of European law over domestic law on the basis that economic competition was the key objective of the treaties.[153] The Maastricht Treaty of 1992 built on this, committing governments to avoiding "excessive deficits," and empowering the European Commission to monitor economies and impose sanctions. Through this and a series of subsequent measures, austerity was enshrined within the legal framework of the European Union.[154] This, Robert Knox notes, "is not simply an incidental part of the EU framework." It is "accorded supreme constitutional status."[155] When Greece was on the verge of default in 2010, the European Union agreed to a bailout package in conjunction with the IMF, with strict conditions such as the "modernization" of the public sector and more "flexible" and "efficient" labor markets.[156] In the aftermath of the Greek crisis, a series of stricter "economic governance" regulations were aimed at getting governments to preemptively self-impose similar measures to "detect, prevent, and correct 'problematic' economic trends" (which is to say, "excessive" budget deficits and "high" unit labor costs).[157] Thus, when Greece's Syriza party was elected on an anti-austerity mandate in 2015, the president of the European Commission could declare that Syriza would be unable to implement its program because "there can be no democratic choice against the European treaties."[158] His argument did not even invoke the idea of economic necessity; he could simply appeal to law.[159]

Lest this be thought to be something specific to the European Union, which Britain might now evade by escaping EU clutches, we should keep in the mind that Britain has a track record of using legal targets to "tie its own hands" in this way. This began to be visible in 1997, with the election of New Labour and the imposition of fiscal rules that the government would maintain a balanced budget or budget surplus while keeping debt at less than 40 percent of the gross domestic product.[160] This self-imposition of austerity through law was entrenched in the wake of the financial crisis of 2008. "Echoing the EU's constitutionalization of austerity," Knox writes, "the 2010 Fiscal Responsibility Act imposed binding legal rules under which the Treasury had to ensure public sector borrowing decreased yearly. In effect, the Labour government attempted to use law to create 'external' compulsions *on itself* to implement austerity."[161] Similar techniques were adopted through the subsequent coalition government's Budget Responsibility and National Audit Act, according to which any future budgets were to correspond to strict fiscal targets. The act also established the Office for Budgetary Responsibility, charged with "objectively, transparently and impartially" analyzing the Treasury's policy for managing national debt and setting fiscal targets. "Thus the Coalition—building on New Labour Policy—attempted to import the legal surveillance techniques of the IMF and EU into UK economic policy."[162] Just as rights set out in the Colombian Constitution were overwritten by actual legislation, legally mandated austerity in Britain has been judged to violate human rights and equalities legislation, as well as human rights conventions ratified by the United Kingdom.[163]

By the turn of the twenty-first century, the sociolegal scholar Boaventura de Sousa Santos was highlighting a worldwide crisis in liberal narratives of a social contract between state and citizens.[164] Ideas of a social contract have been replaced by what Santos calls "neoliberal contractualism"—a multitude of unstable private contracts based on "a mere appearance of a compromise constituted by conditions, as costly as they are inescapable, imposed without discussion on the weaker party."[165] Colombia typifies these dynamics to such an extent that Santos and the Colombian lawyer Mauricio García Villegas have referred to the country as "the reverse of modernity's social contract."[166] Even in Colombia, however, democracy has not been sacrificed to the demands of capitalism, as it was in the Southern Cone dictatorships of previous decades. It is not simply that democratic forces are suppressed, that citizens' rights and protections are suspended in the name of necessity, or even that social and economic rights are rendered toothless by specific laws and policies. Rather, at the same time that democracy is advocated as a global principle of governance, it is hollowed out by a legal architecture that places drastic restrictions on the possibility of challenging corporate power. It is thus "no longer necessary, or even convenient, to sacrifice democracy in order to promote capitalism."[167] The very meanings of democracy and citizenship are being reshaped in accordance with authoritarian neoliberal constitutionalism.[168]

Social Fascism

Santos refers to this worldwide hollowing out of democracy as "social fascism."[169] The "social" element of this seems, for Santos, to be limited to the maintenance of a formal liberal-democratic infrastructure in highly authoritarian political surroundings. Yet this "social" aspect warrants further consideration. Across the world, the hollowing out of democracy has been accompanied not only by emphasis on the rule of law, but also by democratic, social, and humanistic rhetoric configured as an *ethical* rationale for doing whatever also—serendipitously—happens to be demanded by the criteria of efficiency and competitiveness. The intellectual authors of neoliberalism may have considered social and economic rights and anything beyond the most minimal assistance to the destitute a threat to civilization. They may have invoked racist arguments to oppose democratic self-determination of newly independent states. Yet, as we have seen, neoliberal reforms in practice have taken place alongside the extension of economic and social rights, including recognition of ethnic diversity. Neoliberal intellectuals may have deployed the language of human rights to oppose demands for postcolonial redistribution in accordance with a specific vision of human rights focused on securing the investment rights of private capital and the property rights of the wealthy. Yet the human rights that have accompanied neoliberal reforms go beyond this. They do involve recognition of rights to social protection and the territorial rights of Indigenous peoples.

It might be tempting to dismiss this social and humanistic rhetoric as mere "window dressing," used to disguise policies intent on increasing the wealth of the rich at the expense of the lives of the poor, sealed off from democratic oversight and justified through a rule of law that is—from the perspective of formally recognized rights—illegal.[170] This is, without doubt, to some extent the case. The persistence of a language of social welfare, social rights, and Indigenous self-determination is also indicative of tensions between pure neoliberalism and the legacies of liberal democracy and cosmopolitan humanitarianism that neoliberalization must encounter in practice. Neoliberalism, in other words, is unable to avoid the contradictions of classical liberalism to which Marx drew attention. Nevertheless, I do not think we can reduce the social and humanistic rhetoric that has accompanied political expressions of neoliberalism to *just* a combination of window dressing and the tensions between neoliberalism and other political discourses. "'Left' politics, as Bruff notes, "has frequently been guilty of taking the law and the 'social' institutions within capitalism to be somehow neutral, ignoring in the process how 'non-market' social forms have often been central to, not resistant against, the rise of neoliberalism."[171] Building on this, what I want to suggest is that there has been an important shift away over recent decades from these classical contradictions of liberalism and the selective application of rights. An Orwellian world has taken shape in which liberal values and principles are collapsed as far as possible into deadly economic logics.

The shift toward an apparently softer, more socially minded approach in the World Bank has been central here. In part, this was a response to the human consequences of hard-line neoliberalism of the sort envisaged by neoliberal intellectuals. In the mid-1990s, criticism of the devastating effects of structural adjustment generated a strategy change within the bank. Under the new rubric of "poverty reduction," a greater role for state intervention was promoted, while "country ownership" of the agenda, "good governance," "local participation," "rights-based development," and "dialogue" became buzzwords around aid conditionality. Neoliberalism gained a much touted "human face," to the horror of many at the IMF and US Treasury.[172] Yet critics have pointed out that interventions under the label "poverty reduction" are, in reality, strategies designed to create the social underpinnings for productive labor and competitiveness to make targeted countries more hospitable to foreign direct investment. As Paul Cammack was quick to note when the World Bank changed tack, "poverty reduction" means "locking the poor into the market," without any substantive change to policy staples such as privatization or the role of postcolonial states as producers of cheap commodities. Civil society "participation," meanwhile, has largely implied the co-optation of community organizations and NGOs into neoliberal agendas, while "rights-based" development is focused, in reality, not on the economic and social rights of the UDHR, but on civil and political rights (participation, freedom of expression, and so on) plus minimal "basic rights," such as access to food.[173]

There are also important, but rarely acknowledged, connections between the shift toward a "pro-poor" approach within the World Bank and the "social" justifications for neoliberalism in Europe. In the wake of the 2008 financial crisis, instead of arguing that the attachment to "social Europe" must be dropped, austerity has been justified on the basis that "social" institutions such as the welfare state can survive only if they are able to adapt to change.[174] However, as Bruff underscores, "Europe has in reality been neoliberalizing *through*, not against, 'social' institutions of governance since the 1980s." Long before the 2008 crisis, collective bargaining mechanisms had begun to be used to discipline labor rather than treating trade unions as equal partners (as they were considered under the postwar rubric of social partnership among capital, labor, and the state). Likewise, before the 2008 crisis European countries were witnessing welfare retrenchment and a move from welfare to "workfare" (in accordance with a shift in emphasis from the idea of collective entitlement to a social safety net in the face of restructuring toward the individual responsibility to work).[175] British prime minister Tony Blair was a leading proponent of the idea that Europe's social institutions needed to adapt to survive.[176] His New Labour government not only introduced the fiscal rules that paved the way to austerity after the 2008 crisis but also presided over numerous privatizing reforms, such as those that "rapidly accelerated the fragmentation of the NHS [National Health Service] and its permeation by private capital."[177] These reforms, which went with a substantial midterm funding increase, were rationalized on the basis of the need to "save the NHS."[178]

Convergence between European "social" neoliberalism and the humanistic rhetoric of mainstream development discourse can be found in projects such as the "peace laboratories" established at the turn of this century in the wake of state-backed massacres in Colombia. These are regional programs for "development and peace," established as a joint initiative between the Colombian state and the European Union, in association with the World Bank, multinational corporations, and NGOs. They were designed to "explore, with the instruments appropriate to the Social Rule of Law, the paths which Colombian society must go down to reach peace and generate sustainable development."[179] In Magdalena Medio, for example, the rhetoric of the peace laboratory is couched in terms of community "participation" and "dialogue," aimed at generating a culture of peace and "integral rights."[180] In reality, this has involved the insertion of peasants into global markets through the "sustainable" production of monocultures such as oil palm. The "participation" advocated is "a participation on a supposedly equal footing with corporations" through so-called strategic alliances that involve contracts of ten to twelve years, during which peasants must sell palm fruit to the company under an agreement at which the price is determined at the point of sale, meaning that peasants must absorb the risks of falling prices. The company also extracts the cost of seeds and technical assistance from peasant participants in these alliances.[181]

Despite the reference to the Social Rule of Law, the "peace laboratories" embody the "reverse of the social contract" of which Santos speaks. "Strategic alliances" between peasants and corporations are the quintessence of neoliberal contractualism. They are, as one peasant put it in an interview with the investigative journalist Gearóid Ó Loingsigh, like "an alliance between the fox and the chickens: in the end the fox will eat the chickens."[182] While successive governments, the World Bank, and the European Union repeatedly talk about "peace and development," framing development as the antidote to violence, the model of development advocated in the name of "peace" is the very model for which people were killed in the first place. The paramilitary groups who took over entire regions such as Magdalena Medio in close collaboration with the army were never mere armed mercenaries; they were political organizations whose visions of "development" overlapped with those of the government, World Bank, European Union, and international NGOs.[183] Since the 1990s, forced displacement and massacres—as Cardenas and Marín point out—have been accompanied by a humanistic, developmentalist, and conservationist discourse propagated by UN bodies, the World Bank, transnational corporations, and NGOs, as well as paramilitary and state organizations.[184] This is perhaps nowhere more visible than in more recent proposals for land restitution and "post-conflict" development following the 2016 peace deal with defeated FARC guerrillas. Most of Colombia's national territory has been destined for extractive projects to pay for "peace," while displaced peasants have to agree to plant monocultures for export to get their land back or (as is more common) be relocated to "unproductive" land not destined for foreign investment. Thus, the very measures put in place to promote peace and advance justice serve to consolidate what was achieved through state-backed massacres and forced displacement.[185]

The appeal to social and democratic values serves here not to insulate people against economic force, but as means through which violent modes of dispossession are authorized. It is no longer necessary to distinguish between criteria for moral action and criteria for economic action in the style of classical liberal thinkers, for the two become indistinct. This coheres with the aims of the original neoliberal thought collective—to build an institutional and moral framework that could encase wealth and power in the hands of a corporate elite—but it does so in a way that extends beyond their own response to concerns about the civilizational dangers posed by democratic self-determination and systems of social protection. For neoliberals who came together at Mont Pèlerin, the social and economic rights in the UDHR were a threat to a Western civilization founded on commerce and free markets. Today, by contrast, not just *rule of law* but also *democracy, poverty reduction*, and *social welfare* have become part of an increasingly penetrative ethical newspeak that has served to consolidate neoliberal necroeconomics. This needs to be considered on its own terms as a constitutive aspect of how neoliberalization has taken shape in practice. Capitalism, after all, is adept at absorbing everything it encounters, including sites of contestation and critique. With the "social" turn of neoliberalism, we arrive at a juncture in which financial and corporate power has had unprecedented success in shaping global institutions and ethical discourse in the image of an intensely violent global political economy. It is this with which we must contend when considering the politics of human rights.

deadly
colonial ethics

Development Policy-Speak
and Corporate Responsibility
CHAPTER TWO

Sir Geoffrey Chandler, a retired director of Shell International and founder of Amnesty International UK's Human Rights and Business Group, had little success when he first began to invite companies to discuss human rights in 1991. Human rights "were for governments, not for companies" came the unanimous response.[1] Yet just a few years after Chandler's first overtures to his former colleagues, corporate attitudes had undergone a remarkable about-face. By the turn of the twenty-first century, transnational corporations in every sector were signing on to human rights codes of conduct and parroting what was now common sense: that recognizing and respecting human rights was not only morally correct, it was also good business sense.

The sudden shift toward recognition of human rights as a matter of concern for corporations followed a series of high-profile transnational campaigns. It was hailed as a victory for human rights advocates. The period 1995–96 had been dubbed the "Year of the Sweatshop" in the United States after campaigns against use of sweatshop labor by Nike, Gap, Disney, and other companies made the headlines.[2] In 1996, the first proceedings were issued against a corporation in the US courts for human rights abuses committed elsewhere, and similar attempts at litigation began to proliferate. That same year, after a media scandal over its complicity in the prosecution and execution of leaders of the Movement for the Survival of the Ogoni People in the Niger Delta, Shell became the first corporation to accept Chandler's invitation to discuss human rights. In early 1997, British Petroleum (BP) followed suit, establishing a dialogue with a group of British international development nongovernmental organizations (NGOs) after a similar outcry over its links with the Colombian Army and, by extension, with a campaign of threats and selective killings by state-linked paramilitaries against peasant leaders, environmental activists, and trade unionists.

"Reputational disaster provided the stimulus," as Chandler put it. "Shell's experience in Nigeria and, later, BP's in Colombia provided us with a platform and a breakthrough."[3] In particular, BP became a pioneer of corporate responsibility for human rights and one of the founding signatories of the Voluntary Principles on Security and Human Rights for the extractive sector. Since then, an extensive matrix of corporate, sector-based, and global codes of conduct, ethical guidelines, management tool kits, and assessment indices has given form to a global regime of voluntary corporate responsibility for human rights. Companies increasingly have made common cause with NGOs, offering up corporate responsibility as the solution to an array of "global problems," from human rights to sustainable development and beyond.[4]

This widespread corporate uptake of "social responsibility" in the 1990s would seem, at first glance, to be anathema to neoliberal thought. "The social responsibility of business is to increase its profits," Milton Friedman declared in 1970 in an article by the same title in the *New York Times Magazine*.[5] When Friedman wrote, the International Labour Organization had been coming under pressure from the International Confederation of Free Trade Unions to address the social impact of multinational corporations. Shortly afterward, in 1972, the Economic and Social Council of the United Nations passed a resolution calling for "a study of multinational corporations and their impact on the process of development."[6] For Friedman, the very idea that corporations should have a "social conscience" was an affront to a free society. Those in business who proclaimed their purpose as being not just capital accumulation but also promoting "social" ends, such as "providing employment, eliminating discrimination, avoiding pollution and whatever else may be the catchword of the contemporary crop of reformers," Friedman insisted, were "unwitting puppets of the intellectual forces" (i.e., socialism) that had been "undermining the basis of a free society these past decades."[7]

It is important to emphasize that Friedman was not making an amoral argument that corporations had no social responsibilities but a normative case for the pursuit of profit without any additional "social objectives." Neoliberalism was, as we have seen, a moral and political doctrine from its inception. Neoliberals such as Friedman sought not unfettered markets, but "a legal and moral framework to restrain postcolonial sovereignty, protect property and investments, and secure the existing international division of labour."[8] An important part of the context of Friedman's argument was growing international concern with the capacity of corporations to undermine the sovereignty of postcolonial states. Demands from Third World countries for a New International Economic Order included proposals for regulation of the activities of multinational corporations, and this, for Friedman and his colleagues, threatened to undermine the right to trade that was the foundation of all other freedoms and rights. A capitalism that excluded social objectives and social protections was a moral necessity, the only means of ensuring human rights (defined in terms of the absence of "coercive" interference in the market).[9] Thus, for Friedman, directors of corporations should act within the law and in conformity with the basic rules of society embodied in ethical custom, but within those parameters, their responsibility was to make as much money as possible for their shareholders, to whom they owed their primary obligation.[10]

It is now widely accepted that the voluntary corporate responsibility that took shape in the 1990s was a means of continuing "business as usual" and avoiding both litigation and the legal regulation advocated by many campaigners.[11] Corporate responsibility for human rights has been widely denounced as "whitewash," as a "mask" or a "myth" that has little effect in practice.[12] After all, even pioneers of human rights codes of conduct such as Shell and BP have continued to be associated with atrocities. Indeed, activists contesting the harmful social and environmental impact of extractive industries now constitute the majority of victims of selective assassination and forced "disappearance" in many countries around the world, despite the central role played by extractive industries in the recognition of human rights as a matter of concern for corporations.[13] Campaigners and, more recently, the United Nations have responded by emphasizing the importance of judicial remedy for violations, in addition to voluntary means of encouraging corporations to respect human rights.[14] Corporations, so the argument goes, should pay "due diligence" to human rights of their own accord. They must, however, make remedy to victims when they fail to do so.

In this chapter, I suggest that corporate responsibility for human rights is far worse than whitewash: it actively bolsters the legal and ethical framework within which corporations are free to generate premature death. To denounce corporate whitewash is only to scratch the surface of appearances. It is to call attention to the ugly reality covered, but ultimately unaltered, by a veneer of rights talk. The risk is that we overlook the context in which corporate responsibility for human rights emerged, alongside what Dinah Rajak describes as its "profound discursive capacity . . . to transform social relations and projects according to a particular set of corporate interests and values."[15] The recognition of human rights as a matter of concern for corporations occurred at a specific historical juncture, when World Bank and mainstream development thinking was moving away from the market fundamentalism of the 1980s and early 1990s and closer to the original neoliberal emphasis on the legal and institutional preconditions for "development." This, as we saw in chapter 1, relied on a reconceptualization of law as a neutral means of securing economic growth, combined with a morality of self-reliance and entrepreneurialism rather than collective or egalitarian values. What needs to be examined is how human rights became incorporated into corporate activities. How were human rights configured in terms of a particular set of problems, amenable to solutions that could be promoted by corporations—as a matter of good business sense?

The standard account of corporate recognition of human rights as a response to protest is the product of a deeply colonial way of seeing. Transnational campaigns are presented as transmission belts for the struggles of dispossessed constituencies at companies' sites of operation. Everything of significance (the protests, the media scandals) happens "here" (mainly in Europe and the United States) on behalf of Others elsewhere. While some "here" disregard human rights or are co-opted into corporate agendas, cosmopolitan activists demand that corporations recognize the human rights of those Others. Human rights are approached as something abstract that corporations can be urged to respect.[16] Struggles at companies' sites of operation are bracketed out. As a result, we miss the profound discontinuity between those struggles and the demands of transnational activists that corporations respect human rights.

For social movements at companies' sites of operation, the demand is rarely that corporations simply respect human rights. It is the economic model itself that is called into question.[17] Across much of the postcolonial world, the dominant mode of integration into global markets has been what is sometimes referred to as the "extractive-export model," or *extractivismo* (extractivism) in Latin American critical thought. Extractivism encompasses not only oil extraction and large-scale mining but the full gamut of industries that appropriate nature for the accumulation of capital (such as big dams generating hydroelectricity for other parts of the world or agribusiness producing cash crops for export).[18] In continuity with the export enclaves of the colonial era, the bulk of the profits of extractivism go to foreign investors. Local people are a source of hyper-exploitable labor or surplus populations to be displaced. Allegations of both corporate and state complicity in forced displacement and murder have become part and parcel of the extractive-export model. Yet those targeted are targeted for a reason: because of political activism or a way of life that stands in the way of the dominant approach to "development."

The account here seeks to rectify the colonialism of standard critiques of voluntary corporate responsibility by tracing the international trajectory of a struggle central to the emergence of the current corporate concern with human rights: that of peasant organizations against BP in Colombia. In 2007, while I was living in Bogotá in the "international solidarity house" of the Colombian-European Red de Hermandad, I was invited to join a project with peasant leaders who had been forcibly displaced from the country's Casanare region as a result of their mobilizations against BP in the 1990s. The Corporación Social para la Asesoría y Capacitación Comunitaria (Social Corporation for Community Advice and Training [COSPACC]), a Bogotá-based human rights NGO set up by these leaders, asked me to contribute to a book aimed at recovering and preserving historical memory of BP's impact in the region. However, our research trips to the area around the oilfields were to serve a double function: not just gathering details of past events but also providing protective international accompaniment in the context of ongoing abuses, including a spate of recent murders directly at the hands of the army. The coordinator of the book project was Martín Ayala, who had fled Casanare after an attempt on his life on his way home from a meeting at which he had attempted to negotiate with BP on behalf of the peasant population in the 1990s. One of the first people I met in Casanare was the mother of Oswaldo Vargas, a community leader who had been shot dead in front of his young son upon his return from a meeting with BP in 2004, after local campaigners received death threats warning them "No jodan a BP" (Don't mess with BP). Both community leaders had been attacked on their return from meetings with company officials. By the time Vargas was killed, however, BP had become a leading proponent of corporate responsibility for human rights.

In the rest of this chapter, I trace what happened between the attack on Ayala and the killing of Vargas. I consider how the process of engagement between BP and British NGOs after the killings of the 1990s helped to shape voluntary corporate responsibility within the terms of a deeply colonial moral discourse whose effect is to rationalize death in the name of "development." The incorporation of human rights into this scenario is, I suggest, an important ethical innovation, effecting a privatization of human rights that seals corporate activities off from democratic contestation. Those who appeal to the rights of citizenship to contest the extractive model are politically unrecognizable, except as a disruptive presence that must—by one means or another—be made to disappear.

The Violence of Development

In the two decades after BP began oil exploration in the eastern foothills of the Colombian Andes, approximately 2,500 people were "disappeared."[19] Oil extraction at the hands of a consortium led by BP was accompanied, in 1992, by the installation of the 16th Brigade of the Colombian Army in the Administrative Department of Casanare, tasked with providing security to the oil companies. Within weeks of the brigade's arrival, right-wing paramilitaries linked to drug traffickers and landowning oligarchs began to be seen entering army bases, generating fear that here, as elsewhere in Colombia, paramilitaries were being integrated into state strategies of population control.[20] According to human rights defenders who documented the abuses, 1 percent of the population around the oilfields had been killed by the time BP withdrew from the region in 2011.[21]

These figures are dramatic, yet they only begin to capture the devastation. As one leader put it during a community barbecue to which our team had been invited, "We are not just victims of human rights abuses; we are victims of development itself." Selective killings and preemptive "disappearances" of those likely to contest the economic model are just the visible surface of the violence that Arturo Escobar describes as "constitutive of development."[22] This is a violence that has worked its effects in Casanare through the slow strangling of a way of life. It has left its trace in dried-up rivers, eroded farmland and roads, and the severance of the peasant population from its relationship with the land in pursuit of precarious employment opportunities in a region where social investment remains sparse.

Reflections on the violence of development are often retrospective analyses, made after the experience is found impossible to assimilate to the fantasy, after the myth becomes impossible to sustain.[23] The struggles of many social movements are expressed—at least initially—as struggles *for* "development" (albeit for a different development): for better access to health care, stable jobs, and so on. In the early days, many people in Casanare had given BP a cautious welcome. As displaced former community leaders now running COSPACC explained, social organizations—in particular, activists linked to the Asociación Nacional de Usuarios Campesinos (National Peasant Association [ANUC])—had initially focused their efforts on ensuring that the local population saw the benefits of the oil bonanza.[24] More than a decade later, when a human rights defender I was accompanying suggested to a community meeting that they should "demand development," he was met with strongly voiced critique from people who had long since distanced themselves from the use of that concept. Nevertheless, at the inception of these struggles against BP, development was appropriated in contestation of the economic model. Demands were made *for* development, but not as something abstract, to be defined in practice by global and national elites. Development was invoked in opposition to what rural organizations across Colombia often describe as being "abandoned by the state." *Development*, in these terms, was closely articulated with a discourse of rights, framed in terms of popular sovereignty over natural resources and access to the economic and social rights that the National Constitution of 1991 guaranteed to all citizens: social security, stable employment, health, environmental protection, sustainable exploitation of natural resources, and the repair of associated damage.[25]

By demanding recognition of all the rights of citizenship, the peasant organizations may have reinforced the authority of an increasingly murderous state. Nevertheless, these demands had little in common with the "rights-based" approaches that were coming to populate the international development scene at that time. "Rights-based development" not only falls drastically short of the economic and social rights recognized in the Universal Declaration of Human Rights and Colombian Constitution. It also, in so doing, draws a line between the expectations appropriate to "developed" and "underdeveloped" peoples (the latter can expect only civil and political rights and a few additional "basic rights," such as food).[26] The peasant organizations in Casanare were not just asking for a little more participation or better satisfaction of basic needs within the terms of the existing international division of labor. Instead, the demand for rights challenged these colonial dividing lines and exposed the contradictions between the existence of rights in the constitution and the abandonment of the population in practice.

Eventually, commitments were secured from the local authorities for public investment of oil revenues. Meanwhile, BP agreed to undertake a series of works that included repair of environmental damage and the paving of roads eroded by the heavy traffic and shock waves from oil exploration.

When these commitments were persistently ignored, people began to take a more militant stance, organizing a series of civic strikes that blocked some of Casanare's main routes. Over the course of several visits to the region with COSPACC in 2007–8, I had long conversations with surviving members of the community organization in the hamlet of El Morro that had organized the first such strike in January 1994. The strike took the form of a two-week roadblock that prevented equipment from reaching BP's installations. The commander of the 16th Brigade declared the protest to have been organized by subversives. Several of those involved subsequently were killed or threatened or escaped attempts on their lives by paramilitaries. Others were imprisoned on charges of rebellion or had their houses raided by the authorities. Similar patterns of violence were repeated elsewhere. Numerous peasant leaders were killed or forcibly displaced. Eventually, even the strongest peasant organization—the Casanare branch of ANUC—was destroyed.[27]

BP was heavily implicated in the repression. According to the 16th Brigade's commander of military intelligence, the company provided the army with photographs and film taken during meetings with activists. Several of those photographed were later killed.[28] The company had signed a £5.6 million voluntary collaboration agreement with the Ministry of Defense for protection, and had paid £60 million for its own special force.[29] It was also revealed that BP had employed the private security contractor Defence Systems Limited to provide "lethal" counterinsurgency training to the police.[30] Socialist guerrillas of the Ejército de Liberación Nacional (National Liberation Army [ELN]) had, since the mid-1980s, been running a campaign against foreign appropriation of oil revenues. In neighboring Arauca, the ELN had forced Occidental Petroleum to give an annual sum to the church for social projects.[31] BP was having none of that. In line with the US-designed counterinsurgency strategy of the Colombian armed forces, the focus of these counterinsurgency efforts was on "taking the water from the fish": undermining social support for the insurgency by targeting potential sympathizers. The paramilitary commander Carlos Guzman Daza (alias Salomón) stated that "all the oil companies" had given money to paramilitaries in Casanare and linked this directly to the suppression of resistance:

> When peasants organized strikes or protested about any situation that they considered to be affected by the oil companies, the paramilitaries went in to threaten the peasants. There is, or should be, a record of even presidents of community associations who were killed or displaced because they opposed BP's policies in Casanare, and this was done by the

autodefensas [paramilitaries]. And as I say, the paramilitaries never did anything for free. If they gave a service to someone, it is because this someone was financing or giving money or some bribe in exchange for threatening peasants, and people who opposed these policies.[32]

The arrival of the 16th Brigade in Casanare was a precursor to events that were to be repeated across the country. By the second half of the 1990s, paramilitaries operating in collaboration with state forces were taking over vast portions of the countryside, clearing the way for an array of extractive projects through massacres and selective killings in which—as we saw in the previous chapter—various multinational corporations have been implicated. All this took place in the name of "development" and the removal of obstacles to "progress." One morning, in April 2008, I attended a community meeting in a remote part of Casanare, where a number of people had recently been killed or had attempts on their lives carried out by members of the army. A group of soldiers, headed by Second Sergeant Ávila of the 16th Brigade's 44th Battalion, was waiting for us upon arrival. A Colombian human rights lawyer and I explained to the soldiers that this was a human rights meeting and requested that they respect it as a civilian space and move away. They refused to leave, however, and Ávila insisted on positioning himself next to the open window of the school building in which the meeting was being held. The chair of the meeting eventually asked him in to introduce himself to those gathered. When challenged in response about recent murders at the hands of his battalion, Second Sergeant Ávila justified this on the basis of rumors that some of the population were "left wing." "We are the ones who sleep least at night in order to protect you," he insisted.

The Moral and Legal Context of Atrocity

We should not rush to the conclusion that this emphasis on improving and protecting the lives of the population is only a smoke screen for the sacrifice of some to the prosperity and greed of others. Instead, we need to interrogate the mutually reinforcing intersections between the protection of life and exposure to death and the active role of both law and moral discourse within these dynamics. Otherwise, we risk repeating the tacit operating assumptions of mainstream human rights advocacy, where armed violence is presented in terms of an absence (the absence of the "rule of law," or of a suitably strong state). Violence is batted away as something that belongs outside of modernity,

as the work of unintelligible Others that political and economic "modernization" is poised to overcome, the result of a sort of state of nature in which
almost all humanistic intervention is to be welcomed for its potential to
improve lives that otherwise would be—as Thomas Hobbes would have had
it—"nasty, brutish and short." The state cannot, or will not, protect or better
the lives of the population (the argument goes), so "we"—concerned members
of the international community—must go in and do so in the name of the
cosmopolitan values of development and human rights. The focus is on visible acts of violence, not the wider economic and legal backdrop or the moral
discourses that sustain these acts. Violence and humanistic intervention are
presumed to work in opposite directions.

We saw in the previous chapter how mistaken such narratives are. The
atrocities in which so many corporations have been implicated do not occur
in a legal or moral vacuum. The normalization of states of exception is the
product of the active and ongoing operation of state power to suspend ordinary rights and protections in the name of "necessity." Meanwhile, legislative reforms have served to confiscate or deny rights recognized in the
constitution. Colombia is a pronounced example of the intersecting states of
exception that characterize contemporary capitalist legality—"the reverse
of modernity's social contract," as Boaventura de Sousa Santos and Mauricio
García Villegas put it, or an "absent dictatorship," "a laboratory of fascist
sociabilities in democratic political surroundings."[33] During the time I was
working in Casanare, it was commonplace to point out that more people had
been killed under President Álvaro Uribe than during Pinochet's dictatorship
in Chile, despite the formally democratic surroundings and a constitution
that had supposedly established a "Social Rule of Law." Despite a National
Constitution that, on paper, affords citizens more rights and protections than
the constitutions of most democratic states, Colombia embodies a form of
political rule that stands on the threshold between democracy and dictatorship and a political culture in which constitutional exception is considered
normal—even constitutional—as constitutional normality.[34]

All this has been shaped through a heavily racialized moral discourse in
which those deemed to lack the attributes required for success, or who are
considered potentially rebellious, can be killed as obstacles to progress, to
development, in the name of the population itself.[35] This is especially the case
in remote areas such as Casanare: the frontiers or "savage lands" of Colombia,
signified as spaces both abundant in natural riches and constituted by their
violence, as terrain to be appropriated, exploited, and integrated into the
order of modernity promoted by the state.[36] In "savage" territories, where

inclusion as part of "the nation" has long been mediated via integration into the global economy, peasant organizations' appeals to rights expose the contradictions between the existence of rights of all citizens in the constitution, and a political economy of the enclave that has prohibited the occupants of those territories from accessing those rights.[37]

It is also in the context of these porous boundaries between legality and illegality, and of racialized imaginative geographies charting lands with savage populations who require protection from themselves, that we must understand the emergence of voluntary corporate responsibility for human rights.

BP Recognizes Human Rights

The situation in Casanare became the subject of international attention in mid-1996, after a British journalist broke the story of BP's links with the Colombian military.[38] A loose grouping that called itself the Coalition against BP began to organize public meetings and protest actions with the aim of keeping the issue in the public eye. BP at first appeared to flounder, denying the allegations and insisting that "subversives" were waging a smear campaign against it.[39] Then, in early 1997 the Catholic Institute for International Relations entered the fray with a diplomatically worded letter in a British national newspaper. Its author recalled, "Within an hour of the letter being published, BP were on the phone saying that they wanted to talk."

The result was what became known as the Inter-Agency Group (IAG), a coalition of NGOs based in the United Kingdom comprising the Catholic Institute for International Relations, the Save the Children Fund, Oxfam, the Catholic Agency for Overseas Development, and Christian Aid. Over the following two years, the group met several times with BP representatives, carried out short fact-finding visits to Casanare, commissioned independent research, and published two reports outlining its criticisms and recommendations to BP. The company, meanwhile, began to lead the way in propagating the idea that responsibility for human rights was an integral part of a corporation's performance. In 2000, BP became one of the first signatories of the Voluntary Principles on Security and Human Rights for the extractive sector.[40] John Ruggie, the UN Special Representative on Business and Human Rights, has praised BP's human rights training facility for the Colombian Army, stating that the Voluntary Principles were "implemented most extensively at the country level in Colombia."[41]

Leaked email correspondence from BP's policy director to a colleague in Colombia, prior to a visit from representatives of the IAG, makes clear what was at stake for BP in its engagement with NGOs:

> Andres, Well done. I agree with your view that we would benefit by working more with Oxfam in Colombia. They have been a great heklp [*sic*] to us here and are getting closer to us all the time. Your visitors have a lot of influence in the development ngo community in the UK, and hence in how allegations against [us] are picked up or not. Good and closer relationships with Oxfam will be a significant factor in differentiating BP globally. We must consider the possibility of partnerships at country or regional or even global level. Such a partnership would do a huge amount for BP's reputation and be a competitive advantage which would be hard to erode.[42]

After a visit to Colombia in 2007, Ruggie applauded the "positive impact" of BP's human rights training program on the "once notorious 16th Brigade."[43] Meanwhile, back in Casanare, the 16th Brigade was continuing to ensure its ongoing notoriety. Soldiers killed the community leader Angel Camacho, near BP's Cupiagua oilfield, the very month of Ruggie's visit. A report by Colombian human rights organizations recorded at least thirty extrajudicial executions at the hands of the 16th Brigade over the course of that year alone.[44] BP, however, was already a leading light among proponents of corporate ethics. Its community relations program was now presented as a success story of "voluntary partnership with civil society organisations and government authorities in a joint effort to manage social issues and to contribute to sustainable development."[45]

The company's erstwhile ethical advisers apparently did not notice evidence that would suggest that BP was implicated in ongoing abuses. The events in El Morro that had first drawn international attention were repeated at the end of 2002, when another roadblock was organized to protest ongoing ecological damage, hyper-exploitative employment conditions for local people, and BP's continued failure to honor agreements with the community. Over the following months, the organizers received threats telling them not to mess with BP. In April 2004, Oswaldo Vargas, the treasurer of the El Morro community organization that had coordinated the roadblock, was shot dead upon his return from meeting with BP representatives. On my second visit to Casanare, I spent the afternoon talking with another former leader of that organization who had survived an assassination attempt five days after Vargas was killed. He and two other surviving members recounted that, the following year, the president-elect of the El Morro Association of

Community Action Groups was killed, alongside a friend, just a fortnight after he had survived an attempt on his life and asked the army for protection. Cartridges found at the scene of his murder revealed that the killers had used weapons inaccessible to the civilian population.[46] The result, once again, was the flight of many community leaders from El Morro and the disbanding of the El Morro Community Association. Prior to the threats, a representative of BP's Community Affairs Department had declared that he was "tired" of the El Morro Community Association because it did not "let the company work."[47] These comments resonate with Gilberto Torres's analysis of his own torture and forty-two-day detention following his abduction in 2002 by men in a van that belonged to BP's pipeline company Ocensa. "I had become a thorn in the side of the company," Torres sometimes says when he recounts the events, "because of my trade union work." Torres's kidnappers later stated in court that they had been paid US$40,000 by the company to "disappear" him.

An obvious, but inadequate, response to this would be that corporate recognition of human rights is just a public relations exercise. In a fairly straightforward way, BP's efforts to show its concern for human rights did serve to cover over abuses: they did affect whether allegations against the company were "picked up or not" (as BP's policy director put it in his email). Nevertheless, corporate responsibility for human rights does more than simply mask abuses beneath an ethical veneer. It works to shape understandings of ethics and of rights. Human rights cease to be tools of struggle and contestation. They are absorbed into parameters that reinforce the dividing lines between lives that count and lives that do not.

The Virtual Reality of Development Policy-Speak

Peasant organizations in Casanare did not demand rights as the obedient, entrepreneurial citizens that national development discourse sought to incarnate. Demands for the rights of citizenship were made in defense of a peasant class against the economic model. They highlighted the contradictions between the principle of a Social Rule of Law enshrined in the National Constitution and an approach to "development" that precluded access to formally recognized citizenship rights. When international NGOs took up the cause of the rights of people in Casanare, the content of the peasants' demands was emptied out. Rights became abstract values to be added onto an existing state of affairs within a virtual reality of development policy-speak.

This was, importantly, not simply co-optation, but a product of the discursive parameters within which the international NGOs operated. The IAG was far from unwilling to challenge BP. I arranged interviews over Skype with two former members of the group while I was working with COSPACC in Colombia. Both emphasized that they had intended to complement the more confrontational campaigning. I later discussed the matter with the British academic Jenny Pearce, who had visited Colombia alongside IAG members with the aim of gathering independent evidence and holding BP to account. She described how BP was confronted with this evidence at a meeting with high-ranking company personnel:

> We not only told them that they could not claim "not to know" what the army and paramilitary were doing, that we had evidence that the army was lifting roadblocks and letting paramilitaries through to target campesinos working on human rights, for instance, but also we had personally seen a member (a colonel, I think) of the fifth brigade, a brigade accused of massive human rights violations, working in the offices of Defence Systems who provided BP with protection.... As an outcome of that, Defence Systems lost the contract with BP and asked to see me on a later visit to Bogotá and expressed their anger over what had happened for which they held me responsible.[48]

The report that Pearce prepared for the Inter-Agency Group was likewise firm in its criticism, stating that "BP chose not to know" what was going on "and listened instead to apparently 'natural allies' such as the armed forces and political elites." She argued that charges of complicity were justified given BP's reluctance to acknowledge the closeness of its own security personnel to the armed forces, and that intelligence operations among civilians were likely to result in killing: BP, she said, needed to understand that the guerrillas were "only one part of the problem of violence" in Colombia. Pearce underscored that this was "a problem that must be solved politically" and that "the civilian population live in greater terror from the paramilitary right and the army."[49] Nevertheless, the picture painted by the IAG in its public advice to BP was quite different. The former members of the group I spoke to said that, as charities relying on donor support, they had felt unable to publicize Pearce's document.

The IAG's own report was permeated with the colonial distinction between reasonable, developed Self and underdeveloped, irrational Other in need of experts to promote rights on their behalf. As much was assumed in its very title: "Good Intentions Are Not Enough." From the start, the report discounted the possibility that BP was complicit in armed repression and that peasant organizations were being subdued so that oil extraction could proceed uncontested. Colombia was emptied of history and politics, with oil reduced to a "strategic resource" in an armed conflict. The company was positioned as a well-intentioned, if rather ineffective and misguided, "corporate citizen."[50] The problem was, at root, Casanare's own weak "civil society," as the press summary of the report made clear:

> Despite BP Amoco's efforts,[51] the study shows that since it began working in Casanare, health, education and housing services to local poor communities have not significantly improved. Oil revenues have meanwhile boosted the region's per capita GDP above the Colombian average. BP Amoco has seriously underestimated the weaknesses in Casanare's civil society. Illegal armed groups have multiplied and Casanare's poor continue to suffer from escalating political violence and environmental problems. BP Amoco has a right to protect its staff and investment, but the potential exists for its own security arrangements to make matters worse. The IAG believes the company has underestimated the implications of its work in a region of conflict.[52]

The NGOs' recommendations included that BP and subcontractors "establish a code of conduct that addresses fundamental human rights laws and standards and is subject to independent and published audits"; that the company's development initiatives "include a specific poverty-alleviation aim"; that the company's "work to promote civil society [be] focused on transparent, systematic and ongoing consultations with all local stake holders"; and that BP improve its analysis of the relationship between violence and oil wealth.

The IAG's own analysis of the relations between violence and oil wealth was, however, sorely lacking. The group took for granted an orthodoxy on conflict and development constructed around the agendas of governance institutions in the post–Cold War era, which has been ceaselessly repeated by NGOs seeking to maintain influence or secure funding, often in the absence of any evidence.[53] This orthodoxy conjures up a series of "illegal armed actors" with neither face nor history: groupings of economic-rational individuals motivated by either "greed" or "grievance" (or both) and directed in their actions by cost-benefit analyses. "Natural resources" are cast in this narrative as merely "strategic" to their aims. Conflict is marked out as a particular sort of problem, amenable to solutions that favor the perpetuation of (neo)liberal approaches to development and "peacebuilding." This is the case despite a cacophony of critique from across the social sciences.[54] Such criticisms are rarely debated. They are simply ignored within a professional technocracy where this orthodoxy is just "common sense." We enter the domain of simulation: the map precedes the territory.[55] The terrain of conflict can be known in advance, prior to any interaction with the spaces in which those conflicts play out.

The idea that natural resources are merely strategic to financing armed conflict occludes the violence of the extractivist model. It also erases the politics of Colombia's paramilitary groups as state-backed (and often corporate-backed) proponents of that model. Since the IAG wrote its report, it has become commonplace to accept that development (badly done) has often heightened conflict. Critique of hard-line neoliberalism has become routine in debates over peace building and development. Yet even overt critics of neoliberal maxims of free trade and the application of economic reasoning to social activity continue to run on colonial ideological fuel: the task of ameliorating conflict is to be assumed through the supervisory benevolence of international institutions and NGOs. Conflicts might be influenced by global dynamics (illicit trade networks, neoliberal orthodoxy even), but their most significant aspects are "local."[56] The problem of conflict is framed against a backdrop of liberal "normality." The civil peace is merely disrupted by illicit armed actors. Liberal capitalist democracy remains the end for which history was made.

The narrative is endowed with obviousness only through its discontinuity with contexts in which (real, live) "armed actors" operate. It is not just that the politics of groups such as Colombia's state-linked paramilitaries cannot be reduced to criminality or economic motivation. The armed struggles of insurgents likewise resist assimilation to notions of "grievance" framed *within* the terms of liberal individualism. Mobilizations against injustice—whether armed or unarmed—are often pitched against the totality of social relations that produce that injustice. Such struggles demand an unmasking of the concepts through which relations of oppression or exploitation are rendered natural, legitimate, or amenable to "quick-fix" solutions. Even critics of mainstream, top-down approaches to peace and development routinely fail to examine their own imposition of taken-for-granted conceptual frames. Guerrillas in Colombia are read in advance, for example, as those who simply "exploit the grievances of the oppressed."[57] Unburdened by history, out of time and context, they are but abstractions crafted from the categories of policy-speak.

"Armed actors? They might as well replace us with actors!" one senior member of the ELN remarked when our conversation one morning in a high-security prison touched on this mainstream tradition of conflict analysis. "Their theoretical frames do not capture our reality, or that of the population."[58]

The point is not to obscure the violence perpetrated within armed struggle or to romanticize those struggles. It is to recognize the extent to which these abstract categories precede any interaction with the lives and struggles of actual human beings. It is to underscore that "imperialism in representation reflects structural and institutionalized power relations."[59]

From here, rights can be added on—as abstract values within a simulated reality. The IAG urged BP to address the impact of its operations by adopting a (voluntary) code of conduct based on recognized human rights standards. With regard to economic and social rights, the group encouraged BP to promote "civil society" to help "the poor" overcome unsatisfied basic needs and the "dependence" that rendered them vulnerable to the impact of violence and environmental damage.[60] Here, too, we find one of those characteristic tropes of development policy-speak: an amorphous "poor," whose neediness, ignorance, and lack of agency generate a profusion of vulnerabilities and who are in need of expert guidance to realize a better way of life.[61] The NGOs offered their knowledge according to a long-established tradition of "educative trusteeship" over colonized populations, which "aims to change behaviour and social organization according to a curriculum decided elsewhere."[62] That curriculum set out a liberal vision of civil society, understood in terms of "autonomy from the state, self-organization, the capacity to evaluate the performance of local and national political structures and the ability to generate space for free debate and non-violent conflict over a multiplicity of social, cultural and political issues."[63] By implication, the protests against BP were the work of organizations that lacked the capacity for adequate evaluation and did not represent a space of free debate or nonviolence.

The autonomy, analytical competence, and capacity for "free debate" of international NGOs are, by contrast, presented as beyond question. This is the case despite their need to achieve donor support; despite the shaping of their expertise within a colonial regime of representation. A web of truth is woven in which experts are authorized to speak on behalf of "uncivil" others and to inculcate norms of behavior consistent with modern capitalist relations. The language of professional expertise is powerful. Its parameters of legibility are ceaselessly reinforced by institutional practices. Anything that falls outside is neither legible nor credible.

"What about the existing civil society in Casanare?" I ask one former IAG member over Skype, attempting to speak her language. I can almost hear her eyes rolling at the naïvety of my question:

"Lara, there *was* no *civil society* in Casanare."

(I hesitate for a moment, without words. Do I tell her about members of that insufficiently civil society with far more sophisticated analyses of the relations between violence and development than that of the British NGOs? Or what that commander of the ELN would have said about the conceptual and methodological limitations of the doctrine that treats oil as a "strategic resource"? Do I invest those accounts with authority as a result of my own institutionally sanctioned expertise? I bite my tongue. I suspect neither of us will fare well when assessed against these norms of civility.)

In any case, the parameters of debate had already been tested and found to be robust in what they excluded. It was not only aspects of Pearce's report that were considered unpublishable. The IAG had also commissioned a study from Pedro Galindo, a researcher employed by the Union Sindical Obrera (the Colombian Oil Workers Union), which it refused to publicize in its entirety. Galindo had aimed to show, as he put it when we met for coffee in Bogotá in December 2007, "how the oil industry represented the imposition of a culturally and economically alien model onto Casanare society and to put forward the idea that people in Casanare should be allowed to take responsibility for solutions to their own problems."

Galindo was savvy about the colonial politics of knowledge. "I was aware when the British NGOs approached me that I had a very different understanding of concepts that they took for granted, such as 'civil society' and the distinction between 'developed' and 'underdeveloped' peoples," he told me. "However, I had hoped that it would be possible to produce a report that could prompt debate between the two perspectives, which might then generate more respectful attention to the struggles of the peasant organizations."

No such debate took place. The IAG suppressed the report because it contained a discussion of how royalties were calculated to ensure what Galindo described during our conversation as "maximum profits to the multinational and minimal benefits to the population." This the NGOs considered beyond their mandate, which, as one of the IAG members put it during our Skype call, was to address "civil and political rights and how income from royalties could generate sustainable development." The NGOs did visit Colombia and attempt to ascertain the views of people there. However, the mandate to promote human betterment through general notions of development and human rights, within an otherwise unquestioned order, already established a frame within which certain things could not even be expressed. The struggles of people in Casanare were already illegible and thus naturally erased from view. Coloniality at the level of knowledge has powerful material effects.

Civilizing Society

BP did go on to emphasize the promotion of civil society. In the mid-1990s, the oil companies in Casanare had already set up an NGO—the Fundación Amanecer (Dawn Foundation)—to "help position the oil industry as a generator of development."[64] We should not overstate the reach of such initiatives. Nor have they been particularly successful in improving people's life chances. Nevertheless, the Dawn Foundation's activities are instructive, given that they embody an approach to "promoting civil society" compatible with that of the British NGOs. There were two occasions, early on in the time I was working with COSPACC in Casanare, that social organizations held large community meetings to address the ongoing killing of civilians by the army. On both occasions, foundation representatives had turned up uninvited to urge people to participate in their projects instead of organizing around human rights. We wanted to know more about their own understanding of their work, but we could not expect foundation employees to talk openly to anyone linked with social organizations. It was decided, as a result, that I should approach the Dawn Foundation in my individual capacity as a British researcher, framing my questions in policy-speak, and that I should then travel to Casanare to meet with foundation representatives in disguise, with my then partner on hand as security backup in constant contact with the team back in Bogotá.

During the day in October 2007 that I spent with the Dawn Foundation visiting some of its projects, foundation representatives explained how their programs were designed "to develop peasants' business capacities" and create "an entrepreneurial culture." They aimed to build "social capital"—for example, through collective applications for microcredit among groups of *socios* (stakeholders or partners).[65] As one employee put it in an interview during that visit, "We are trying to change the mentality in the Casanare countryside . . . from peasant to owner, producer, entrepreneur." These stakeholder-partners are—like the armed actors in conflict orthodoxy—just a collection of economic-rational individuals who come together to pursue private goals. Where each individual is responsible for managing (inevitable) risks, the struggles of a peasant class fade into pursuit of the skills to mitigate those risks. Meanwhile, BP is a "corporate citizen"—a "founding stakeholder," a "partner for development" with the population.[66]

Peasants, for Dawn Foundation employees, were childlike subjects in need of guiding hands to become fully mature and rational. "Here is where they hang their little hammocks," the foundation's director commented as she showed me around an agricultural training camp as if it were a kindergarten. "This one is a bit of a naughty boy who doesn't always do what we tell him," she said of one farmer with a nuanced critique of the advice that he should sell his produce to a supermarket chain. When the director left us alone for a short period, this "beneficiary" gave an apt summary of the foundation's approach: "First BP destroyed the social fabric. Now they try to create a new one in their image."

The childlike, yet-to-be-civilized population was also assumed to be the source of violence because of its inadequate levels of civility. In the words of BP's associate president, the company's presence promised to help eliminate violence "by improving the value of people so that they believe in the value of life."[67] Those who resist are not only dismissed as not understanding what is good for them. They can also be labeled subversives from whom the population must be protected. The promotion of civil society merges with militarized counterinsurgency. Death is authorized to protect and improve life.

It was not only leaders of actual protests who were killed. Those identified as *probable* leaders of *possible* future resistance in areas targeted for oil-based "development" were preemptively mopped up and made to "disappear." In January 2003, a few months before oil exploration began in the municipalities of Recetor and Chámeza, paramilitaries took over the village of El Vegón and proceeded to summon and "disappear" more than sixty people. Their victims were those profiled as likely leaders of possible future protests: peasant leaders, university students, the local doctor, the schoolteacher.[68] It is no exaggeration to say that people have been killed so that they will demand no more than the corporate-NGO vision of civil society.

Violent Locals and Bungling Cosmopolitans

Members of the Inter-Agency Group did acknowledge risks that the dialogue might be used to "rights-proof" BP's operations. "We felt we had to do *something*," one IAG member explained. "If even a few lives were saved, it was worth it," said another. Perhaps, in the short term, some lives were saved by the termination of the contract with Defence Systems Limited. What the British NGOs did not grasp, however, was that the very form of their expertise already served to "rights-proof" violent dispossession. It did so by squeezing human rights to fit within the extractivist model.

The only advice the NGOs were prepared to make public was permeated with the unspoken but assumed distinction between the botched cosmopolitanism of corporate executives and the state of nature in which deprived, and potentially dangerous, "local populations" reside. The NGO letter in the

Independent that prompted BP to initiate the dialogue assumed from the start that BP took its social responsibility "very seriously." Members of the IAG emphasized that BP's policy director (and author of the leaked email) was "very credible and liberal," to the extent that he was even a member of Amnesty International. "I met [BP CEO] John Browne in person, and he was genuinely open to being challenged," said one NGO representative, who observed that BP seemed to find the allegations "bewildering and offensive" and to show willingness to take on the NGOs' views. "BP did move," another said. "They developed a sophisticated understanding of human rights."[69]

Sir Geoffrey Chandler explained his approach to corporate executives on behalf of Amnesty International UK in similar terms: "The best of them have their own principles and morality, and those who work in [multinational corporations] are no more or less moral than ourselves."[70] Reflected in these comments is a sense of responsibility that emerges from superiority—human rights as the "burden of the fittest," as Gayatri Spivak might have it.[71] Those Others, over there, could not reasonably have negotiated with success (or successfully negotiated with reasonableness?). "We" have the benefit of expertise. The white men in suits are, at heart, "our boys"—reasonable, decent, open to being challenged about their mistakes.

It was within these colonial parameters for locating violence and defining capacities for action that BP could credibly deny the allegations. The Colombian interinstitutional report that had sparked such a furor in the British press could be dismissed as "an ad hoc local thing" without even being read.[72] The company was just the victim of "greed" and resentment on the part of insurgents.[73] Michael Gillard, the journalist who broke the story, recalled when we spoke in December 2007 that he, too, was a target of this line of argument: "For BP, it was helpful to try and undermine my journalism by suggesting I was orchestrating the campaign's activities and that, in turn, one of Colombia's guerrilla groups was pulling my strings. I was first alerted to this smear campaign in 1997 after talking to an oil journalist in Houston who'd been briefed by Roddy Kennedy, [then BP CEO] John Browne's Chief Press Officer. I later heard through various sources that BP was smearing me as the ELN's man in Europe." As Gillard put it, BP's response was "a classic strategy of creating a division between so-called 'reasonable' activists that they felt they could do business with and so-called 'unreasonable' ones, who were subtly labeled as militants and guerrilla sympathizers."

The idea that the campaign was spawned from irrational or dangerous political agendas was a potential death sentence, not only in Colombia, but also for Colombians supporting the campaign in Britain. Asdrubal Jiménez, an exiled lawyer, was also named as a member of the guerrillas.[74] His compatriots were afraid to associate with him for fear of reprisals, and his family was thrown into panic that his refugee status would be revoked.[75] Freddy Pulecio, an exiled leader of the Colombian Oil Workers Union who had faced an attempt on his life in Colombia while he was working on the issue of BP, was named in the press as a subversive manipulating the campaign.[76] When she spoke on Skype to one of COSPACC's research team in 2007, an exiled representative of ANUC was still afraid of reprisals, more than ten years after learning that she had been named as a guerrilla in a draft document that BP had planned to publish (before the IAG had convinced the company that it would be inappropriate to do so).

Opponents of corporations are not always labeled subversives in ways that feed so directly into armed repression. It has, however, as Rajak notes, become standard to label them "unethical." As more and more NGOs, lobbying groups, and even unions have been drawn into a burgeoning corporate-civil society network, campaigns against corporate abuses are routinely dismissed as uncivil, opportunistic, and more interested in "throwing stones" than in "making progress."[77] Colonialism takes the form of a language of cosmopolitan common interest: human rights are not only good for humans; they are also good for corporations, which are, by serendipity, perfectly placed to transcend the irrationality and corruption of "local contexts." This is the task of what Chandler described as "the community of interest between responsible governments, good companies and NGOs."[78] After all, at least the corporate-NGO nexus is "doing something," whatever companies' previous "mistakes." As David Rice, BP's erstwhile policy director, put it, "We've learnt from our mistakes, not least because we've been challenged by NGOs."[79]

The notion of prior "mistakes" is part of the performance of corporate "citizenship." Confessions of past misconduct or errors of judgment pave the way for executives to set out new regimes of best practice developed in partnership with NGOs.[80] BP was a leader here. Denials of intentional wrongdoing were quickly tempered by the acknowledgment that BP had "made mistakes" by entering Casanare without a full understanding of the context.[81] To err is human, and these were mistakes from which BP had "learnt."[82] The actions of "local" armed actors and blundering corporate executives might both result in death, but—in terms resonant with Himadeep Muppidi's discussion of media representations of Saddam Hussein and George W. Bush—"only one of them functions in the arena of humanity and politics (of bungling, learning, living, accommodating, getting along) while the Other is in the realm of nature and necessarily outside of politics and history."[83]

The Architecture of Impunity

The colonial imaginary that invests corporate recognition of human rights is not merely symbolic (unfortunate but of little matter if lives are saved). It is a girder in the architecture of impunity. It reinforces the dividing lines between those who count and those who can be killed without anyone being held to account for a crime. Corporations do not merely recognize "human rights." They allocate humanness differentially—to some and not to others—through the practice of recognizing rights. The subject recognized as a holder of rights, already reduced under liberal modernity to the figure of the citizen, collapses into that of the "stakeholder" in corporate operations that remain beyond question.[84] This does not mean we should romanticize citizenship rights or the fact that their gradual extension in the nineteenth and twentieth centuries masked racialized, class-based, and deeply patriarchal power relations. Nevertheless, the idea of citizenship rights as the basis of state power has a degree of malleability that opens up the possibility of struggle over who is included and on what terms.[85] This is where citizenship rights are entirely distinct from the private allocation of rights to "stakeholders." The problem is not just that fewer rights are recognized. The very conceptual matrix within which the recognition of rights occurs precludes any possibility of struggle over what those rights might mean. It entails, in its very formulation, a privatization of human rights, premised on the incontestable existence of those processes of capital accumulation within which the holders of privatized rights can have a "stake." Resisting those processes in the name of the rights of stakeholders in corporate operations is logically impossible. It implies resisting a tautology.

These privatized human rights are entirely consistent with neoliberal concerns to encase the market within a legal and moral framework that can restrain postcolonial sovereignty, protect the commercial rights of multinational corporations, and maintain a colonial international division of labor in the absence of colonial institutions. By usurping the economic and social rights of citizenship to which the peasant organizations appealed, recognition of the rights of stakeholders offers no challenge to a conceptualization of rule of law as a neutral, merely technical means of encasing wealth and the rights of investment. Thus, this regime of privatized rights actively bolsters the legal and moral framework in which corporations are free to generate premature death. It is also, as I explore further in the next chapter, the apotheosis of a broader shift that Radha D'Souza identifies in global governance mechanisms, according to which rights are no longer "justiciable principles" but are reduced to the status of "statistically measurable goals."[86] By turning classical liberalism on its head and insisting that economic freedom was the basis of political freedom (and not the reverse, as eighteenth-century liberals argued), it was, D'Souza contends, neoliberal thinkers who propelled a reconceptualization of rights not only away from social and economic conceptions, but also away from the liberal legal maxim that "every wrong must have a remedy."[87]

The 2011 *United Nations Guiding Principles on Business and Human Rights* recognized that voluntary corporate responsibility can detract from abuses and urged states to "address obstacles to access to justice."[88] As I show in chapter 4, UN treaty bodies likewise have placed greater emphasis in recent years on the need for states to investigate and punish corporate human rights abuses. However, the idea that voluntary responsibility for human rights should be complemented by access to judicial remedy where voluntary measures fail misses the point. Voluntary corporate responsibility for human rights is the product of a legalized state of exception that gives companies license to generate death with impunity. The idea that companies are ethical actors only adds to this scenario. Allegations of crimes fade into acknowledgment of all-too-human "mistakes," reinforcing the status of far-off Others as less than human. Corporate recognition of human rights, set against prior "mistakes," bolsters victims' exclusion from human justice, as those who can—in Giorgio Agamben's terms—"be killed without the commission of a homicide."[89] By writing the economic model out of the domain of contestation, and by simultaneously affirming that model as open to being made ethical, recognition of the rights of corporate "stakeholders" rationalizes a situation in which anything can be done to those who occupy the position of Otherness in relation to "development" and "progress."

It is not just that those who protest are framed within this narrative as irrational and dangerous. The very framework renders the everyday violence of development illegible as forms of injury for which anyone can be held to account. The erasure of a way of life, the destruction of land, and the recasting of peasants as precarious worker-entrepreneurs are now "benefits" of development. Anything else is simply beyond the ambit of rationality. When people resist this scenario, they have no rights at all. Human rights codes of conduct are not a buffer against socioeconomic dispossession or armed repression. They are a further instance of dispossession, representing the enclosure of rights supposedly offered as guarantees to all.

privatizing workers' rights

Social Partnership
in a Neoliberal World

CHAPTER THREE

Western trade union organizations have tended to be vocal advocates of the state welfarist vision set out in the 1948 Universal Declaration of Human Rights (UDHR). After World War II, while "development" became a means of keeping the Global South within the confines of US hegemony, postwar recovery and the containment of communism in Western Europe were achieved through huge packages of US aid, alongside a "social pact" among capital, labor, and national governments. In this context, the economic and social rights abhorred by neoliberal thinkers were fundamental to trade unions internationally. When Friedrich Hayek later criticized the UDHR, he argued that it was "couched in the jargon of organization thinking which one has learned to expect in the pronouncements of trade union officials or the International Labor Organization [ILO]."[1] From its establishment under the Versailles Treaty in 1919, the ILO had emphasized the importance of (male) workers and their families' having an adequate "standard of living." Article 25 of the UDHR was in fact drafted by the ILO, setting out a vision of family-based welfare that embodied the ILO's founding premise: that labor conditions involving "injustice, hardship and privation to large numbers of people" would lead to "unrest" and imperil the "peace and harmony of the world."[2]

Postwar social partnership was underpinned theoretically by institutionalist political economy, which centers on the idea that both capital and labor can benefit from the right institutional mediation of relations between them—including strong unions.[3] Yet for all the rhetoric of common interest underpinning it, postwar social democracy offered no substantive challenge to the international division of labor that neoliberal thinkers also sought to uphold. Welfare states relied on the spoils of empire, now redirected to European working classes, where supposedly universal welfare was, in turn, shot through with "informal colour bars" across industry and society.[4] Meanwhile, the International Confederation of Free Trade Unions (ICFTU), established in 1948 with support from the US Central Intelligence Agency, went to lengths to discipline left-wing militancy in Western unions and to promote "Free West" trade unionism in the Global South.[5] While this was driven by an explicitly anticommunist agenda in the context of the Cold War, the policy of the ICFTU was largely in continuity with the policies of imperial states to promote docile unionism in the Global South.[6] The International Trade Secretariats (precursors of today's global unions, which bring together unions internationally across specific sectors), already bastions of "moderate" trade unionism largely under the control of European states, were also incorporated into the ICFTU.[7]

When the rug of the postwar social pact was pulled from beneath the feet of those once settled in its comfort, international trade union bodies initially floundered. They then shifted focus: from state-based legal and institutional frameworks for securing workers' rights to international institutions and multinational corporations. This was framed as raising social partnership "from the national to the global level."[8] The ILO set the agenda in 1999, establishing a vision for "decent work" along these lines that has since been incorporated into the development discourse of the international financial institutions, as well as into the United Nations' Millennium Development Goals and subsequent Sustainable Development Goals.[9] The aim was to garner support for minimal international standards so that globalization could be made to "work for everyone," with a strong emphasis on encouraging multinational corporations to support a baseline of labor standards.[10] Global unions were central to this new vision of global social partnership. Cautious about the potential of voluntary approaches to enable companies to decide their own standards, global unions have sought to negotiate agreements directly with multinational corporations. While these agreements may include a mutually negotiated code of conduct—and most now include reference to preexisting international human rights instruments and principles—their primary focus is the establishment of "an ongoing relationship," designed to "solve problems" and to "work in the interests of both parties."[11] In 2002, the ICFTU's Dwight Justice characterized the strategy in these terms: "There is always at least one appropriate trade union organization to engage any multinational company," because "every multinational company has an appropriate social partner in an ITS [a global union], which is the legitimate representative of the workers' side of its industry."[12] The International Union of Food, Agricultural, Hotel, Restaurant, Catering, Tobacco and Allied Workers' Associations (IUF) signed the first ever global framework agreement with Danone in 1988 and went on to forge a path through agreements with Accor in 1995 and Chiquita in 2001.[13] By late 2014, well over a hundred multinationals had signed a global framework agreement with one or more of the global unions.[14]

What I want to consider here is how, despite this institutionalist rhetoric, "global social partnership" represents a further example of the privatization of rights. Like corporate social responsibility, it embodies a version of human rights discourse that does active work in consolidating neoliberalism as a particular sort of moral and legal project, even as it moves away from the prescriptions of neoliberal intellectuals. Critics of "decent work" have noted that the agenda "replicates and even exacerbates the underlying structural tensions within the global labour movement."[15] Worse still, it does so in the absence of the significant bargaining power of Western unions that characterized the postwar era.[16] Global framework agreements have been criticized along similar lines, as "largely . . . 'top-down' instruments, the usefulness of which has seldom moved beyond the institutionalized context of the social partnership in which they are negotiated and signed" (i.e., between the global union and the head office of the multinational), albeit with some effectiveness when union power resources are "openly invoked to challenge corporate power" via militant workers' struggle and transnational campaigning.[17] While I agree with the thrust of these criticisms, we need to think beyond their terms of reference to capture the shift in how human rights are comprehended within so-called global social partnership and how this helps consolidate a neoliberal legal order.

Existing studies of global framework agreements and the efforts of global unions and their affiliates to secure "decent work" tend not to consider workers' struggles taking place outside and beyond these parameters. In particular, scant attention is paid to unions who continue to mobilize against capitalism and to advocate alternatives to a global political economy dominated by the interests of multinational corporations. Debates on the prospects for labor internationalism from the 1990s made ample reference to "social movement unions," whose aims go beyond traditional collective bargaining to include wider social justice concerns.[18] The historical role of unions of the Global South in twentieth-century anticolonial struggle is also well recognized.[19] In discussion of global framework agreements, however, there is a tendency to assume that labor unions all want the same thing: to strengthen the position of labor to improve workers' pay and conditions. Thus, the success of a particular strategy for bolstering workers' rights can be assessed in relation to the extent to which it has improved pay and conditions and whether it has shifted the balance of power between labor and capital. However, as Louisa Acciari emphasizes in a study of eight decades of struggle of Black female domestic workers in Brazil, we should be open to how workers mobilize rights discourse in ways that do not simply demand inclusion within an existing framework but challenge the very framework through which rights are recognized.[20] We need to be alert to what may be hidden by abstract categories such as "labor" and pay attention to *how* workers claim rights in struggle. In this chapter, I take up these questions by reference to a trade union struggle deeply embedded within wider social movement struggles in Colombia. This is the struggle of the Colombian Food Workers Union, with which I worked closely on an international campaign against Coca-Cola that was launched a few years after the events of the previous chapter.

The focus of the Colombian Food Workers Union has always gone well beyond the defense of workers' rights as conceived within mainstream frameworks. "A struggle for pay and conditions alone won't solve the wider problems of the community," as the union's president, Javier Correa, put it when I was accompanying the union's Bugalagrande branch in southwestern Colombia during its 2006 negotiations with Nestlé. The union seeks to improve workers' pay and conditions in the immediate term, but its aim has always been to develop proposals and engage in a collective struggle with peasant and Indigenous groups for an alternative mode of food production, focused—in Correa's words—on "land redistribution, agrarian reform, the democratization of landholdings, food sovereignty, and an end to hunger." At that time, however, the union was not only in a labor conflict with Nestlé and a global campaign against Coca-Cola. It was also at loggerheads with the IUF, the global union that pioneered global framework agreements. The IUF had vocally opposed the Colombian Food Workers Union's campaign against Coca-Cola from the outset. Yet the IUF also has a track record of robust negotiation and the mobilization of union resources to challenge corporate power, and cannot be easily dismissed as "pro-company" in the sense that some campaigners at the time suggested. As such, the story of the Colombian food workers' campaign and the IUF's opposition to it provides us with a way in to explore questions about how workers claim rights and how they are recognized as subjects of rights. It helps us glimpse conflicts and tensions between different frameworks within which rights are allocated to—or claimed by—different subjects. Thus, it provides us with insights into the politics of "global social partnership" that are easily missed when we think in terms of abstract collective subjects such as "labor," "capital," and the balance of power between them.

Labor Unionism against the "Empire behind the Multinationals"

Since it was formed in 1982 as a *sindicato de industria* (industry union) for the whole of the food production sector, the Colombian Food Workers Union has engaged in militant activism over working conditions, with tactics including strikes, pickets, rallies, and hunger strikes. From the 1970s, the union and a predecessor union with which it subsequently fused made significant gains for both Coca-Cola and Nestlé workers.[21] In contrast to the hyper-exploitative conditions that had existed in the mid-twentieth century, with scanty wages, a long working day that forced many workers to sleep in the factories, and no right to time off, unionists secured recognition of the right to organize and forced bottlers to negotiate a series of collective conventions that led to a gradual, but substantial, improvement in conditions—at least until the 1990s, when the reforms of labor law discussed in chapter 1 took place.[22] Like the peasant organizations around the oilfields of British Petroleum (BP), the Food Workers Union's demands for rights have drawn attention to the distinctions between rights recognized on paper (in the constitution and in ILO conventions) and the absence of those rights in practice. We might say, in Jacques Rancière's terms, that the union has demanded rights as a sort of supplement, an excess to the established allocation of places and functions.[23] Nevertheless, going beyond Rancière and others who have highlighted the disruptive potential of rights, the union's demands for rights do not just expose the contradictions of dominant normative schemas so as to open possibilities for something else to emerge or to incite democratic contestation over the terms of inclusion within the established order. They are staged within struggles that reveal the fiction of the "free" worker under capitalism as a subject of rights. The union has necessarily conducted its mobilizations with one foot within the existing order of things, negotiating with employers to improve immediate material conditions and with the aim of gaining (or holding on to) access to rights set out in the constitution and by the ILO. Yet this has not precluded an oppositional discourse that refuses the premises on which the demand for these rights is based. The union overtly defines employers as representatives of an exploitative capitalist class and the multinationals for whom they work as perpetrators of an ongoing colonialism.

The Food Workers' struggles also go beyond labor relations, drawing attention to the systemic violence of capitalism in the form of widespread hunger and the obliteration of other modes of food production and distribution. This work has involved carefully researched critique of the prevailing, extractivist mode of food production, popular education initiatives, and building international solidarity for the demand that populations should have sovereignty over food production and food culture. A particular focus of this international solidarity has been a campaign against Nestlé in Switzerland, denouncing the multinational not just for violations of workers' rights, but also for perpetuating a model of food production that implies hunger for much of the world's population. At a day-to-day level, the union's local branches are involved in practical initiatives to address hunger and to support alternative networks of food production and distribution. For instance, in the Caribbean coastal city of Barranquilla, where I accompanied union leaders after they had received death threats during the international campaign against Coca-Cola, the Food Workers Union helps peasant farmers to transport organic produce to a market in the city so it can be sold at a price that is affordable for the urban poor. In Bugalagrande, the union provides training in urban agriculture and runs community kitchens to meet the immediate needs of those who are otherwise unable to obtain adequate food. All of these initiatives are combined with deep links with peasant and Indigenous struggles. Indeed, during several days of a teach-in where the Bugalagrande negotiating committee prepared to meet with Nestlé factory management, leaders' briefings on negotiation technique alternated with strategy discussions on this wider struggle, led by the union's primary researcher.

All this is illustrative of a wider tradition of labor unionism in Colombia, which combines critique of capitalism with a deep-rooted understanding of the links between capitalism and colonialism, including a colonial politics of knowledge that continues to categorize the problems of poor and nonwhite populations in ways that enable their destruction, exploitation, or subjection to civilizing interventions. We saw in the previous chapter how a report along these lines from the Colombian Oil Workers Union drew attention to this colonial politics of knowledge and power and contested British nongovernmental organizations' (NGOs) understandings of "civil society" and "development." For the Food Workers, as for the Oil Workers, the response has been the trade union genocide that I described in chapter 1. The Bugalagrande teach-in during the negotiations with Nestlé was where I spent coffee breaks with Oscar López, who in a subsequent round of negotiations was shot dead during a hunger strike. Barranquilla was where Adolfo Múnera was killed and where paramilitaries threatened union members on the instructions of bottling plant management because they were "interfering with Coca-Cola's business."[24] It was also where students who helped me with a report on state terrorism in Colombian universities told me that they had been detained and tortured for supporting the Food Workers' strike against casualization, and where the fifteen-year-old son of Limberto Carranza—a leader of the local branch of the union—was abducted and tortured while paramilitaries phoned his father and threatened him for his trade union activities. There is not space here to recount the numerous cases of death threats, arbitrary imprisonment, attempts on union members' lives, and kidnapping or attempted kidnapping of their children that have taken place during these struggles against casualization—as well as the murders of union leaders. Múnera was the seventh Coca-Cola worker and López the fourteenth Nestlé worker that the Food Workers Union reported killed by paramilitaries.

It is important that we understand the union's campaign against Coca-Cola in the context of this wider struggle. The story that forms the substance of the discussion here begins in 2001, when lawyers acting on behalf of the union lodged a civil action in the Southern Florida District Court against the Coca-Cola Company, two Colombian bottlers, and named company directors, demanding relief and damages for human rights violations committed by paramilitaries. The lawsuit itself was designed as a vehicle of *denuncia* (which in Spanish connotes both lodging a complaint and rendering visible the matter for complaint). In the immediate term, the negative publicity against Coca-Cola was intended to halt the paramilitary offensive. However, the union also hoped to draw international attention to systematic practices of multinational corporations and—as Correa put it during a meeting in April 2006—"to expose the empire behind the multinationals." It was in this spirit that the international boycott campaign was also conceived. The following year, while they were still waiting for a decision on whether or not the lawsuit could proceed, the Food Workers and their supporters held three "People's Public Hearings"—in Bogotá, Atlanta, and Geneva. At the final hearing, participants agreed on a series of demands that set out a political vision of what full reparation would entail. Alongside measures to protect workers' rights, they included numerous initiatives aimed at giving visibility to past events, including photographs and biographies of murdered trade unionists on all Coca-Cola bottles. The union also demanded a reversal of casualization facilitated through the repression, as well as the repair of all ecological damage in the company's areas of operation.[25] The demands were accompanied by an ultimatum: if Coke did not respond positively within a year, an international boycott would begin. In July 2003, while the Food Workers were still awaiting a decision from the court as to whether their case would be allowed to proceed, they launched the boycott.

The IUF versus the Colombian Food Workers

A week before the boycott began, the IUF issued a statement from its affiliates in condemnation. For the IUF, the campaign threatened to "damage . . . the credibility of all those seeking to secure union rights in the Coca-Cola system."[26] This was, in part, a response to misleading information regarding abuses against Coca-Cola workers in other countries that were not accurately reported by the Food Workers' supporters.[27] However, IUF affiliates also openly questioned whether there was really evidence of company involvement in some of the murders in Colombia, including that of Múnera.[28] In private correspondence, the IUF general-secretary acknowledged there was substance to at least some of the Food Workers' allegations.[29] However, as he put it when asked about the matter in a meeting with the campaign group UK Students against Coke, the disagreement was "not exclusively about the facts." What mattered was Coca-Cola's policy going forward.[30] For the IUF, the only "credible" objective was the pursuit of a mechanism for sustained engagement with the company, backed up by a "credible threat of action" where necessary.[31] Unlike the British NGOs that entered into dialogue with BP, the IUF did not approach corporations as well-meaning ethical actors. It did not disguise its assessment that Coca-Cola, like "most other transnational companies," would "seek to weaken an agreement, block an organizing drive or bust a union," given half a chance.[32] Despite this, however, the IUF felt that it was on the path to finding a mechanism for more sustained engagement. According to Ron Oswald, then the union's general-secretary, the IUF's previous campaign efforts with Guatemalan affiliates in the 1980s had forced Coca-Cola to do what it had previously said was impossible: to accept responsibility for the actions of its bottlers (who operate under a franchise system). Accordingly, the IUF issued a strong statement against Coca-Cola's defense in the legal case that it was not responsible for its bottlers.[33] Nevertheless, throughout the Colombian Food Workers' campaign, the IUF encouraged unions worldwide to oppose the boycott, dismissing the entire campaign as based on "sweeping, unsubstantiated allegations."[34]

The IUF's position was supported by many British unions representing Coca-Cola workers, all of whom acknowledged that they relied on the global union's expertise and had not investigated the allegations themselves.[35] This was due, in part, to a shared commitment to ideas of global social partnership. Brendan Barber, then the president of Britain's Trades Union Congress, was not only a prominent advocate of the idea that globalization could "made to work for everyone" by strengthening multilateral institutions and promoting decent labor standards in multinational corporations.[36] He was also the president of the British trade unions' NGO Justice for Colombia, which quickly began to oppose the boycott.[37] When students at British universities took up the task of persuading the National Union of Students (NUS) not to renew its purchasing agreement with Coca-Cola, the NUS purchasing consortium—NUS Services Limited—rejected a pro-boycott motion tabled by university student unions. Instead, they began a process of "constructive engagement" with Coca-Cola on the IUF's advice while leaders of the NUS national executive spoke out publicly against the boycott.[38] In the context of the dialogue that ensued, NUS Services asked Coca-Cola to commit to biannual meetings with the IUF to negotiate a global agreement on labor standards. In March 2005, Coca-Cola sat down with the IUF and signed a joint statement in which both parties committed to ongoing engagement on human rights and labor rights issues.[39] The IUF then claimed that this rendered the Colombian Food Workers' campaign superfluous: *if* the campaign did have a more sensible aim of getting Coca-Cola to introduce a "serious and accountable mechanism" of permanent assessment and discussion of its policies, then the IUF had "already moved on to the next stage" through engagement with the company.[40]

The intervention of the IUF was ultimately successful in derailing the boycott by undermining international support for the Food Workers. In Italy, one of the countries where the campaign was most active, several left-leaning municipalities had voted to boycott Coca-Cola and, in the run-up to the 2006 Winter Olympics in Turin, had refused to allow the Coke-sponsored Olympic torch to process through the areas under their jurisdiction.[41] To resolve the situation, Coca-Cola had agreed that a verification commission composed of Italian civil society groups could visit its Colombian bottling plants.[42] Just weeks later, however, Coca-Cola reneged on the agreement: the IUF and Coca-Cola invited the ILO to inspect the company's Colombian bottling plants *instead* of the proposed verification commission.[43] For the Colombian Food Workers, the prospect of an Italian verification commission had been significant gain for their campaign. The intense pressure on the company had at last generated the possibility of independent research that could confirm before international opinion that the abuses had taken place. The ILO, by contrast, can investigate complaints against companies only on a voluntary basis. As a result, the substitution of an independent commission with an ILO investigation was a significant blow for the Food Workers. In early April 2006, when I had coffee with Correa at the union's Bogotá headquarters, he was despondent. He feared that the union's allegations would be put to one side in favor of a box-ticking audit process. This, as I show, was a fear in which he was eventually proved correct.

On top of this, the campaign was now unraveling in Britain. A couple of weeks before, in March 2006, the question of whether NUS Services should renew its purchasing agreement with Coca-Cola had been put to a vote at the NUS annual convention. As a result of efforts to discredit the campaign by the NUS leadership and some British trade unionists, the motion to support the boycott had been lost by a narrow margin in favor of a countermotion that rejected the boycott in favor of ongoing "constructive engagement" with Coca-Cola. The countermotion also included a proposal that the NUS work in solidarity with Colombian trade unionists, students, and civil society through Justice for Colombia and the British Amicus, Transport and General Workers, and GMB unions.[44] In a particularly disturbing turn of events, a Colombian trade unionist who had been invited to speak at the conference by the anti-boycott lobby while visiting Britain with Justice for Colombia reported that his hosts had requested that he end his speech by asking students to vote for proposal for "solidarity with Colombia." He insisted that they had taken advantage of his lack of English and not told him that this included resolutions opposing the Coca-Cola boycott.[45] On hearing of the incident, his union wrote a letter confirming its support for the Food Workers' campaign.[46] However, by then the damage had been done. Many students subsequently reported that thinking they were hearing the position of the "Colombian trade union movement" had led them to withdraw their support and vote against the boycott.[47]

The campaign was thus in a substantially weaker position, and Correa was due to travel to the United States to meet the union's lawyers in a few days' time. The lawyers, for their part, were aware that the campaign could not continue indefinitely. On top of that, for technical and political reasons that I discuss in the next chapter, it appeared unlikely that the US courts would allow the Food Workers' case to go forward.[48] The lawyers thus moved quickly to secure a settlement. Four months later, I was in the union's Bogotá offices with members of the national executive committee when the proposal came through for a binding agreement with Coca-Cola that included a "non-disparagement" clause committing the union to stopping the international campaign. Given the state of the campaign, and the benefits of a potential settlement, the union reluctantly agreed to sign. However, in mid-2007 the Food Workers withdrew from the process, turning down a substantial financial compensation package because Coca-Cola's lawyers insisted that the settlement be conditional on an undertaking from the union never again to name Coca-Cola as responsible for the violence they had suffered. Had their aim been simply to secure financial remedy, the outcome would have been satisfactory. However, a campaign that sought to expose the empire behind the multinationals could never have been resolved with an obligation to keep quiet about past crimes.

The relationship between the IUF and Coca-Cola did yield some short-lived results. In stark contrast to Coca-Cola's earlier denial of responsibility for its franchisees' operations, all of the members of the IUF's negotiating team in the biannual meetings with Coca-Cola that began in 2005 represented workers contracted by franchisees within the bottling system from across the Asia Pacific, Latin America, North America, and Europe.[49] The IUF never signed a global framework agreement with the company, but it secured recognition of trade unions, as well as of a process by which its members could raise human rights concerns. By 2018, however, the Coca-Cola Company was, according to Oswald, reverting to the line that it was not responsible for the actions of its bottlers.[50] In June 2018, the IUF publicly declared Coca-Cola a "serial human rights offender" in several countries. Despite the IUF's having established a mechanism through which unions could inform the company of ongoing human rights violations, Coca-Cola had "failed to take any meaningful action to remedy the abuses." For the IUF, Coca-Cola's "systematic human rights due diligence failure" now made it "complicit in these abuses, and a rights abuser in its own right."[51]

Social Partnership in a Neoliberal World

The differences between the IUF and the Colombian Food Workers Union were, in part, tactical differences about the most effective way to improve working conditions. However, they were also differences regarding ends. The

Food Workers sought to draw attention to an empire given form through systemic violence. It sought not just to improve the conditions of workers, but to help build and strengthen grassroots movements against neoliberalism, capitalism, and imperialism. The IUF's more modest—and, it would say, more "credible"—goal was to secure decent labor conditions for workers in the Coca-Cola system. Although some campaigners denounced the IUF as simply "pro-company," the reality is more complex. As was the case in Guatemala, it was worker mobilizations supported by the IUF that eventually led Coca-Cola's bottler to recognize trade union rights in Pakistan via an agreement that followed intense negotiations among the IUF, the Turkish bottler operating in Pakistan, and Coca-Cola representatives from Atlanta. The struggle in Pakistan was, in turn, inspired by the success of workers at Unilever who, supported by the IUF, had managed to transform a situation in which only twenty-two of some eight hundred workers had permanent contracts and a union recognized by management, creating many hundreds of jobs and a huge increase in union membership. The relationship with Unilever, like that with Coca-Cola, never included a global framework agreement. However, whether or not an official agreement exists, the IUF is clear that only the relation of forces between workers and the company can prevent the company from withdrawing from the agreement or from its relationship with the global union.[52] In this regard, the IUF approach represents the sort of method that scholars of global framework agreements have identified as most likely to achieve the type of agreement that can be effective on the ground.[53] Moreover, although the IUF was the first global union to sign a global framework agreement, it was also the first to put a moratorium on such agreements during an internal discussion between 2009 and 2010. This internal discussion was focused on the risk identified here: that corporate recognition that workers have rights could, in isolation, easily supplant mechanisms for ensuring that workers can access those rights. Since then, the IUF has moved toward making the signing of agreements conditional on the implementation of the agreement across a multinational's production networks and supply chains—even if this makes a global framework agreement harder to achieve.[54] To describe the IUF as simply "pro-company" fails to capture not only its support for its affiliates' struggles, but also its efforts to prevent multinationals from being able to use agreements for merely cosmetic purposes.

Nevertheless, any assessment of the IUF's approach to promoting "decent work" must confront the fact that the global union spearheaded a campaign against the Colombian Food Workers. It might be tempting to see this stance as a product of the internal dynamics of trade unionism in Colombia. Opponents of the Food Workers' campaign frequently made reference to the supposed anti-boycott position of other unions in Coca-Cola, with no mention made within this game of numbers of the fact that the Food Workers Union still outnumbered those affiliated to all these other unions put together, or that the other unions were IUF affiliates established explicitly as less militant alternatives to the Food Workers.[55] It was also often claimed that the largest Colombian workers' confederation, the Central Unitaria de Trabajadores (Central Union of Workers [CUT]), opposed the Food Workers' campaign when this was not, in fact, the case.[56] Yet without knowledge of the situation on the ground, it was easy for the Colombian Food Workers' struggle to fall foul of the abstract proxies so common within the discourse of Western labor unions. In their efforts to deter support for the Food Workers, the IUF and British unions made repeated appeals to the supposed position of a "Colombian and international labor movement," which was presented as more authentic, and more representative of the workers of the world, than "the small union that has called for a boycott of Coca-Cola."[57] Justice for Colombia, the British trade unions' NGO, was—in a double statement of coherence—stated (again falsely) to be "the only UK solidarity organization" that "the Colombian union movement" recognized.[58] The proclaimed "unanimity" of the anti-boycott views of unions representing Coca-Cola workers in the United Kingdom, Ireland, and United States could then be said to represent the position of a coherent "Colombian and international labor movement," of which the IUF was the authentic voice.[59] Yet this "Colombian and international labor movement" was a fabrication, a sign that aimed to be the thing it stood for. It was, like the waxwork model of a painting that Umberto Eco describes in *Travels in Hyperreality*, "a real copy," offered so that the observer will no longer feel any need for the now almost invisible original fresco (the actual struggles of actual human beings).[60] In reality, the positions for and against the Food Workers' campaign represented deep political divisions between unions who still espoused anti-imperialist and anticapitalist politics and those who had adopted the agenda of trying to "make globalization work." These divisions, entangled as they were with colonial legacies of state terrorism and armed dispossession, are precisely what is missed when we attempt to derive the politics of struggle from an abstract account of challenges facing "labor" or "the international trade union movement."

The Food Workers' campaign took place in the context of trade union genocide on an enormous scale. One consequence of this was that many workers sought to engage in forms of self-organization that did not involve social movement organizing or any overt challenge to the neoliberal economic model. The result, as the CUT's director of human rights put it while we were having coffee together at the time of the boycott, is that "many trade unions in Colombia have lost their ideas; they no longer even have a position against the paramilitaries."[61] The IUF was represented in Colombia at that time by the president of the Sindicato Nacional de Trabajadores de la Industria Agropecuaria (SINTRAINAGRO), an agricultural union renowned for having formed a "social pact" with banana plantation bosses, the military, and paramilitaries in the region of Urabá.[62] Thanks to Chiquita Brands' generous funding and provision of weapons, Urabá was a region central to the development of paramilitarism. By entering into an alliance with the perpetrators of genocide, the union's leadership was able to achieve limited improvements in banana workers' conditions. Meanwhile, however, members of the union who rejected the alliance were gradually eliminated from the union or killed by the paramilitaries with whom the union's leadership was in alliance.[63] It was in Urabá, too, that paramilitaries drove the Food Workers Union from Coca-Cola's Carepa bottling plant, killing union leaders and then rounding up union members to tell them that they also would be killed if they did not sign letters of resignation printed on company computers and collected by company management. In the aftermath of these events, a new union—the IUF-affiliated Sindicato Nacional de Trabajadores de la Industria de los Alimentos y Bebidas de Colombia (National Union of Workers in the Food and Drinks Industry of Colombia [SICO])—was established at the bottling plant with the help of SINTRAINAGRO. When asked about this at a meeting with British students supporting the Coca-Cola boycott, IUF general-secretary Ron Oswald stated that he considered it "courageous" of SINTRAINAGRO "to have turned to the state for support."[64] The IUF's position was that it was possible— even in contexts such as Urabá—for unions to "build a framework of rights. It was greatly dangerous, but possible," as Oswald put it later. As far as the IUF was concerned, the Food Workers' opposition to its affiliates and public denunciation of the Urabá "social pact" only contributed to this danger: "If you label a union as being close to the paramilitaries, you put a target on their back."[65]

Oswald's description of the IUF's Urabá affiliate as having "turned to the state for support" might sound like a disingenuous way of describing an alliance with brutal right-wing death squads. It is, in fact, insightful when we consider that these groups were never mere armed mercenaries. They were—and remain—deeply political organizations, often espousing a development discourse that has reflected that of the government and international institutions.[66] Carlos Castaño, one of the leaders of Colombia's largest paramilitary group, the Autodefensas Unidas de Colombia, described a three-phase paramilitary model along these lines. The first phase was the "liberation" of large zones from the insurgency and their supporters (anyone who raises a voice in dissent being counted as a supporter) and imposing processes of land concentration and an authoritarian social structure. Phase two was "bringing wealth to the region" through "development" projects such as employment creation, the building of schools and health centers, technical assistance, and loans for production, all "carried out with the knowledge and legalization of government bodies such as the Colombian Institute for Agrarian Reform." The third phase was "legitimation and consolidation": "Once potentially subversive elements of the population have been eliminated and their support bases destroyed," the Colombian sociologist Libardo Sarmiento wrote in 1996, "the paramilitaries believe they will cease to be a 'loose cannon of the State.' . . . They will have put in place the necessary structures for the victorious expansion of national and multinational capitalism and the 'modernizing' State will be able to install itself with the co-operation of the private sector, non-governmental organisations and the 'organized' communities."[67]

While Sarmiento made these observations in relation to another area central to the development of paramilitarism—the Magdalena Medio region—it is through a study of Urabá that Humberto Cárdenas and Álvaro Marín highlight the extent to which paramilitary violence has been accompanied by a humanistic and conservationist discourse, propagated by the United Nations Educational, Scientific, and Cultural Organization (UNESCO), the UN Food and Agriculture Association, the World Bank, international NGOs, and multinational corporations. This is the logic that Cárdenas and Marín denote "defending life by sowing death."[68] Workers' ability to build a minimal, but still not insignificant, "framework of rights" is entirely consistent with this overall scenario. The IUF affiliate at Coca-Cola's Carepa bottling plant, SICO, has not achieved anything like the conditions that the Food Workers Union achieved before the paramilitary onslaught. But it has improved their working conditions, eventually succeeding in converting temporary contracts into permanent ones, which is hard to imagine possible had no union been established to replace the Food Workers.[69] None of this is anomalous to the consolidation stage of paramilitary strategy, and the IUF's role in the process is comparable to that of other international bodies.

However, we also need to be clear that none of this reflects an entirely Colombia-specific phenomenon. It would be a mistake to view the IUF's opposition to the Coca-Cola campaign as solely the product of internal dynamics in Colombia. On the contrary, state-backed terror in Colombia represents a particularly brutal means of fostering the social and institutional conditions of a competitive market, akin to the approach that Hayek praised in Chile.[70] Seen in this light, a "social pact" among trade unionists, paramilitaries, state institutions, and business is a far from counterintuitive phenomenon. On the contrary, it is another manifestation of what Boaventura de Sousa Santos and Mauricio García Villegas call social fascism—an authoritarian configuration of power in which formally recognized rights are ousted and replaced by nonstate legislators in the context of a neoliberal international investment regime. For Santos and García Villegas, as we saw in chapter 1, Colombia is the supreme example of these globalized dynamics: "the reverse of modernity's social contract."[71] Across the world, however, trade union bodies have sought to accommodate themselves to neoliberalism, not always through alliances with far-right armed groups, but through the wider agenda of "making globalization work," promoting "decent work" in the context of a violent international rule of law that has made access to once recognized rights impossible.

The divergent positions of the Colombian Food Workers and the IUF with regard to this wider agenda are reflected in their distinct approaches to addressing past abuses. For the Colombian Food Workers, the demand for *reparación integral* not only included reversal of the labor casualization made possible through extreme violence. It was—as we have seen—inseparable from a series of demands focused on giving visibility to what had already occurred. This public recognition of past abuses was fundamental to the union's struggle and to its wider opposition to the empire behind the multinationals. The IUF's approach to past violations of human rights, by contrast, was more focused on "a remedy that establishes a space in which people can exercise those rights."[72] It is important to clarify here that this does not imply overlooking the past: the IUF has been outspoken about the problem of impunity and repeatedly insisted that the individual perpetrators of abuses against trade unionists should face prosecution.[73] The IUF has likewise long supported moves toward a strong international regulatory framework on corporations and human rights and has never viewed the negotiation of agreements with companies as a substitute for this.[74] Nevertheless, while the IUF is clear that such a regulatory framework would strengthen the position of unions with regard to multinational corporations, the "best concrete mechanism" that it considers available in the absence of this is to establish a process of dialogue and negotiation with the company. Finding a mechanism for dialogue was, in practice, difficult to reconcile with the Food Workers' emphasis on public recognition of corporate complicity in past abuses. Indeed, the IUF's support for an ILO investigation as an alternative to the Italian verification commission coheres with this order of priorities. The ILO's Tripartite Declaration on

Multinational Enterprises makes no formal provision for allegations against companies to be investigated, which means that multinationals volunteer for such investigations only "where the reputational damage to the company so requires."[75] Thus, as Correa had predicted, the ILO did not address the Food Workers' allegations. Instead, the investigation considered matters such as whether collective agreements with workers existed, whether a code of ethics was in place, what percentage of workers was subcontracted, and so on. While the report noted the comparatively disadvantageous conditions of subcontracted workers and evidence of "a tendency to encourage workers" against unionizing, no mention was made of the Food Workers' allegations of murders, threats, attacks on family members, and locking up workers in hotels and forcing them to resign, included in the Food Workers' own complaint to the ILO.[76] What the ILO actually conducted was less an investigation than an audit, in which allegations of gross human rights violations fell beyond the purview of its method.

Indeed, the focus on negotiating agreements with companies has meant that the IUF has been drawn into protecting corporate reputations on more than one occasion. In 1999, union leaders in Guatemala were attacked by armed men following the announcement of sackings of more than nine hundred workers. These sackings were the result of three banana plantations having been sold by a Fresh Del Monte Produce subsidiary, in violation of the collective bargaining agreement with the union. A court in Guatemala later determined that the narco-paramilitary Mendoza gang, to whom Del Monte had sold one of the plantations, was behind attacks in which union leaders were locked up at gunpoint and forced to resign from the union. In the face of ongoing threats of violence, the IUF affiliate representing the workers requested international support. According to Oswald, the IUF then mobilized affiliates around the world to put maximum pressure on the company, eventually bringing Del Monte to the negotiating table.

The outcome was an agreement that guaranteed that as many of the workers who wanted to do so could return to work at the plantations and remain members of the local union. The agreement also protected the union's right to represent them and bargain on their behalf. However, leaders of the union had been forced into internal exile in Guatemala and could not safely return to the region where the plantation was based. The IUF succeeded in pushing Del Monte far beyond the terms of its initial offer (to provide employment in other Central and Latin American countries), enabling these union leaders to relocate to the United States and train with the IUF affiliate in the hospitality industry as union organizers, with financial support from Del Monte. As part of the final settlement, however, the Guatemalan union—and therefore the IUF—agreed that neither it nor the IUF had specific evidence that the violence against the workers was "instigated or organized by the company at its corporate level."[77]

Because the agreement with the multinational was signed by the Guatemalan union and the IUF, rather than by the individual workers, lawyers were still able to file a lawsuit against Del Monte after the workers arrived in the United States (again, this was ultimately unsuccessfully for technical reasons).[78] However, while the Colombian Food Workers' campaign was underway, the IUF actively sought to prevent Coca-Cola from being subjected to further litigation in relation to ongoing abuses of workers in Guatemala, which included illegal sackings and threats to the workers' lives. In April 2005, just weeks after Coca-Cola signed the agreement with the IUF, armed men forced their way into the home of the union activist José Armando Palacios, threatening to kill his wife and children if Palacios continued with his union activities. Less than a month later, when it was clear that he would not be intimidated into giving up his union work, Palacios was fired without cause from his job at the Coca-Cola syrup plant in Guatemala City. Palacios spent the next eight months fighting for reinstatement and rallying support for nine other members of his union who had been illegally fired from a Coca-Cola bottling plant owned by the same company.[79]

The IUF's Oswald had been seeking to secure the reinstatement of Palacios and other workers, as well as a security package for Palacios and guarantees with respect to union rights. However, when some of the other workers accepted "higher than average severance packages," Oswald reluctantly concluded that reinstatement for Palacios was no longer an option and that what remained was to address Palacios's situation.[80] In early 2006, while he was in hiding after narrowly escaping an assassination attempt, Palacios was approached by a lawyer acting on behalf of Coca-Cola and asked to "name his price" for "dropping all legal claims against Coca Cola and agreeing to maintain permanent silence about what the company and its bottler had done to him."[81] Palacios, who refused the offer, remained in hiding and was hoping to flee to the United States. Oswald now anticipated a "major complication." While Coca-Cola had not raised the matter specifically, Oswald was concerned that the company's lawyers might "question whether the possibility exists that, should [Palacios] leave for the US on some kind of negotiated agreement but then be approached by a certain DC-based lawyer with promises of significant sums of 'settlement' money, they might face another legal suit."[82] The "DC-based lawyer" was Terry Collingsworth of the International Labor Rights Fund, who was already acting against Del Monte on behalf of the exiled Guatemalan banana workers, as well as against Coca-Cola on behalf of the Colombian Food Workers Union. Oswald expressed this concern in an email to Bob Perillo, who at the time was the Latin America liaison for the US Labor Education in the Americas Project (US/LEAP), an NGO with close links to the US trade union movement. Perillo later stated in an open letter that the directors of US/LEAP succumbed to the pressure from the IUF and "found a near-perfect solution to the problem of how to protect Coca Cola from legal action," by persuading Palacios to accept a Michigan-based lawyer (who, he said, had admitted that she lacked the capacity to actually sue a large corporation) to negotiate with Coca-Cola on his behalf.[83] (Perillo by then had resigned from his job on ethical grounds because, in a remarkable conflict of interest, one of the board members of US/LEAP was also acting as a consultant to Coca-Cola.)

All of this is illustrative of the profound limitations of agreements negotiated between global unions and multinationals (whether consolidated in a global framework agreement or not). Unlike the regime of social partnership that characterized postwar welfare states, agreements between global unions and multinationals are little more than unstable private agreements. We must be alert to the warning that Ian Bruff issues in a discussion of authoritarian neoliberalism: "Institutions that are viewed (by way of their genesis in previous eras) as a form of social protection against the often-wrenching nature of socioeconomic restructuring could well be the means by which such change establishes itself."[84] During the decade or so after the Food Workers' campaign, IUF affiliates had a mechanism through which they could raise human rights concerns directly with Coca-Cola. Ultimately, however, in the absence of any binding legal framework, the whole arrangement depends on the balance of forces between unions and the company. In a globalized legal environment that stacks the odds in favor of corporations, it is of little surprise that a global union might be compelled to make trade-offs in pursuit of some sort of framework within which workers can exercise their rights. While trade-offs might appear prudent where they allow substantial gains in terms of jobs, working conditions, or measures to protect individuals' safety, the short-lived nature of the IUF's successes with Coca-Cola illustrates the precarity of these arrangements. While the IUF insists that such agreements should not displace the longer-term goal of binding regulations on corporations, the question that needs to be asked is whether negotiated agreements, premised (at least in part) on corporations' desires to protect their reputations, might not in fact undermine this longer-term goal.

Encasing Wealth

Bruff's warning highlights the risk that what looks like means of establishing social protection are in fact means of what Quinn Slobodian calls "encasing" capital.[85] The entire neoliberal project, as I emphasize throughout this book, was focused not on the market per se but on redesigning states, laws, and other institutions to keep wealth in the hands of a minority deemed capable of using it, and to secure an international division of labor after the demise of older colonial institutions. Repetition of the categories of social partnership without engagement with the legal and moral aspects of the neoliberal project readily masks these dynamics. This is a problem beyond the pursuit of global framework agreements. The ILO reaffirmed its commitment to "social partnership" between capital and labor when it set out the Decent Work Agenda.[86] Benjamin Selwyn identifies the same institutionalist inheritance in more recent scholarship coming out of the ILO, according to which minimum labor standards and strong worker representation are said to "contribute to successful resource allocation, leading to rising firm profitability and more rapid economic development."[87] The emphasis of the Decent Work Agenda is on how workers can benefit from increased firm-level competitiveness, leading researchers within and beyond the ILO to reframe the whole question of workers' rights in terms of "social upgrading," directly linking improvements in workers' conditions to corporate innovation.[88] Nevertheless, when we look beyond the institutionalist rhetoric of social partnership and mutual gains, the rationale behind the ILO Decent Work Agenda reveals clear synergies with the original neoliberal concerns noted earlier. It is noteworthy that the World Bank now shares the ILO's view that capitalist development can be fueled by the existence of strong unions. Likewise, the World Bank's International Finance Corporation demands that its funded projects comply with the ILO's core labor standards. Yet the International Finance Corporation simultaneously defines "almost all labour regulations . . . as undue impediments to 'doing business.'"[89] For Selwyn, these sorts of dynamics indicate the vulnerability to co-optation of the Decent Work Agenda into a post-Washington agenda that implies, in Paul Cammack's terms, "locking the poor into the market." "Effective unions," Cammack underscores, "eliminate the need for large-scale state regulation and intervention, and help firms to extract more surplus value from workers; they do not distort labour markets, or protect jobs."[90] If we shift the lens, however, we find far more at play here than the risk of "co-optation" of an otherwise institutionalist agenda.

Within the Decent Work Agenda itself, the rationale for workers' rights is presented in terms of the needs of a competitive market as opposed to the legal norms and state regulation through which proponents of social partnership traditionally sought to "re-embed the market."[91] This was explicit when the ILO director general first set out the Decent Work Agenda in 1999, insisting that "market forces," including "social preferences" that might influence markets, are more important to economic outcomes for both workers and companies than "mediation through social actors, legal norms or State intervention."[92] Yet economic outcomes are largely determined by a regime of international economic law that was designed, in accordance with Hayek's own ideas of "free markets as socially embedded," to encase wealth where it could not be touched by democratic legislatures and "to deepen the power of competition to shape and direct human life."[93] Workers' rights reconfigured in terms of the needs of a competitive market are not just entirely consistent with the neoliberal encasement of wealth within an international legal order designed to privilege the rights of competition and investment. They also represent a reconfiguration of workers' rights away from hard law and state regulation in what might be considered an innovative addition to original neoliberal concerns to create the social, moral, and institutional foundations for a competitive market order. Agreements between global unions and multinational corporations play out within this same terrain. The IUF also spoke the language of institutionalism when it put forward its charter of demands to Coca-Cola in the spirit of mutual gains, arguing that "decent labour relations are necessary for a successful, sustainable business."[94] Yet in the absence of the social law and labor law that characterized the postwar social pact, rights are, in effect, privatized, made contingent on what a global union can negotiate directly with the multinational company.

Thinking about workers' rights in terms of abstract categories ("labor," "firms," "market forces," "competitiveness," and so on) obscures all of this. With the challenges facing "labor" read off an account of abstract and impersonal economic forces, the world economy appears, in André Drainville's words, as "a thing on a separate plane," something to be grasped in its totality in advance of consideration of how subjects are produced within it.[95] Abstract categories such as "labor," "the workers of the world," "the international trade union movement," and so on take the stage as "false subjects caught up in false universalities," "cosmopolitan proxies" that substitute actually existing subjects bound up in the realities of place and context.[96]

This abstract political-economic thought also obscures its own racism by making racism appear to be a separate "political" phenomenon rather than a constitutive part of the various socially and legally constructed and regulated ways in which labor is subordinated to capital.[97] In Britain, for instance, colonialism shaped the labor movement from at least the late nineteenth century, when cooperative labor organization was incorporated into efforts to defend the British imperial order while nonwhite colonial subject populations were deemed lacking in the qualities associated with self-organized English workingmen.[98] In the interwar period, elite concern with the promotion of disciplined trade unions was absorbed directly into colonial policy. Britain's Trades Union Congress even joined the Colonial Labour Advisory Committee, sending officials to the colonies "to help focus unionism strictly on wage improvement and the amelioration of work conditions"—albeit without the expectation of the political enfranchisement that their white counterparts enjoyed.[99] In continuity with prewar policy, the Labour government that implemented universal welfare promoted trade unions and limited local self-governance in its African colonies without so much as a gesture toward parliamentary rule.[100] The ease with which British trade unions accepted the authority of the IUF regarding the "unsubstantiated" nature of the Colombian Food Workers' allegations reflects this history, just as it reflects a shared common sense about the challenges facing "labor" that occlude this history.

With attention to actual ways in which labor is subordinated to capital substituted by "false subjects" inhabiting "false universalities," it is easy to miss the fact that, within the logic of the framework agreement, the worker as the subject of market-rationalized "rights" is no longer the worker as citizen. Unlike (predominantly white male) workers in the context of postwar social partnership, workers as subjects of these precarious rights are not citizens protected by legal norms. Despite ongoing attachment to institutionalist ideas of mutual gains and partnership between capital and labor, rights as *external* (legal, regulatory) limits on what can be done in the name of economic necessity disappear. Workers come to hold rights exclusively on the basis of how much corporations' extraction of surplus value is aided by recognizing those rights. The ground for recognition of workers' rights is internal to the logic of economic force (to be found, for example, in the "social preferences" of consumers who might desire that companies treat their workers well). When required by "market forces," workers can still be allowed to die with impunity. This may occur slowly, through inadequate safety and bodily exhaustion. However, in contexts such as Colombia, where colonial legacies of exception shape the subordination of labor to capital to an extreme, the economic politics of letting die readily morphs into direct killing for demanding more substantive rights.

The Politics of Truth

It is in this context that we should understand the Colombian Food Workers' desire to expose the empire behind the multinationals. I do not wish to suggest that the campaign tactics of the Food Workers and their supporters were beyond critique. There are, of course, limitations to a consumer boycott. In the United States, the consciousness-raising aspirations of the campaign were often submerged beneath a discourse of ethical consumption and sensationalist story of "Killer Coke," as if the latter were an aberration set against the standard conduct of multinationals.[101] This problem was less pronounced in Britain and elsewhere, where the campaign was promoted by activists with closer links to Colombian social organizations. It was still not absent, however, and I was involved in numerous discussions with the Food Workers and with British, German, Swiss, and Italian members of la Red de Hermandad throughout the campaign regarding how to raise awareness of the wider issues and of the nature of the Food Workers' struggle. Litigation also proved a Janus-faced instrument, given the inadmissibility of the Food Workers' understanding of reparation within legal narratives that approached remedy as a financial transaction. Yet despite all of this, the Food Workers did succeed in creating a great deal of awareness internationally about corporate and state-backed violence, in Colombia and beyond.

If all that had been at stake for Coca-Cola workers was improvement in their pay and conditions in the short term, then it could be argued that the IUF made the correct assessment of what was mostly likely to generate benefits for workers across the Coca-Cola system (at least, until the company reverted to the idea that it was not responsible for its bottling plants). It may also be that such agreements do currently represent unions' "best concrete mechanisms," in the absence of enforceable regulations. However, the question still has to be asked: At what price do such mechanisms come if they require global unions to agree to measures that will protect companies' reputations? At what price do they come if they inhibit remedy in the sense that the Food Workers understood it: as entailing provisions focused on public recognition of the multinational's responsibility for what happened in the past? Within the parameters of global social partnership, there is a risk that questions of what happened and who is responsible fade into the background. We see this in the IUF's public dismissal of the allegations against Coca-Cola (despite recognizing in private that at least some of those allegations had substance). We see it even more clearly in the attitude of the British students who entered into "constructive engagement" with Coca-Cola, approaching the allegations as, if not unsubstantiated, then at least irrelevant to strategy and trivializing the Food Workers' allegations with the claim that they did not "want to be judge and jury."[102] There was, after all, no final authority to issue a judgment on what may have occurred.

This stance was only reinforced by the request that an ILO audit replace the more judicial-style investigation of the proposed Italian verification commission. If audit mechanisms can quantify and standardize suitably, then it is unlikely that the life-and-death reality of work and struggle will even register with consumers to impact the "social preferences" and "market forces" hailed in the Decent Work Agenda as determinants of workers' rights. The actual effects of policy decisions are covered over, separated from actual lives and deaths, serving to maintain the collective fiction that companies are socially responsible in a manner similar to that of the various corporate, sector-based, and global codes of conduct with their associated means of measuring compliance through managerial techniques of audit. The late Mark Fisher captured these dynamics with the term *market Stalinism*. Within the managerial logics that have come to characterize neoliberal governance, symbols of achievement come to matter more than actual achievement. Initiatives matter only insofar as they register at the level of auditable appearance. A short-circuiting occurs, so that work is more focused on generating and massaging auditable representations.[103] Here, too, in other words, we find the shift in the function of human rights that Radha D'Souza identifies: a conversion of rights from judiciable principles into "normative standards to guide administrative action."[104]

We must consider the Food Workers' refusal to accept a settlement from Coca-Cola in this light. Some of the union's supporters asked why. The campaign was exhausted, and the proposed settlement agreement would not have stopped its members from speaking out about future abuses. Yet it was through their refusal to surrender truth about the past that the Food Workers held open the possibility of unraveling a neatly stitched-up world, in which the profitmaking activities of corporations are the basis of rights. Whether human rights litigation against corporations has any prospect of contributing to this end is the question to which I turn in the next chapter.

elusive justice

Capital, Impunity,
and Counterlegality

CHAPTER FOUR

Some years ago, I worked briefly at the London headquarters of Amnesty International. I still remember the frustration of a senior member of the Latin America team when supporters asked why they should be demanding that human rights abuses from almost thirty years ago be investigated and the perpetrators prosecuted. "People just don't understand the significance of impunity," he grumbled. Impunity, understood as the systematic failure to bring perpetrators to justice, is a core concept for the international human rights movement. The 1990s did not just see the promotion of privatized human rights by corporations but also a move by human rights nongovernmental organizations (NGOs) such as Amnesty away from a focus on naming and shaming and the release of political prisoners toward "fighting impunity."[1] "Anti-impunity" relies on the idea that would-be perpetrators will be deterred from committing abuses if they believe they will be prosecuted in the future. If we do not want crimes against humanity, war crimes, and genocide to recur, the argument goes, then individual criminal liability must be established and those responsible for these crimes must be held to account. With the establishment of the International Criminal Court under the Rome Statute of 1998, the fight against impunity began to be consolidated as a dominant view of global justice.[2] Thus, while corporate codes of conduct and other compliance-based mechanisms were configuring human rights as goals to guide administrative action, we must also bear in mind that—at the level of individual liability—human rights were simultaneously being reasserted as judiciable principles.

Over the intervening years, the anti-impunity and corporate responsibility agendas have merged, with campaigners making increasing reference to a problem of "corporate impunity." In 2014, the United Nations Human Rights Council adopted a resolution committing it to developing a binding human rights mechanism for corporations, reigniting old Third Worldist demands for the corporate obligations that had been smothered by the Ruggie agenda (see chapter 2).[3] The treaty was heavily opposed by Western states and the corporate lobby. As a result, successive drafts have disappointed campaigners. Nevertheless, the turn to corporate impunity raises questions that are as relevant to the demand for binding human rights obligations to be placed on corporations as they are to the Colombian Food Workers Union's lawsuit against Coca-Cola or Gilberto Torres's proceedings against BP. What does it mean to tackle corporate impunity in the context of an international legal order designed to maximize the profits of corporate investors? Furthermore, is this reassertion of human rights as justiciable principles strategically useful for social movements seeking to challenge corporate power?

The problem with the prevailing anti-impunity discourse was summed up by the director of research for the Colombian Food Workers Union, Carlos Olaya, when we were catching up over coffee at the union's Bogotá headquarters shortly before Christmas 2014. The Colombian government was by then in peace negotiations with the Fuerzas Armadas Revolucionarias de Colombia (Revolutionary Armed Forces of Colombia [FARC]) guerrillas and had undertaken to create a transitional justice mechanism that, the union feared, would only entrench impunity for state crimes. When our conversation turned to the question of what it meant to fight impunity, however, Olaya underlined the limits of a focus on the culpable individual as a perpetrator of human rights abuse, saying, "Are we simply to prosecute this general or that minister who gave the order? Are they really the ones responsible? Of course, they have part of the responsibility. But the oligarchic families won't be taken before the tribunal. Nor will the shareholders of the transnational corporations that made this possible. So what are we talking about? We would have to prosecute an entire class."

As I show in more detail in the next two sections of this chapter, the exclusive focus on the responsible individual reflects a model of criminal justice designed precisely to prevent the harm caused by capitalism from being addressed as a justiciable wrong. What is more, these problems are amplified when it comes to attempts to address corporate impunity. The corporation is a legal construct designed precisely to ensure that owners and beneficiaries of corporate activities escape liability. As we saw in chapter 3, the payment of financial compensation to victims is the main way that the courts understand remedy in cases of corporate human rights abuse—normally with the sort of confidentiality agreement that compelled the Colombian Food Workers to turn down a settlement from Coca-Cola. Contrary to dominant human rights narratives, "impunity" cannot be counterpoised to legality. Still less can it be counterposed to "justice" as understood by the law.

Some would argue on this basis that the Food Workers' attempt at litigation against Coca-Cola was a mistake. The legal scholar Grietje Baars, for instance, rejects "cause lawyering" against companies as a neocolonial practice that serves to domesticate class struggle. Baars considers efforts to persuade victims to bring lawsuits to be akin to the attempts of nineteenth-century corporate colonizers to "spread capitalist law."[4] Nevertheless, what is clear from Olaya's comments, against the background of the Food Workers' use of litigation, is that those seeking to use the law to hold companies "to account" for abuses may have sophisticated analyses of the limitations of the law, yet they nevertheless seek to use the law strategically within wider processes of struggle. This brings into relief the question that I address in the second part of this chapter: How, and on what terms, might it be possible to use human rights law without undermining wider struggles against capital and against the legal order underpinning corporate power?

As I was mulling over this question in the months after my conversation with Olaya, I was asked to spend a week on a speaking tour with Gilberto Torres, the former leader of the Colombian Oil Workers Union whose kidnapping and torture at the hands of paramilitaries I discussed earlier in this book. In June 2015, lawyers acting for Torres had filed a case against BP in the High Court in London. In November of that year, Torres visited Britain to launch a campaign that sought to link his case directly to the broader dynamics of structural injustice that had given rise to his kidnapping: the murders of almost 2,500 others living around the oilfields, and the plunder and ecological devastation that had destroyed a peasant way of life. During our road trip, and in the various pubs and bars in the cities we visited that week, Torres and I repeatedly came back to the question of what it means to use the law strategically in these circumstances. We came to the conclusion that, while there was an implicit understanding—at least in our own circles—of the violence of legality and its implications for attempts to address corporate impunity, this had not been subject to sustained collective discussion. We therefore decided to get some funding for a series of workshops with social movement leaders and lawyers on just this theme, an effort that Torres, at our first Bogotá workshop in 2017, billed as an exercise in "building collective critical thought."

The second half of this chapter draws heavily on that process. It links the reflections offered in the workshops with Colombian social movement leaders and lawyers to my analysis of an "alternative justice" mechanism in which I was involved while I was living and working in Colombia: the session of the Permanent Peoples' Tribunal on Transnational Corporations and the Rights of Peoples that was held between 2006 and 2008. Through attention to these struggles invoking human rights I consider how social movements have made strategic use of law to highlight the colonial and capitalist underpinnings of dominant legal narratives while also using legal argument as a site of normative innovation. Rather than seeking "justice" within the terms of the law, these strategic uses of law should be understood as part of an ongoing struggle to expose the violence of the legal order and to rethink legality "from below"—by challenging the understanding of the human subject at the heart of modern law and providing alternative parameters of legibility for the harm caused by capitalism.

"Justice" Is Not the Other of Impunity

In chapter 1, I considered two broad constellations of meaning around the term *rule of law*. One centered on rejecting arbitrary power and defending the individual against tyranny; the other centered on protecting private property and the existence of a deeply unequal division of wealth. A concern with defending individuals against arbitrary power was the founding impetus of international human rights NGOs such as Amnesty International. Amnesty's early campaigns, Christine Schwöbel-Patel writes, "were to a great extent directed toward *releasing* political prisoners: amnesty, not fighting impunity, was the primary objective."[5] The shift toward anti-impunity in the 1990s can also be seen to reflect a concern with a rule of law that applies equal protections and penalties to everyone, including the perpetrators of human rights abuse. However, it also needs to be understood in more direct relation to the other constellation of meaning around *rule of law*. It is significant that the embrace of anti-impunity coincided with the foundation of the World Trade Organization, which was itself the product of the counteroffensive against Third Worldism by followers of Friedrich Hayek that sought to reclaim the idea of rule of law as an enforcer of private property and competition and human rights as the rights of property and investment. The strengthening of the judiciary and "access to courts across frontiers" was central to this redefinition of *rule of law*.[6] This, as Schwöbel-Patel emphasizes, not only paved the way for a global structure of courts and quasi-judicial mechanisms all claiming to speak on behalf of humanity; it was also aligned with the rise of anti-impunity and the emphasis on individual accountability—a significant move away from human rights as challenging state power.[7] Schwöbel-Patel thus extends Slobodian's analysis of neoliberalism as a legal-institutional order by highlighting the role of the anti-impunity vision of global justice in further "encasing the market."[8]

Schwöbel-Patel analyzes in depth how the International Criminal Court (ICC) has marketized a particular vision of "global justice" that relies on racialized narratives of good and evil and cements the integration of criminal and trade law.[9] As Tor Krever also underscores, the ICC's "selective and highly-politicized interventions" have dovetailed neatly with imperial agendas while at the same time helping institutionalize the impunity enjoyed by those acting on behalf of powerful Western states.[10] Indeed, Krever highlights the continuities between the anti-impunity agenda taken up by Western powers at the end of the Cold War and the problematic application of law at the Nuremberg Trials, often hailed as the founding moment of the battle against impunity. Despite being the first time in history that individuals were held liable for international crimes, at Nuremberg "the principles of valid law, impartially and legally established jurisdiction were trampled underfoot, along with basic matters such as *habeas corpus*, the right to appeal and the admissibility of evidence." The trials were little more than show trials, with indictments that included "newly minted crimes—'war of aggression,' 'crimes against humanity'—that breached the principle of *nullem crimen, nulla poena sine lege* (no crime, no punishment in the absence of law), amounting to *ex post facto* criminalization" while the victors were not only granted impunity but cast as the defenders of peace and humanity.[11]

There is a risk, however, that by homing in on the ICC's selective application of law, against the principle of impartiality, the law itself gets off the hook. There are deeper problems with dominant narratives about impunity, rooted in the legal concepts, categories, and forms of reasoning that have been established to hold actors responsible for harmful acts, which Olaya summed up so poignantly during our conversation over coffee in 2014. Because of the focus on individual perpetrators (this general or that minister who gave the order to kill), the responsibility of the beneficiaries of the armed imposition of a neoliberal model is "disappeared," made to vanish without trace.[12] In the aftermath of large-scale human rights abuse there is often what Scott Veitch refers to as a staggering "asymmetry between extensive suffering and findings of responsibility for it," precisely because of how "legal categories for establishing responsibility also enable responsibilities to be disaggregated, dispersed and—crucially—in the process, disavowed."[13] The combination of law's normative claim to correctness, the enforceability of legal standards, and the priority given to law in normative social hierarchies all work to "establish the ability of law to operate as a key mode of organising responsibilities" and "*simultaneously* allow for and legitimise the proliferation of their clandestine counterpart: irresponsibility."[14] Put bluntly, law can function "as a kind of amnesiac, a guarantor of total impunity" precisely because of how it can dominate the terms on which responsibility can be made possible."[15]

The focus on criminal liability of individuals reflects one of the foundational tenets of modern public law. Yet this overwhelming focus on the culpable individual was the result of legal reforms in the eighteenth and nineteenth centuries designed precisely to exclude the harm caused by capitalism from being taken into account. As the subject of criminal law was redefined in terms of the rational individual, "earlier notions of 'collective' crimes generally, including those applying to partnerships and corporations, were absented from the new economy of punishment."[16] Furthermore, the focus on the culpable individual made it impossible for defendants charged with theft to make recourse to the once common defense that the true crime was the unequal distribution of wealth that had left them with no choice but to steal.[17] Such arguments would imply that appropriation of property from those with more than they need may be not a crime but the partial rectification of criminal levels of inequality and thus justified as part of the public interest.[18] Penal reformers such as the Scots legal scholar and judge David Hume (not to be confused with the philosopher) reversed the argument, defining the interests of the owners of capital as the public interest. Not even abject poverty could justify violating the "interests and bonds of society," defined in terms of private property.[19]

It is here that we find the origins of one of the firmest doctrines of modern criminal law: the idea that motive, or any other concept that might reveal the social content of an act, is irrelevant to criminal responsibility. Thus, Owen Thomas writes, "The exclusion of motive neutralised any claim that those very same 'interests and bonds of society' might be complicit in constituting the circumstances in which the defendant behaved."[20] Instead, crime was defined as a matter of individual choice, if the individual is compos mentis and can make that choice rationally. Where an individual had knowingly transgressed the law, and was in control of these actions, an infraction had been committed and punishment was both justified and required. The question of criminal liability could be boiled down to the question of the state of mind of the individual (known in law as *mens rea*).[21] Rich and poor alike were prohibited from stealing and from various other categories of property offenses given shape at this time. The law was not arbitrary but consistent and proportionate. It thus embodied formal principles of liberty and equality while simultaneously meeting the demands of the (unequal and coercive) capitalist order in which these principles were asserted.[22]

The exclusion of motive not only serves to criminalize actions necessary for survival in the face of vast inequalities of wealth. It also inhibits possibilities of prosecuting what might otherwise be called the crimes of the powerful. Thomas has explored this in relation to the use of judicial methods in public inquiries in Britain: into allegations of institutional police racism and into alleged deception by the British government when it made the case for the invasion of Iraq in 2003. Both inquiries, Thomas notes, were initially accused of whitewash because they focused on the *intentions* of the actors involved and were thus unable to hold any individual to account. In both cases, these accusations led to the appointment of a second inquiry that explained the phenomenon through *unintended* consequences: "The inquiry alludes to institutionalized and normalized cultures of behavior that directly lead to a wrong but for which no individuals can be held directly responsible."[23] Thus, Thomas concludes, judicial methods are ultimately unsuited to understanding the complicity of powerful actors in recognized harms, because they are unable to interrogate how certain cultures of behavior were made possible. A style of investigation that focuses only on individuals and their states of mind excludes important factors that inform human agency. "The constituents of our subjectivity, of our motives, are missing."[24] This, Thomas continues, prevents us from considering how harmful practices "are made possible, maybe even necessary, by ways of thinking and acting that are endemic to the liberal state and society."[25]

This is precisely the problem captured by Olaya. The sole focus on individual perpetrators misses the systemic nature of abuses, making it impossible to raise *any* questions about the responsibility of those who profit from selective killings, massacres, and forced displacement, or about the everyday managerial decisions and calculations of risk and benefit that sustain this violence. Olaya's point was not that responsibility should simply be deflected onto "the system" (in which the causes of atrocity are so diffuse that no individual can be held to account). Of course, he said, individual perpetrators have some of the responsibility. The problem is not the idea that individuals are responsible for their acts but the individualistic normative framework that makes it possible to formulate the question in these binary terms (either the aberrant individual or "the system"). Indeed, juridical individualism justifies its own narrow limits, in part, by warning that the alternative (blaming the big fuzzy system) would be less robust, precise, and fair. "What is particularly significant about modern Western subjectivity," Alan Norrie underscores, "is its insistence upon individual*ism*: individual autonomy and responsibility *to the exclusion of* the individual's actual location between the personal and the social."[26]

This individualistic normative framework not only narrows the understanding of responsibility for harm. It also places limits on how harm is conceptualized and, indeed, what harms can be recognized as injuries (*injuria*, injustice) for which anyone should be found responsible. "For those whose suffering is beyond the legal relation, there can be damage, but no injustice," as Veitch puts it.[27] Not just responsibility, but the injury itself is "disappeared." Gustavo Rojas-Páez has explored this with regard to the catastrophic impact of the Cerrejón open cast coal mine in northeastern Colombia mentioned in chapter 1. In 2015, following the deaths of 4,770 Wayuú Indigenous children from hunger and malnutrition, the Inter-American Commission on Human Rights ruled that the Colombian state must implement "precautionary measures" to ensure adequate food and drinking water for populations affected by the mine.[28] That the deaths of Wayuú children have continued is, in part, the product of difficulties with the enforcement of judicial decisions.[29] Nevertheless, Rojas-Páez underscores, the more fundamental problem is that dominant narratives of human rights are unable to recognize the underlying causes of the harm they purport to address. The commission was able to recognize harm to individuals, but not the Wayuú people's claims that extractivism itself is a cause of harm, or that the river diverted and dammed to provide water for use by the mine and agribusiness had been privatized. It was likewise unable to contend with the spiritual significance of nature or with the particular harm of the deaths of mothers, whose deaths have an important meaning within the Wayuú's matrilineal cosmovision. More broadly, the commission was unable to challenge the idea of "natural resources" as commodities available for extraction and large-scale commercialization or to see humans other than as sovereign individuals with nature at their disposal.[30] This scenario, for Rojas-Páez, "represents nothing less than a continuation of the principle of *terra nullius*"—the idea of uninhabited lands—"that facilitated and legitimized colonial genocidal expansion in the past."[31] Although the commission's report describes a situation marked by social and environmental harm, it fails to question the practice of the extraction and commercialization of resources. Nor does it question associated "colonial understandings of humanity's relationship with nature and the notion of economic development surrounding it," which continue to lead to the extermination of Indigenous peoples.[32] The result, Rojas-Páez underscores, is "the chronic impunity of the crimes committed by the powerful."[33]

Corporate Accountability as an Aspect of Corporate Impunity

These problems are only confounded when the corporation is the focus of efforts to establish liability. It is easy to forget that corporations themselves are legal constructions. The figure of "the corporation" was consolidated in law by the late nineteenth century through legislative measures designed specifically to shield owners and shareholders from liability for financial losses generated in the course of the company's activities.[34] "Although the basis for legal personhood has always varied widely across time and across national jurisdictions," David Whyte explains, "there are two aspects that are generally held in common in contemporary liberal democratic states. First, corporations are recognized by a particular state or sovereign authority as 'entities' distinct from the people who own or control them; and second, they are able to conduct commercial functions as if they were individuals (most notably, to enter into commercial agreements as contracting parties)."[35] As such, the corporation is a "structural form of impunity."[36] The corporate "person" can—as Baars underscores—take the hit for capitalism so that the system itself, and real people profiting from harm generated through corporate activities, are immunized from liability.[37] Shareholders do not even need to know about issues such as labor conditions, security arrangements, or the ecological impact of the company's operations.

The consolidation of the legal figure of the corporation also went alongside efforts to differentiate corporate crime from "real" crime.[38] Whyte has discussed this in relation to the sliding scale of fines that the English Factory Acts imposed on masters culpable of offenses against workers. The courts quickly found a means of normalizing these crimes via the category of "strict liability," which means that liability for an offense can be established without need to establish fault or to identify a specific "guilty mind" (or minds) that led to the offense. Shifting focus in this way also made it possible to make "the corporation" (rather than its individual members) the liable entity—something that had become routine by the twentieth century.[39] The idea that corporate wrongdoing is different from real crime has important implications when it comes to allegations of human rights abuse. As things stand, only individuals can be prosecuted as perpetrators of human rights violations. A company can be held accountable for a civil offence—or tort—linked to violations of human rights normally by alleging harm caused by "negligence" arising from breach of a "duty of care" (rather than, for example, torture or violation of the right to life).[40] Whereas criminal proceedings normally fall under public law (which deals with relations between individuals and states), tort litigation against corporations falls within private law. Pursuit of remedy for human rights abuse is thus premised on the idea of two formally equal parties in dispute, despite profound inequalities of power and resources. This generates immense material obstacles for victims. The process of litigation itself is an entirely unfair fight, in which corporations can employ expensive teams of lawyers and respond with legal threats and counterlitigation against victims' lawyers.[41]

Furthermore, even if litigation is successful, this can be a Pyrrhic victory because of what Baars aptly characterizes as a "commodified responsibility relationship."[42] Victims risk penalties if they do not settle at the earliest opportunity, meaning that the process can force victims' lawyers to accept confidentiality and non-disparagement clauses of the sort that were unacceptable to the Colombian Food Workers Union.[43] A "calculable price tag" is put onto harm, which can then be brought into corporate calculations of profit and risk.[44] In the aftermath of their refusal to accept Coca-Cola's offer of settlement, union leaders offered similar reflections: the court process was conceived as an economic transaction, and even the very substantial sum of money on offer was the antithesis of reparation if it meant the union could no longer speak out about the harm its members had suffered and the causes of that harm.

Tort proceedings reify and legitimate the legal fiction of "the corporation" as the surplus-value extracting machinery of capitalism.[45] Yet when it comes to the evidence required to demonstrate fault on the part of the company, the figure of the corporate person breaks down, and specific individuals must be identified who carried out the acts in which the company is alleged to be complicit. This makes matters even more difficult, as the complexity and secrecy of decision-making within corporate structures means that it tends to be very difficult in practice to identify the links between the abuses and individual actors within a corporation.[46] Thus, Torres's case in the London High

Courts was eventually dropped because, without identification of specific individuals, neither Torres's account of being kidnapped in a van belonging to BP's subsidiary Ocensa nor the testimony of paramilitaries that they had been paid US$40,000 by the company to "disappear" Torres helped to attribute the acts to the company. All this can make litigation not only an extremely expensive business, but one that has limited chances of success in court. What is more, the principle of shareholders' limited liability not only protects individual shareholders but also enables multinational corporations to deny responsibility for operating subsidiaries. For instance, BP tried to argue that it had no responsibility for Torres, given that he was employed by Ocensa.[47]

Recent developments in legislation and case law have been directed at making this sort of argument more difficult. In 2017, France became the first country to bring into force legislation establishing a *devoir de vigilance* (duty of vigilance) on large French companies, not just to formulate a transparent plan regarding all human rights risks and other risks of serious harm within its supply chain, but also to implement this plan effectively.[48] There is, however, as the solicitor Paul Dowling notes, a risk that reforms within the "due diligence" and "duty of care" framework will provide companies with an incentive to further decentralize their activities (or, at least, give an impression of having done so). The very idea of a duty of care also serves—in Dowling's words—to "impose an artificial moralism on an entity that is preordained to obey only economic motives."[49] Thus, the very means through which liability is established feeds into the wider discourse of global "corporate citizenship" whose deadly implications we saw in chapter 2. This problem has been replicated at the time of this writing in the first three drafts of the United Nations' binding treaty on corporations and human rights. The proposed treaty does contain elements that mitigate technical obstacles to multinationals being held civilly liable for abuses, setting out a framework in which a company can be held liable for foreseeable harm arising from operations over which it "had control or was sufficiently related."[50] Nevertheless, successive drafts have not only failed to address the problems of international financial institutions and the trade and investment agreements that prioritize corporate rights over human rights, even though this has been a major focus of the interparliamentary working group established to provide input into the treaty. The direct human rights obligations on corporations that campaigners argued were vital to enable the prosecution of companies have also been avoided, as has the middle ground advocated by some campaigners: corporate international criminal law.[51] Instead, the drafts of the treaty have built on the "human rights due diligence" norms in the existing United Nations

Guiding Principles on Business and Human Rights, further bolstering the idea of the corporation as moral actor. Even innovations that go beyond seeking to strengthen compliance-based approaches and the false moralism of "due diligence" remain caught within the strictures of corporate personhood. For instance, Dowling—one of the lawyers acting on behalf of the victims of Cerrejón mine—has drawn on French jurisprudence to develop arguments for the strict liability of corporations for harm caused by a risky activity (such as coal mining) from which the company profits.[52] This evades the need to prove fault associated with notions of due diligence but nevertheless invokes a notion of liability designed to protect bosses and shareholders by differentiating corporate wrongdoing from real crime. Even then, getting a court to accept this level of innovation would be an enormous achievement.

Likewise, if campaigners were to succeed against the odds in securing binding human rights obligations on corporations or corporate international criminal law, it is likely that the legal figures of rational individual and corporate person would still shape the attribution of liability so as to shield senior management involved in criminal acts—as well as shareholders. In common law jurisdictions, it is possible to hold a corporation criminally liable when an "individual within the organisation can be identified with sufficient knowledge of the offence and with the necessary responsibility and authority" to be considered the "controlling mind" of the company. The corporation itself is treated as rational individual in which the state of mind of directors or managers "is the state of mind of the company and is treated by the law as such."[53] However, this provision has rarely been used to prosecute corporations in practice because, as Steve Tombs and David Whyte emphasize, the identification of a (guilty) "controlling mind" does not capture the dynamics of much corporate crime, in which acts are undertaken in the knowledge that harms are likely to occur, or the harm is the result of omission, or the result of decisions across a chain of action.[54] In other words, we come back to the problem that Thomas underlines. Juridical individualism—the focus on the "guilty mind"—cannot capture how harmful acts are made possible by ordinary cultures of behavior that are endemic not only to the liberal state and society, as Thomas emphasizes, but also to the corporation as an entity designed for the extraction of surplus value.

Outside of the English-speaking world, the main form of law is civil law, which relies on written codes rather than legal precedent. Here, the figure of the corporate "person" historically has been taken to exclude the possibility of corporate criminal liability altogether on the constitutional principle that one person cannot be "vicariously liable" for an offense perpetrated by another. There have been some more recent moves toward criminal liability of corporations where a crime has been committed on behalf of or in the interests of a company and where the company—even tacitly—ratified the conduct. Nevertheless, it is significant that these latter measures for corporate criminal liability have been developed to deal with corruption, a potential obstacle to the smooth functioning of capitalism.[55] Even if international law were to be developed in this direction to accommodate corporate criminal liability for human rights abuse, it is likely that these provisions would be merged with existing compliance-based measures.[56] Provision for corporate criminal liability within a compliance-based framework risks further protecting senior managers and the corporation itself by deflecting responsibility downward to workers, who then become the most likely targets of any enforcement action.[57] The corporation itself would most likely be subjected to a financial penalty, entrenching the right to trample on rights as something that corporations can in effect purchase, while the figure of corporate "person" remains intact. The implications are, as Baars sums it up, "planned impunity" for the corporate "structure of irresponsibility."[58]

Strategy and Tactics

What is perhaps remarkable, given this scenario, is that social movements still use the law to address atrocities linked to multinational corporations. They do so, furthermore, despite being aware of the asymmetry between the production of harm and legal means of allocating responsibility for it. Often, social movement lawsuits against corporations are referred to by lawyers and activists as "strategic litigation." However, as Robert Knox has emphasized, so-called strategic uses of law tend in reality to focus on short-term tactical questions rather than the strategic question of "how—or even whether—the left can utilize international law in such a way as to advance the interests of the oppressed and the exploited."[59] This brings us back to the question posed at the start of this chapter: On what terms might it be "possible to use the law *without* fatally undermining longer term structural considerations"?[60] There are, of course, all sorts of good tactical reasons for seeking to counter "impunity" within the terms of the law. If the aim is to prevent the most egregious forms of direct violence from recurring, then tackling the impunity of individual perpetrators can have an important deterrent function. Likewise, a potential benefit of extraterritorial litigation against companies is often said to be the publicity generated by such cases, which can do much to deter further abuse.[61] Negative publicity does matter to companies—to such a degree that Coca-Cola was keen to try to buy the silence of critics even *after* the Colombian Food Workers' case had been thrown out on technical grounds.

Yet is there not still a risk that would-be "strategic" use of law will serve to recast the issues within the terms of dominant legal narratives? While the Colombian Food Workers may have considered their lawsuit to be a vehicle of *denuncia*, a means of making an empire visible, we must address the possibility that what the legal process provides is not visibility but blinkers, shaping understandings of the world that inhibit structural change. Culpable individuals can be prosecuted, or the fictive "corporate person" be forced to account for its wrongdoing. After that, however, the matter is closed. A line is drawn. The rule of law is reaffirmed as neutral and benign, and corporate transgressions are presented as aberrations within a rule-governed system.

The Food Workers Union and its supporters had to repeatedly contest the narrative that Coca-Cola was simply an unethical company. The anthropologist Lesley Gill, who spent time with the Food Workers and followed the union's campaign in the United States, writes about how union members found that the only way to get support when they traveled to the United States was to speak about human rights "with a U.S. accent," within the terms of a "U.S. human rights frame which voided references to capitalists and the working class, or the rich and the poor, and simply asserted that Colombian trade unionists had the right to free association without the threat of constant terror."[62] This was less the case in Europe, where union leaders found people more "open."[63] The campaign across Europe was coordinated by member groups of la Red de Hermandad, who had closer links with the Food Workers. As I mentioned in chapter 3, several of us were engaged throughout the campaign in conversations with the Food Workers' leaders about how to give visibility to their wider struggle: for alternative political economies of food production and against an extractivist model generating hunger, displacement, and ecological destruction, as well as hyper-exploitation of labor. Indeed, beyond this pedagogical process, which took shape through various events and social forums around Europe, conversations with leaders of the union at speaking events across Europe were the beginnings of much longer-term relationships of solidarity that saw people from various European countries travel to Colombia to work with the union and with other social organizations in the network.

It is at this point that I want to come back to Torres's visit to Britain in 2015 to launch a campaign linking his case directly to wider struggles against an economic model that had been the larger context of the killing of almost

2,500 people around BP's oilfields, ecological devastation, and the destruction of a peasant way of life. The very fact that these campaigns ran alongside litigation against both Coca-Cola and BP is a reminder that legal narratives do not exercise automatic monopoly over the story that is told. In the case of BP, the Oil Justice campaign had been conceived by Torres; his lawyers; the British antipoverty charity War on Want; and the Corporación Social para la Asesoría y Capacitación Comunitaria (Social Corporation for Community Advice and Training [COSPACC]), the organization set up by displaced peasant leaders that I worked with in Casanare. From the outset, Torres's British lawyers had recognized the limitations of litigation aimed at securing compensation for a minority, and had wanted to think with Torres and other victims what it would mean to pursue remedy for the population as a whole. The stated aims of the campaign in publicity materials were not just "to hold Big Oil to account where corporate crimes have been committed," but also "to develop a new and unique community-led model to obtain justice for the entire community, not just compensation for a minority." The goal of the campaign was "to rebuild and empower communities," not only by bringing cases, but also through pedagogical work in Casanare. The role of COSPACC was important here: training members of these communities in investigative and paralegal work and facilitating collective analysis of the economic interests behind the violence. This work was explicitly linked in campaign flyers to the broader goal of "creating lasting structural change" by lobbying for changes in the existing legal framework that had enabled plunder with impunity.

Those who led the campaign were clear about the limited ability of law to address the injustice perpetuated in the context of oil extraction. They insisted that litigation had to be accompanied by what Sebastian Ordoñez, a Colombian refugee involved in the Oil Justice campaign and who later joined the staff at War on Want, described as "a more holistic view of justice."[64] This included recognition of the harm that had occurred by "unmasking a reality" given shape not only through illegal acts of violence but also through legalized plunder. That was why I was asked to accompany Torres on his tour: no one from COSPACC had been able to come from Colombia, and I had worked with COSPACC on research that addressed in depth that wider reality of plunder and dispossession in Casanare. That is not to say that any of us had reflected together on what it meant to use law strategically prior to launching the campaign. It was after our first speaking engagement in Oxford, on the road to Bristol, that Torres and I began the conversation that led us to seek funding for a series of workshops to bring people in our networks together to discuss that question in depth. Within the Oil Justice campaign itself, these conversations were nascent and ongoing—as they had been within the Colombian Food Workers' lawsuit and accompanying boycott campaign against Coca-Cola.

In this light, we see notably strategic elements to litigation within both the campaign against Coca-Cola and the Oil Justice campaign. Strategic interventions, as Knox defines them, critique and seek to undermine the logic of the system.[65] They are informed by deeper analysis and understanding of systemic power relations and constitutive violence, making the pedagogical interventions surrounding litigation as important as the legal process itself. A similar understanding was expressed by social movement leaders and lawyers at a workshop hosted by Torres in Bogotá in late 2017, after we had secured funding to bring people together to discuss these questions. The Colombian legal scholar Gustavo Rojas-Páez and I had prepared notes for discussion, summarizing some of the problems with the law that I discussed in the first two sections of this chapter. For most of those gathered at the workshops, litigation was considered a useful tactic for exerting pressure to stop corporate-backed acts of direct violence. Many also felt that the development of robust corporate criminal law was important, if this could pierce the corporate veil and mean real material costs for directors and shareholders— for example, through custodial sentences being imposed on boards of directors and through the cancellation of the legal personhood of companies. However, as one of the leaders of COSPACC put it, there was also a need for a pedagogy that could challenge the ways in which dominant legal narratives legitimize harm. This was part of the process of unmasking a reality, a process that was conceived not merely in symbolic terms but also as something to be accompanied by critical pedagogical work among affected constituencies, as part of the process of building and sustaining a social movement.[66]

What, however, is the relationship established to the law within this combination of strategic litigation and social movement pedagogy? Because of the barriers created by existing legal frameworks, the Oil Justice campaign was frustrated in its efforts to lobby for legal reforms that would generate structural change. Nevertheless, the need to dismantle an international legal order crafted to the benefit of a corporate elite was something repeatedly emphasized by social movement leaders and lawyers during the 2017 workshops as a fundamental aspect of strategic use of law.[67] If law and legal categories are constitutive of productive relations, then legal change is essential to undermining the material basis of the harm perpetrated through corporate activities. Struggle for legal reform may take place within the parameters of the system, taking for granted capitalist social relations and the ideology of rule of law, but this is not the only way in which legal struggles can be approached. Legal struggle can also be the fabric of struggles to transform social relations. Despite his critique of liberal declarations of rights, Karl Marx himself recognized the transformative potential of law in relation to workers' collective struggle for legislation to limit the length of the working day. What was crucial to Marx, Knox highlights, was that this was the product of workers' overcoming individualism and fighting together "as a class" to "compel the passing of a law, an all-powerful social barrier that shall prevent the very workers from selling, by voluntary contract with capital, themselves and their families into slavery and death." Thus, "In place of the pompous catalogues of the 'inalienable rights of man' comes the modest Magna Charta of a legally limited working day, which shall make clear when the time which the worker sells is ended, and when his own begins."[68]

We can see collective social movement struggles for reforms of international law in a similar light: as part of a process of forming an international movement, but also as a means of pushing for concrete mechanisms that can put a stop to certain forms of harm that the international legal order currently facilitates. In October 2018, as part of the project with Torres, I traveled with Ordoñez and Rojas-Páez to the Thematic Social Forum on Mining and the Extractivist Economy, a four-day event organized in Johannesburg by a network of social movement organizations from Africa and Latin America. We were to present a draft of the coproduced book that had resulted from our Colombia workshops and get feedback on it from a wider array of social organizations. Prominent in the organization of the forum was the Global Campaign to Dismantle Corporate Power and Stop Impunity, a coalition of more than two hundred grassroots groups affected by the activities of multinational corporations across the world. While Global Campaign has been a strong voice of advocacy within the intergovernmental working group negotiations for the United Nations' binding treaty, its interventions have not been confined within the parameters of seeking to fill regulatory gaps in the existing legal order. Global Campaign has not only lobbied for the inclusion of direct human rights obligations that would give human rights clear priority over trade and investment treaties; it has also coordinated a worldwide process of consultation over a Peoples Treaty on the Control of Transnational Corporations, based on an "international law from below."[69] The idea of international law from below draws attention to the fact that international law has been shaped from "above," by colonial powers and corporations. It presents efforts to change international law as inseparable from a collective social movement critique of the law as it exists.

In the Bogotá workshops, there was also widespread recognition that the need to reshape law entailed rethinking ideas of harm and of the culpable individual subject in terms other than how they have been conceived within an international legal order designed to underwrite capitalism. This was described by one of the leaders of COSPACC as a need to "broaden the temporal understanding of harm," to present a view of crime "not as an act committed in a momentary event, but as an ever present possibility, with historical roots and generative conditions." This, other participants commented, implied a challenge to the individualism at the heart of the law and a greater focus on the historical and structural origins of harm, as well as a need to approach law "through another epistemology," and to "articulate a dialogue between the dominant language of human rights and the epistemic and political claims of historically marginalized peoples of the world."[70]

All this points us to key aspects of the strategic use of law: using law and legal argument while also seeking to undermine the idea that the law is neutral, benign, or definitive of "justice"—via both social movement pedagogy and legal argument itself. Yet given the extent to which existing legal narratives and concepts shape what sort of argument can be made, it is important to consider how and in what forums it might be possible to generate forms of legal argument that do seek not merely to make a critique of specific features of the law but also to expose and counter the violence authorized through prevailing legal narratives. For this, I now turn to consider how such modes of legal argument have been advanced alongside and apart from official processes of litigation, through mechanisms of alternative justice such as popular opinion hearings and, most significant, hearings of the Permanent Peoples' Tribunal (PPT).

Counterlegalities

The Permanent Peoples' Tribunal is an unofficial international court that emerged from the international tribunal on US war crimes in Vietnam, convened by Bertrand Russell and hosted by Jean-Paul Sartre in 1966–67. While the PPT aims to exert pressure for the crimes of the powerful to be "brought to justice," it is also a site of critical legal innovation that draws attention to forms of violence obscured by dominant legal narratives. The tribunal, as Rojas-Páez puts it, "recognizes that international law is an incomplete project and raises concerns about the fact that judicial bodies such as the International Criminal Court do not include within their jurisdiction economic crimes perpetrated by complex networks including transnational corporations and states."[71] The 2018 Thematic Social Forum on Mining and the Extractivist Economy was preceded by the third session of the Southern African Permanent People's Tribunal, the last of a yearlong series of hearings into the responsibility of multinational corporations, international financial institutions, and states for human rights abuse, the destruction of livelihoods, and environmental devastation. However, the session of the PPT in which I was closely involved was that on Transnational Corporations and the Rights of Peoples in Colombia. Between 2006 and 2008, the PPT held a series of six two-day hearings in Colombia relating to different thematic areas: food and agriculture, mining, biodiversity, oil, public services, and Indigenous genocide. I worked with the Food Workers Union on the preparation of material for the food and agriculture hearing in 2006 and with COSPACC on the oil industry hearing in 2007. At each hearing, expert judges received extensively documented evidence and heard numerous testimonies from witnesses. At the end of each hearing, a verdict was delivered according to the provisions of national and international law. These verdicts are not, of course, legally binding, but "they can," Rojas-Páez emphasizes, "set a precedent for future legal actions."[72] What I want to suggest here is that the PPT was a site of expression of what I call *counterlegalities*: modes of legal argument that invoke existing jurisprudence but do so in a way that exposes violence authorized and concealed by dominant legal narratives.

One important feature of the 2008 final ruling of the PPT was that it shifted the definition of international crimes such as genocide away from prevailing interpretations. The ruling condemned numerous multinational corporations (as well as the Colombian government) "for their direct or indirect participation, by action or by omission, in the commission of genocidal practices."[73] Alongside the destruction of Indigenous groups, the ruling referred to genocide against political groups, including the Colombian trade union movement. In other words, it recognized the concept of "political genocide," which has long been considered the "blind spot" of the Genocide Convention, despite having been recognized in later developments of customary international law—and in Colombia's own criminal code.[74] The more significant innovation, however, relates to the question of genocidal intent. In its predominant interpretation, genocide is "a crime of 'special' or 'specific' intent in which the perpetrator seeks the whole or partial destruction of a protected group."[75] The ruling, however, referred to genocide against Indigenous groups "by action *or by institutional omission*" to attend to the needs of those groups.[76] This separation of the crime of genocide from specific intent takes up an existing critique of prevailing interpretations of genocidal intent: that culpability for genocide should be extended to acts undertaken with knowledge of the destructive consequences of those actions, even in the absence of a specific genocidal purpose.[77] By linking genocidal intent to systematic failure to prevent or address conditions of life destructive of a group, the PPT was able to denounce economic policy decisions as genocidal because they failed to address the destructive consequences for Indigenous peoples.

There were related innovations regarding what constitutes a crime against humanity. The ruling condemned numerous multinationals for participation as "authors, accomplices, or instigators" in crimes that conform to the standard definition of crimes against humanity, including murder, extermination, imprisonment, torture, rape, and forced disappearance.[78] The reference to "accomplices" stretches the received understanding of the perpetrator of a crime against humanity. In contrast to genocide, in the case of a crime against humanity it is not necessary for perpetrators to share the overall goal behind a systematic attack on the civilian population; the perpetrator need only to have acted with knowledge of that context. A perpetrator must, however, have intentionally committed the specific act—of murder, torture, and so on.[79] By incorporating the idea of corporate "accomplices," the ruling paves the way for a wider interpretation of culpability, according to which a person may not have carried out the specific act but, nevertheless, have been complicit in it. This opens the way to extending culpability for crimes against humanity in ways that better capture the complex dynamics of corporate crime than is possible through the identification of a (guilty) "controlling mind."

The significance of these extensions of the concepts of genocide and crime against humanity should not be underestimated. Both crimes are considered peremptory norms of international law, which is to say that they are not open to appeal or to challenge. Through its innovative jurisprudence, the PPT was able to give greater significance to the murders of trade union leaders and to institutional actions that meant the extermination of Indigenous groups (whatever the specific intent of individuals). One implication of this was that the PPT was able to recommend in its ruling that the International Criminal Court open an investigation, having demonstrated a link between corporate operations and serious international crimes that fall within the remit of the ICC.[80] This was in itself a challenge to the dominant vision of global justice highlighted by Schwöbel-Patel.[81] Yet the ruling went beyond this, condemning corporate involvement in crimes against humanity and genocide as an indictment of the entire neoliberal model promoted by international financial institutions and the World Trade Organization (WTO).[82] It recommended that people's sovereignty, dignity, and rights be given precedence over private economic interests; rejected the privatization of fundamental life resources; and insisted that the international community take a legal and ethical attitude toward hunger and toward the inhuman living and working conditions denounced by plaintiffs akin to that taken against torture, extrajudicial execution, and so on.[83] What is more, the ruling at several points denounced the international economic legal framework that facilitates not only genocide and crimes against humanity but also conditions of life that should be considered as abhorrent as these crimes.[84] Testimonies presented within the hearings went even further. In the case of Coca-Cola, for example, alongside testimonies relating to crimes conforming to the standard definition of crime against humanity (murders of union leaders, mass detention of workers and their resignations forced at gunpoint, imprisonment on false charges and torture at the hands of the police, and so on), workers spoke of the inhumanity of pay and conditions that meant long treks to work and twenty-hour shifts; of disabilities worsening until they could no longer work; of life in destitution after being forced to resign their contracts; of deaths of workers from stress and exhaustion. Submissions to the PPT persistently used the term *crime against humanity* to refer not only to a new normality of degrading labor conditions and the slow deaths of workers, but also to the drying up of rivers and the destruction of the land engendered by extractive projects. Indeed, it is noteworthy that in publicity materials created by Colombian social organizations, the two-year session of the tribunal was referred to as the "Colombia Session on Transnational Corporations and Crimes against Humanity" (as opposed to "the rights of peoples").

It is important to reflect on the politics of these attempts to dislodge dominant legal narratives by means of legal argument. While the law is malleable and open to adaptation, we have seen in the discussion in this chapter just how quickly new developments in law—such as those that address corporations and human rights—are adapted to the interests of capital. Capitalism is a system of ongoing transgression and innovation that persistently incorporates what was previously outside. It may be possible to make theoretically cogent legal arguments to the effect that even the consequences of ordinary economic decisions should be judged as crimes against humanity, genocide, or even, as Norrie has suggested, "social murder," but this does not mean that such an argument will be readily accepted by a court.[85] Courts do sometimes accept more modest innovations. For instance, similar arguments about complicity in crimes against humanity to those made by the PPT have more recently been developed within the criminal courts of Argentina to prosecute corporate functionaries who facilitated the murder, detention, and torture of workers as "necessary participants" in crimes against humanity on the basis that any systematic practice involved in the commission of a crime against humanity was part of that crime.[86] This was the outcome of decades of mobilization by victims' organizations on "economic complicity" with the dictatorship. Even then, legal innovation went nowhere near a critique of the neoliberal economic model and legal order imposed by means of those crimes against humanity.[87] Indeed, any potential of the law to respond to such concerns is undercut by concrete determinations of legality that underwrite plunder and exploitation.

In this light, we need to understand the counterlegalities advanced through the PPT not merely as practical attempts to develop jurisprudence, as expressions of what the law should be, or as even statements of the law's openness or the dislocation at the heart of law that offers a future "justice to come."[88] As Emilios Christodoulidis insists, "A mere promise that there *will be* a further dislocation appears crucially inadequate ... because legal reasons, institutional solutions, capitalist determinations *now* are actualisations *now* of a conceptual schema that is held in place (now) by the promise of its future redress."[89] The political force of these counterlegalities can be better grasped via the concept of a "strategy of rupture," coined by the controversial French lawyer Jacques Vergès in relation to his defense of the Algerian militant Djamila Bouhired, who in 1957 was accused of terrorism for planting a bomb during the struggle for independence from France. Vergès's strategy was to reject the characterization of the defendant's actions as criminal. Rather than appealing for sympathy from the court, he undermined the legal terms of reference that the court was appointed to uphold. He sought to demonstrate the criminality of the colonial order itself, denouncing torture of political prisoners and presenting an account of the defendants as fighting against colonial brutality.[90] While Vergès coined the term *strategy of rupture* in his book *De la stratégie judiciare* (1968), he was far from being the first to use such an approach.[91] Nor should we romanticize Vergès's anti-imperial ambition, given that he was notorious for his subsequent deployment of a similar strategy in his defense of the Nazi Klaus Barbie. (In relation to Barbie, the defense "consisted in maximal use of the '*tu quoque*,' [the "you too" fallacy] in a way that would bring the French in direct confrontation with their hypocritical denunciation of a crime that underpinned their own colonial legacy.")[92]

What is characteristic of a defense of "rupture," in Christodoulidis's analysis, is that it seeks to confront the system that underlies the prosecution's case. It embodies a logic of immanent critique that forces the system "to face up to its stated principles, to equality, to procedural fairness," and so on, but in a way that *"forces* it *beyond* what it can possibly 'contain' within its economy of representation." Thus, the act of resistance "registers without being absorbed, integrated or co-opted into the system against which it stands."[93] While *rupture* is commonly associated with the strategy of defense in criminal law, Brenna Bhandar has identified a similar logic in court judgments such as that of the 2011 Indian Supreme Court ruling in *Nandini Sundar et al. v. State of Chhattisgarh.* In it, the court itself denounced capitalist development policies as the cause of armed resistance, in effect "shatter[ing] the illusory and unreal sovereignty of the individual who is technically and formally considered an equal member of the political community, but simultaneously subject to untold levels of social and economic inequality in the private sphere."[94]

In the hearings of the Permanent Peoples Tribunal, it was not in the defense but in the ruling and prosecution that a strategy of immanent critique was deployed. The counterlegalities advanced through the PPT targeted not the hypocrisy of the other party, but the inability of dominant legal narratives to recognize certain forms of harm as justiciable wrongs. By ruling that the economic model itself is productive of genocide and crimes against humanity, that its day-to-day consequences should be considered international crimes akin to torture or murder, the tribunal's final judgment offered an implicit challenge to the very idea of rule of law as something neutral or benign. Corporate wrongdoing is exposed not as an aberration, but as constitutive of the system and, by implication, made possible through a neoliberal model of rule of law. This is even more pronounced in the redefinition of *crime against humanity* made within the hearings themselves, which extended the concept to include the conditions of life generated by casualized labor and the ecological damage caused by corporate operations. Denouncing the ordinary operation of the system as a crime against humanity reflects precisely the sort of logic of rupture that Christodoulidis identifies: forcing the system beyond what it can contain by generating a contradiction that "makes impossible a response *in* and *by* the system."[95] Instead of "crime against humanity" providing "the overarching context that might contain legal debate over its proper instantiations," the category itself "becomes the stake of a confrontation that is political, unmitigated and unmitigable by law."[96]

The impossibility of a response in and by the system was even more explicit in the series of "public people's hearings" held by the Colombian Food

Workers in Colombia, Switzerland, and the United States while the union awaited a decision on whether its extraterritorial litigation could proceed. As I mentioned in chapter 3, these hearings culminated in demands for "comprehensive reparation" that went far beyond anything that would be considered reasonable within the terms of the law. Alongside demands for financial compensation and for all Coca-Cola personnel involved in the repression to be sacked and handed over to the Colombian justice system, the list included a series of measures to repair the wider forms of harm enabled by the repression of the union. Reparation could be made only by reversing the neoliberal labor reforms imposed through the violence. Workers who had been forcibly displaced or sacked were to be reinstated; all workers were to receive permanent contracts; and ecological damage in all of the company's areas of operation was to be remedied. The union and its supporters demanded that a monthly pension be awarded to the families of the murdered unionists equivalent to the monthly income of the president of the Coca-Cola Company, and that a commitment be made to finance all medical or psychiatric treatment that victims and their families needed because of the repression. Damages were to be paid not only to all victims of paramilitary violence and false imprisonment but also to the union as a collective entity—in compensation for "economic, social and political damage"—and Coca-Cola was explicitly to finance trade union promotion and education campaigns by the union.[97] The demands for reparation also included measures aimed at giving perpetual visibility to what had happened: public apologies from the president of Colombia and the president of Coca-Cola and photos and biographies of murdered trade unionists on all Coca-Cola bottles, as well as funding for work to preserve historical memory of what had happened. Compliance with the demands was to be monitored by a committee comprising representatives of Colombian social organizations and Coca-Cola, and the issues were to be given ongoing visibility through an annual two-hour television report by the union that was to be funded by the company. These demands highlighted the law's incapacity to offer an adequate remedy or an adequate conceptualization of justice. A friend from another Colombia trade union organization offered similar reflections when we met for a drink in 2017. In the wake of trade union genocide, this friend said, "true reparation is recovering the trade union movement, recovery of the social fabric, not anything that can take place through the state's mechanisms of 'justice.'"

Thinking back to the COSPACC leader's comments about the need to shift the temporal understanding of harm, we should note a very different temporal logic to this use of law from that evident within narratives of justice as means of seeking redress to foreclose on the past. There is no possibility of drawing a line behind past events, as if those events were transgressions within a rule-governed system. Rather, it is the present order of things that is condemned. Far from posing the question as to how victims might move on from the harm they had suffered, that harm is presented as systemic, ongoing, the product of past acts of direct violence and sustained through the ordinary operation of the rule of law. Nor do we find the glib allusions to a future redress that might one day emerge through the judgment of these crimes in the present, as found within narratives of "transitional justice."[98] This was explicit in 2021 when the PPT returned to Colombia, this time to consider not corporations but the matter of Political Genocide, Impunity, and Crimes against Peace in the wake of the 2016 peace agreement between the Colombian government and the FARC guerrillas. Rejecting the characterization of an internal armed conflict and transition to "peace," the 2021 ruling condemned the Colombian state for "continuous genocide" aimed at the partial destruction of the Colombian national group via the construction of an "enemy within," seeking to show that the actions of the state met all the criteria of genocide—including that of genocidal intent as conventionally understood.[99] Here, too, there was no possibility of redress within the terms of the system, since the aim of the genocide had been to change the social fabric by destroying Indigenous and Afro-descendant cultures, as well as the political characteristics of trade union, peasant, student, and human rights organizations, precisely to facilitate the vision of development now proposed as a path to peace.[100] What is more, the ruling made clear that the genocide was ongoing, denouncing the killing of forty more people and the disappearance of an additional four hundred in the three months between the hearings and the final ruling. The narration of state crimes in the past tense was a form of disavowal, the expression of a "repetition compulsion" in Sigmund Freud's sense, an expression of the psychic toll of terror. The rallying cry "Never again!" was "a persistent act of denial, insisting over and over on the inexistence of what it has been impossible to stop."[101]

Alongside the articulation of counterlegalities as rupture, as immanent critique, as pedagogy, there is, however, a parallel expression of counterlegality visible within the PPT that is focused on developing jurisprudence within the parameters of legally cogent argumentation. In this regard, it is significant that, unlike in some of the cases presented in the hearings, the 2008 final ruling of the PPT did not denounce day-to-day living and working conditions as "crimes against humanity."[102] The fact that the PPT precluded such an interpretation can be understood in the context of its efforts to press the ICC and other courts to address the crimes of the powerful as violations of peremptory norms of international law. Claims of structural violence are far more vulnerable to being dismissed precisely because they do not allow for judicial methods of tracing cause and intent.[103] Yet we need to consider these efforts to provide a precedent for future rulings in the context of the tribunal's wider insistence that living and working conditions generated by the existing organization of global political economy should encounter the same legal and ethical stance as acts already recognized as international crimes. Likewise, by denouncing the legal framework that places private economic interests over people's sovereignty, dignity, and rights, the tribunal recognized the role of law in underwriting the very forms of harm it was judging. The PPT embodies a tension: recognizing the transformative potential of law and thus seeking to push international law in a direction that might begin to address the crimes at the heart of the system, even as it exposes the impossibility of a response in and by that system or within the prevailing understanding of rule of law.

Law and the Critique of the Present

What can we take from this regarding the strategic use of law to address so-called corporate impunity (better expressed as the legally formed ability of capital and capitalists to profit via the perpetration of immense harm)? Two key aspects of strategic use of law emerge from the discussion. The first aspect is the pedagogical work to expose how harm is underwritten by the existing "rule of law." Much of this takes place outside of legal argument, as we have seen with the campaigns and pedagogical initiatives running alongside litigation against Coca-Cola and BP. Nevertheless, within mechanisms of alternative justice such as the PPT, legal argument can be deployed as a means of immanent critique in ways that draw attention to systemic aspects of violence and challenge the excessive focus on the individual (or corporate "person") as the locus of liability. There is much in common here with the defense strategy of rupture, although the focus is not on establishing the hypocrisy of the prosecution or the court, but on highlighting contradictions that mean that cases such as these rarely get before a court precisely because of the asymmetry between the causes of harm and means of establishing responsibility for it. The idea of a neutral rule of law, or of a benign, rule-governed system that corporations sometimes transgress, is rendered untenable in the process, although this does not mean that the law is abandoned.

Forums such as the PPT also seek to develop jurisprudence through careful legal argument in a direction that can better address the harm caused by capitalism at the same time that they draw attention to the causes of that harm. This mode of argument operates between the poles of the tension at the heart of the rule of law: the law is exposed as a tool of domination at the same time that the law's "logic of equity" is mobilized to push the law beyond and against the interests to which it has been harnessed.[104]

The second aspect is intricately related to the first: a shift in the temporal understanding of harm, from past event to an enduring feature of the present. Of course, past atrocities are also condemned. There is no suggestion within the PPT rulings that past crimes should not be reckoned with or those responsible held to account. Nevertheless, the rulings made clear that no judgment of these crimes could provide a means of foreclosing on the past. The judgment of past crimes was thus inseparable from critique of the present order of things, including the political economic and legal order that enables large-scale harm at the same time that it "disappears" responsibility. The animating force of "Never again" was shown to be rooted in disavowal of what is still happening—as is the idea that human rights can be added onto the present order of things through voluntary corporate responsibility or global framework agreements. In the next chapter, I have more to say about the centrality of disavowal to dominant approaches to human rights—and the implications of this for political struggle beyond the strategic use of law.

from pernicious optimism to radical hope

Human Rights
beyond Abstract Values
CHAPTER FIVE

Elizabeth Povinelli begins her book *Economies of Abandonment* with a story by Ursula Le Guin, "The Ones Who Walk Away from Omelas." In Le Guin's magical tale, Omelas is an almost perfectly happy city, but the happiness of those who live in it depends on one small child being constrained in a broom closet, naked, beaten, left in her own excrement, covered in sores. Some people have only heard stories of the child; some go to see the child for themselves, while others try to justify the situation. Some, however, walk away from the city of happiness, one by one. For Le Guin, the ethical imperative is not liberal empathy—putting oneself or imagining oneself in the child's place. It is to know that one's own good life is already with the child in that fetid broom closet and, "as a result, either you must create a new organisation of enfleshment by compromising on the goods to which you have grown accustomed . . . or admit that the current organization of enfleshment is more important to you than her suffering."[1] Either way, Povinelli writes, "every member of Omelas must assume some relationship among his or her present personal happiness, their solidarity with the present happiness of the millions inhabiting Omelas, and the present suffering of one small human being."[2]

Povinelli recounts Le Guin's tale to counter what she considers a predominant ethical logic of our times: normative judgments are made by reference to some future state of affairs so that any assessment of suffering in the present can be postponed by reference to a projected future good. There is, says Povinelli, a "tense-based ethical grammar" characteristic of late liberalism, wherein large-scale suffering and predictable premature death is "best understood from the perspective of the redemptive end from which this death gets its meaning."[3] Normative evaluation of suffering in the present is deferred to some indefinite point in the future, which will provide the necessary vantage point from which to see things in perspective. Until then, we must defer assessment or justify the situation by reference to some abstract future good. Even if we know what is happening, it is better not to look too closely; better, perhaps, to act as if we do not know. There was something akin to this in the asides and whispers of those early neoliberal thinkers, discussed in chapter 1, at least in those fleeting moments when the question of life itself was addressed. "The knowledge that the ideal of a market utterly free of state interference requires . . . the exposure of life to death and the courage to turn away from the imploring hand of famine or to strike it down if it should violate the laws of property and the rationality of the market," Warren Montag insists, "drives the great works of neo-liberalism as they strive simultaneously to suggest, deny and justify what they deny."[4] A similar logic is at play in dominant discourses of "development" today. It is rarely that inhuman working conditions, forced displacement, and the devastation of ecologies and communities are explicitly justified in the name of a better future (although death squads in Colombia, as we have seen, routinely referred to "development" as the rationale for their actions). Nevertheless, that presumed future good occupies the conceptual horizons of policy as an implicit justification of suffering while responsibility for that suffering is "disappeared."

What I think the foregoing chapters have revealed, however, is a different ethical logic, prevalent not so much among the architects of policy as among those who seek to ameliorate its consequences. Rather than indefinitely postponing the assessment of present suffering, the ethical potentiality of the present is affirmed. Rather than engaging in critique and contestation of structures premised on exploitation and oppression, human rights are promoted as abstract values that can be tacked onto the present situation, a feature of the durative present, part of the self-definition of the present order. This operates quite comfortably alongside the logic of deferral that Povinelli describes. In the attitude of British nongovernmental organizations (NGOs) toward British Petroleum (BP), for instance, the assumption of "good intentions" (at least on the part of the white and the wealthy) shaped intervention to such an extent that postponement of judgment was barely necessary. Suffering was treated not as a byproduct of the existing legal order, but as the result of aberrations ("mistakes," "gaps" in governance, or the acts of the yet-to-be-civilized). There is a similar affirmation of the present at play when trade union organizations insist that labor must adapt to neoliberalism, or when the International Labour Organization suggests that market forces can underpin rights. So, too, in dominant narratives of transitional justice and "anti-impunity," a line is drawn between a discredited past and a present state of affairs so that the present is narrated—in Robert Meister's words—as a time "after evil," or "a virtual reality in which one acts as if everyone had good will" while full redress is deferred to a future moment.[5]

Both attitudes to present suffering—the deferral of judgment and the affirmation of the present's capacity to be made ethical—involve, in the terms of Le Guin's allegory, a failure to address the relationship between the child in the broom closet and the happiness of the citizens of Omelas. What we can see in the policies of "engagement" promoted by the British Inter-Agency Group (IAG) and International Union of Food, Agricultural, Hotel, Restaurant, Catering, Tobacco and Allied Workers' Associations (IUF), and in the various initiatives designed to ameliorate the violence perpetrated through corporate operations, is a mode of ethical intervention in which abstract values are pasted onto what is already present, papering over the cracks so that the child in the broom closet is hidden from view.

While Povinelli talks about "ethical grammars," we could just as well think in terms of moral-psychological strategies of avoidance or denial, modes of attachment to fantasies that make it possible—even necessary—to evade the relationship between the present order of things and the suffering on which that order is premised. In this chapter, I characterize what I call a "pernicious optimism" that animates the promotion of human rights as abstract add-ons to the present. The desire to affirm the ethical potentiality of the present takes the form of attachment to a fantasy that subsumes any possibility of addressing the relationship between the ethical intervention and the harm perpetuated toward that intervention's intended beneficiaries. This does not, however, lead me to advocate despair, to suggest that all that is left is to denounce what exists without the illusion that it is possible to transform the world. Instead, through reflection on struggles for alternatives to capitalism, I outline how human rights can be part of a grittier and more open-ended process of charting ethical coordinates in the face of devastation, where the violence of dominant human rights narratives is clearly on display.

The Pernicious Optimism of "Feel-Good" Ethics

Writing in Britain a little more than a decade ago—shortly after trade unions had succeeded in defeating the Colombian Food Workers Union's campaign against Coca-Cola—Mark Fisher coined the term *capitalist realism* to make sense of a juncture at which it had become impossible to so much as imagine an alternative to capitalism. Margaret Thatcher's slogan "There Is No Alternative," he said, had become a "brutally self-fulfilling prophecy."[6] We may know very well that capitalism is ruthless in human terms and ecologically unsustainable. We might take an ironic distance from it, even engage in protest. We might know, but we continue to act as if we do not. Capitalism, after all, "can proceed perfectly well without anyone making a case for it."[7] Capitalism need not be celebrated, or even defended: its ideology exercises a hold not simply at the level of conscious belief, but as an unconscious fantasy structuring our social reality.[8] The result, Fisher wrote, was a pervasive sense of political exhaustion and cultural sterility in which capitalism "seamlessly occupies the horizon of the thinkable."[9] We might associate this with a pessimistic outlook, given that the impossibility of an alternative is accepted with a sense of inevitability. Indeed, it may seem odd to suggest that we should characterize the attitudes of NGOs that sought to persuade BP to promote human rights, or of the trade union and student leaders who entered similar processes with Coca-Cola, in terms of optimism. They would be more likely to think of their attitude as realism, in contrast to the wishful thinking of peasant farmers who sought to challenge an entire economic model or workers who wanted to tackle "the empire behind the multinationals." The comments of a British trade union leader prominent within the anti-boycott campaign reflect precisely this self-understanding: the Colombian Food Workers needed to "get in the real world." They were naïve if they thought that their campaign could make any material difference to workers' conditions.[10] Yet what I want to explore is how, even here, the pessimistic expectation that bad things will continue to happen is accompanied by apparently paradoxical expressions of confidence about what can be achieved, despite it all. If actually existing capitalism occupies the horizon of the thinkable, then the "real world" can at least be declared good or amenable to positive intervention.

The process of constructive engagement between Britain's National Union of Students (NUS) and Coca-Cola provides a particularly stark example of this. The NUS Services Ethical and Environmental Committee published a series of documents that repeatedly referred to the allegations against Coca-Cola as if they could not really be true, praising the various "positive initiatives" undertaken by the company, such as a new "development fund" for communities in Colombia.[11] A few years after the international boycott ended, a video entitled "The Importance of Ethics to Students" appeared on the NUS website, setting out the achievements of engagement with Coca-Cola.[12] The company's move toward developing a global human rights policy is listed there alongside "better efficiency for different types of equipment provided in student shops and bars," as if human rights and students' consumption of soft drinks were on par with each other. All forms of "positive initiative" become equivalent. Everything becomes indistinct. Enjoy "the Coke side of life" and support human rights. The result is an ethics focused on the appearance of things. As Fisher put it, "Morality has been replaced by feeling."[13] What matters is not whether something is good or bad but whether it is good or bad for the individual engaging in a certain behavior. Ethics itself becomes a lifestyle choice, a proclamation of values that can be tacked onto anything, like a logo.

Western moral thought has rarely attended to its relationship to colonialism, or to how dominant iterations of the moral agent have tended to take for granted a particular understanding of the human as rational individual engaged in judgments of value, which also functions to police the parameters of the category of the human.[14] Nevertheless, there has been a critical aspect to Western moral philosophy, embodied in ideas of deliberation, conscience, and even virtue, that is obliterated when "values" are the order of the day. This is precisely what we see in those forms of ethical intervention that seek to promote human rights as add-ons to a global legal order that privileges property and commercial rights above all else. This fetishism of abstract values demands disavowal of the relationship between atrocity and the deadly legal-economic order that is the backdrop to humanistic intervention. It serves to patch the seams through which critique might emerge (and with it, lives, struggles, and suffering that cannot be assimilated to the fantasy). A widespread ethical newspeak simulates a world in which companies are responsible, in which governments exist to look after their citizens, and in which law exists to protect us from tyranny. Human rights as abstract values can be harnessed to other, equally abstract categories of social-humanitarian policy-speak, fueling aspirations for programmatic fixes on behalf of peripheral others who are—as we have seen—obliterated in the process (almost certainly at a symbolic level and sometimes at the level of life itself). It is not necessary—or even possible—to confront a reality in which interventions to protect human rights might in fact fuel systemic violence. "Justice" can be reduced to an agreement between parties. Conduct is assessed according to a series of tick-box schemas geared toward managing appearances and helping consumers feel good about their purchases and lifestyles.

In their campaigns on global issues, many NGOs seek actively to mobilize this "feel-good" ethics. As Amnesty International UK's director, Kate Allen, summed it up when launching the NGO's well-known "Protect the Human" campaign: "It has never been more important to stand up for human rights and now it has never been easier, by wearing a badge, going online, watching a film or taking part in an exhibition, you can show your support for our message."[15] Indeed, the 1990s not only saw the rise of the corporate code of conduct, global framework agreements, and the "anti-impunity" movement. The same period, Christine Schwöbel-Patel emphasizes, "saw a mutually influencing relationship emerge between marketing and global justice." Not only were global brands "looking enviously towards NGOs and other civil society groups because they had *meaning* already available."[16] Branding and marketing also proved adaptable to countercultural and anticapitalist aesthetics.[17] In Schwöbel-Patel's words, "Feel-good can be bought."[18] Allen's comments reflect a wider marketing-based approach to campaigning. Rather than sustained political organizing, the idea is to "sell" people an idea or a project, offering easy actions that can make them feel optimistic about their capacity to effect positive change. Do not depress people; do not make them feel negative. Do not engage in ideological critique but simplify the message so that goals appeal to what people already believe or feel (or, at least, what they desire to believe or feel).[19] To some extent, this is the unavoidable product of institutional constraints. To garner public support—be it financial, practical, or in terms of public opinion—it makes sense that NGOs speak a language that replicates the prevailing ideology. The British NGOs involved in the dialogue with BP were restrained by the fact that they were "household names" and had charitable status. Their mandate was to promote civil and political rights and to consider how royalties from oil extraction might contribute to "sustainable development," and they felt that they could not get involved in more confrontational campaigning.[20]

The approaches of the British NGOs that lauded BP's "good intentions," as well as of trade union representatives who campaigned against the Colombian Food Workers, relied on suppression of what was known to be the case. The British NGOs knew that BP executives were aware of links between the company's Colombian operations and death squads and that company executives, in turn, had also "chosen not to know."[21] The IUF knew that there was substance to the Food Workers' allegations and that its affiliate in Urabá had links to the same paramilitary groups that had perpetrated trade union genocide. Yet they publicly dismissed the allegations in their pursuit of a framework for dialogue with Coca-Cola. Here we see the paradox that so fascinated Sigmund Freud: that of disavowal, of simultaneously knowing and not knowing, captured in the formulation "I know well . . . but all the same."[22]

Disavowal, Stanley Cohen emphasizes, need not involve denial of a phenomenon; it might only involve denying its significance.[23] Thus, with respect to Le Guin's allegory, disavowal does not mean denying the existence of the child. It is a matter of the relationship one establishes to what one knows. For the British NGOs, the significance of what they knew was readily downplayed on the basis that, as one representative of the IAG put it, "If a few lives were saved, it was worth it." "All the same, we have to do *something*," goes the refrain. Thus, the NGO representatives could avoid confronting a reality in which their own interventions—and the abstractions through which those interventions were framed—might, in fact, have made the population around the oilfields even more vulnerable to being killed. The IUF could acknowledge in writing that some of the allegations did, in fact, have substance, but the significance of this was downplayed. Instead, the campaign against the Colombian Food Workers, alongside the IUF's encouragement of British students in a policy of "constructive engagement" and the simulation of a coherent "international trade union movement," served to solidify the fantasy that was the flip side of disavowal of "the facts" and to draw others into a "real world" that nevertheless had to be actively constructed.

Lauren Berlant described a relation of "cruel optimism," which exists when something we expect and desire—a fantasy of the "good life" or a political project, for instance—becomes harmful to us or impedes the aim that drew us to it in the first place.[24] Berlant's specific interest was in why people continue to adhere to conventional, hetero-familial, upwardly mobile fantasies of the good life—when these fantasies have become so unstable, fragile, and costly that the attachment ends up doing them harm.[25] Her cruel optimism addresses the harm we end up doing to ourselves by continuing to hold on to fantasy, to "hoard idealizing theories" in the face of the retraction of the promise of postwar social democracy in the United States and Europe, and the resultant "impending crises of life-building and expectation whose sheer volume so threatens what it has meant to 'have a life' that adjustment seems like an accomplishment."[26] My focus here, by contrast, is on how certain fantasies of ethical action on behalf of others can end up doing harm to the targets of intervention, impeding the aims of those who seek to act ethically in a subtle and insidious way. This is what I call "pernicious optimism": "pernicious" because the desire to affirm the ethical potentiality of the present takes the form of a fantasy that blocks out the possibility of addressing the relationship between the ethical intervention and the harm perpetuated through it. Rather than harming the subject of the optimistic attachment, pernicious optimism results, primarily, in harm being perpetuated toward others: the intended beneficiaries of intervention. Often these harmful effects are not immediately visible or clearly traceable to the ethical intervention itself. Yet the attachment to the fantasy is such that it inhibits sustained reflection on how harm might be generated.

Disavowal is central to the construction of a virtual reality in which pernicious optimism takes hold. It feeds the kind of reified thought in which actual lives and struggles are subsumed beneath abstract categories such as "civil society" and "the international trade union movement," to which equally abstract "human rights" can be added. In the case of the IUF, this was inseparable from continued attachment to a fantasy of social partnership, clinging to the categories of a bygone social configuration long after the demise of the postwar social pact. Representatives of the so-called international trade union movement know very well, of course, that the postwar social pact is no longer in existence even in its European former heartlands. Yet, all the same, they have conjured a "real world" in which social-democratic principles can be recovered at a global level. Labor just has to adapt to globalization, so the story goes. There is, as a result, no space to talk about how rights are pinned to particular sorts of human, within boundaries that mark out who is entitled to a long life and who can be abandoned to a slow death. Meanwhile, the imperatives of the "rule of law," "the market," and "good business sense" are reframed: not as generative of mass suffering, but as part of the solution to that suffering, the basis of corporate responsibility for human rights. Where direct acts of violence lead to harms that are legally recognizable as injury, and human rights advocates seek to hold perpetrators "to account," the deeper significance of those harms is disavowed through mechanisms of reactive justice that serve to draw a line behind past evils and to reaffirm the soundness of the present order of things.

Human rights as abstract values have been a keystone of this perniciously optimistic mode of humanistic intervention. It does not, however, follow that we should reject human rights on this basis, any more than we should reject human rights as inherently capitalist or inherently colonial. Rather, we should be cautious toward the deployment of abstract values more widely, sensitive to what may be disavowed in the adherence to a fantasy. "Whatever the *experience* of optimism is in particular," Berlant writes, "the *affective structure* of an optimistic attachment involves a sustaining inclination to return to the scene of fantasy that enables you to expect that *this* time, nearness to *this* thing will help you or a world to become different in just the right way."[27] Indeed, it is worth emphasizing that so-called radical left politics is also vulnerable to its own perniciously optimistic attachments. Maybe what is disavowed is not the existence of suffering or even its root causes, but secret convictions, unwanted desires and beliefs similar to those captured in in George Orwell's comments in 1937 on class difference. "We all rail against class distinctions," Orwell wrote, "but very few people seriously want to abolish them." On the contrary, "every revolutionary opinion draws part of its strength from a secret conviction that nothing can be changed."[28] Along similar lines, Slavoj Žižek likens the attitude of many leftists to that of smokers who are so sure that they can give up smoking when they choose to do so that "the possibility of change is evoked to guarantee that it will not be acted upon." The need for an alternative to capitalism is invoked as "a kind of superstitious token that should achieve the opposite."[29]

The same might be said of some variants of decolonial thought. I previously mentioned Silvia Rivera Cusicanqui's condemnation of the "elitist" tendency of lauded decolonial scholars to reify and romanticize Indigenous ontologies and epistemologies in a manner that occludes the "counterhegemonic strategies" at play in actual struggles. Rejecting modernity outright, Rivera Cusicanqui comments, is an easy move for those not encountering dispossession and deprivation as part of their everyday reality.[30] In those who romanticize decoloniality from the comfort of secure positions in the university, we find the sort of reified thought that feeds on fantasy. Just like the fetishism of abstract values, these perniciously optimistic attachments on the part of "radical" thinkers are—as Žižek puts it—"a sign of theoretical cowardice, functioning as a fetish that prevents us from thinking through to the end of the deadlock of our predicament."[31]

However, Žižek's own proposal in response to this scenario is as detached from actual struggles against dispossession and oppression as the proposals of the scholars whom Rivera Cusicanqui criticizes. We should, he insists, gather the strength to despair: "It is only when we despair and don't know what to do anymore that the change can be enacted—we have to go through that zero point of hopelessness."[32] Rather than advocating despair, keeping with Žižek to the course of a long-running current of bleakness in European critical thought, it might serve us better to do what Rivera Cusicanqui advocates: consider strategies of struggle in contexts in which disavowal of capitalism's devastating consequences cannot be sustained.

Human Rights beyond Abstract Values

Struggles such as those that converged around the Permanent Peoples' Tribunal (PPT) session on Transnational Corporations and the Rights of Peoples in Colombia embody the reverse of the pernicious optimism of much mainstream human rights activism. The denunciation of human rights abuse made through the hearings of the tribunal reflected precisely the ethical imperative that Povinelli draws from Le Guin's story. The world of consumption, "development," the "Coke side of life" (in the words of one advertising slogan) is shown to be inseparable from its constitutive underside: exhaustion; impoverishment; inhuman labor conditions; worsening disabilities; the suicide of Guillermo Gómez; the murders of José Manco, Luís Giraldo, Luís Gómez, Isidro Gil, and Adolfo Múnera; the abduction and torture of Limberto Carranza's fifteen-year-old son; the attempted abduction of William Mendoza's four-year-old daughter.[33] The world "Beyond Petroleum"—a marketing slogan of BP at that time—was shown to include Dulcelina Sanabria's desperate wait for her teenage sons, Jefer and Gustavo Mora Sanabria, when they did not return one day from buying cheese, then her trip to the morgue to identify their bodies, dressed up after death to give the impression that they had been left-wing guerrillas killed in combat. It included the kidnapping and torture of Gilberto Torres, who had become, as he put it, a "thorn in the side" of the oil companies because of his trade union work. The destruction of human life was also shown to be inseparable from the destruction of the land, crimes against humanity inextricably linked to crimes against nature. The promise of "development"—and the extractive model on which a future "peace" was said to depend—was the promise of more deaths like those of thousands of children who had died around the Cerrejón mine. The victims of human rights abuse here were not mere victims, inviting liberal empathy. They were named explicitly as lives wounded and destroyed by the everyday, often entirely legal operation of the political-economic model on which the "good life" of its beneficiaries depends.

What is important to underscore, however, is that the session of the PPT was not a stand-alone process but deeply embedded within social movement struggles for alternatives to capitalism. In addition to using human rights strategically to expose the violence of the existing legal order, these struggles strive to find ways to sustain and reproduce life that are less harmful and less predatory on people and planet, but with a remarkably open-ended set of normative coordinates that are quite at odds with the optimistic attachments on display in some streams of "radical" thought. The network that coalesced around the PPT has also been deeply involved for many years in a series of place-based peasant, Black, and Indigenous struggles seeking to enact alternatives to "development" in the here and now. Known as *planes de vida* (plans of/for life), they are processes that emerged across Colombia in the face of state- and corporate-backed plunder and paramilitary terror. My relationship to the *planes de vida* has been somewhat different from my involvement with the Colombian Food Workers Union, strategic litigation initiatives, or the process of recovering historical memory in Casanare (where there was no active *plan de vida*). While I was living and working in Colombia with la Red de Hermandad, a regular topic at our weekly meetings was the work of supporting and connecting different *plan de vida* processes. The Coordinador Nacional Agrario (CNA), a grassroots national coordinating body of peasant, Black, and Indigenous groups and part of la Red, has been an important force building links among the *planes de vida*. During our meetings, CNA representatives gave regular updates on different processes in different regions of the country. In the run-up to the final hearing of the PPT in 2008, the network brought people from across Colombia for a two-day forum to discuss and share experiences of their *planes de vida*. This was facilitated by a friend of mine who had recently served a long prison sentence on charges of "rebellion" because of his role as a popular educator with a *plan de vida* process in oil-rich Arauca, which borders Casanare. In the run-up to the forum, which I had a small role in helping to organize, my friend recounted the story of the Arauca process for several hours over wine. The *plan de vida* process with which I had the closest, albeit intermittent, links was that in Catatumbo—a remote, predominantly rural region toward the northern end of Colombia's border with Venezuela. A delegation from la Red visited Catatumbo in November 2007 in the context of a spate of extrajudicial assassinations and other atrocities at the hands of state forces over the previous ten months.

The nature of the *plan de vida* process was most clearly articulated over a shared meal with members of the rotating leadership of the Comité de Integración Social del Catatumbo (Committee for the Social Integration of Catatumbo [CISCA]). Catatumbo, which means "house of thunder," is inhabited mostly by Barí Indigenous people and small-scale peasant farmers, and

CISCA is an umbrella body that draws together local peasant and Indigenous associations. These populations, as one of the leaders of CISCA put it, have been "abandoned by the state for all their social programmes. The only thing they have offered us is repression and militarisation in the service of natural resource extraction."[34] Since the end of the 1990s, inhabitants of the region had suffered several years of occupation by state-backed paramilitaries, during which thousands of people were killed and thousands more were forcibly displaced from their homes. While this was, as usual, framed as a counterinsurgency offensive, it was in reality, as Gearóid Ó Loingsigh emphasizes in a book written with CISCA, the result of the majority of the victims' being considered part of "a surplus population sitting on top of natural riches."[35] By the time of my visit, paramilitaries had begun demobilizing and the burden of repression had been handed back to official state forces, as was the case in Casanare.[36] Nevertheless, over the previous three or four years, many of those driven from their homes by paramilitary terror had begun to return to the region, with Indigenous and peasant organizations beginning to discuss how they could work together in defense of life and territory. A community meeting of more than four hundred people in 2004 had resulted in the formation of CISCA as a coordinating body designed, in the words of one of the committee's leaders at that time, "so that we can pursue our dream of continuing to live in Catatumbo and resist the state's attempts to displace us from the land so that multinational corporations can exploit natural resources."

It was in pursuit of this dream that CISCA began a process of "building thought in a collective way" to develop concrete proposals "for remaining on the land and for defense of life, in a way which includes everyone in Catatumbo—peasant farmers, indigenous people, women, children, old people, workers, teachers," as another CISCA leader put it. She explained that the *plan de vida* was pitched from the start against dominant ideas of "development."[37] Yet crucially, as with other *planes de vida* across the country, CISCA also refused the idea that the construction of an alternative should follow a ready-made blueprint or be framed in terms of a fixed set of concepts imported from theory or leftist doctrine. "The *plan de vida* is not a document," this CISCA leader underscored. "What is this proposal called? Is it 'socialism'? Is it 'communism'? A proposal with its own name and number plate? No, it doesn't yet have a name, but definitely it is not capitalism. It is not about how to accommodate ourselves to the strategies of capital." "Life" and "territory" were initially invoked as empty names that, as she put it, "we then had to fill with content. What does it mean to defend 'life' and 'territory'? . . . What is 'territory' in itself, and what do the people want?"

One important influence on *planes de vida* has been the concept of *buen vivir*, an expression of the cosmological visions of Indigenous peoples of the Andes (roughly, "living well together," implying harmonious relations among one another and between humans and nature).[38] However, it is important to emphasize that *buen vivir* is not invoked as a predefined category. On the contrary, as the CNA underscored in 2011 in the booklet *Construyendo nuestros planes de vida* (Building our plans for life), "It is worth being clear that there is no finished concept of *Buen Vivir*. Rather, different communities have developed their own concepts in accordance with their own cultures and territories."[39] *Buen vivir* is open-ended. It is mobilized and defined in the context of struggle, as part of a process of thinking "life" collectively outside of what the CNA describes as the "straitjacket" of development discourse, in which life "can be more or less reduced to being born, growing up, consuming, reproducing oneself and dying" and that "locates us according to statistics, as if our lives were a straight line."[40] As my popular educator friend commented during our long conversation about the Arauca process, the critique of development also engendered critique of the notion of the human it entailed—the sovereign and self-interested subject—while the "convergence in space time" between peasant struggles and those of Indigenous peoples led to a redefinition of life as "a dynamic equilibrium between the physical, the biological and the human," as well as a critique of linear conceptions of time.

Filling "life" and "territory" with content has also meant, in the words of one of the CISCA leaders, asking, "What are the conditions experienced by the population in this territory?" Within all the *plan de vida* processes, addressing these questions has implied an ongoing process of collective "diagnosis" of how the problems people face have been shaped historically and how they are connected to wider dynamics at a national and international level. The processes of diagnosis of social and political conditions that are part of the *planes de vida* have little in common with the modes of analysis also commonly referred to as diagnosis: contextual studies carried out by state bodies, multilateral organizations, and NGOs to guide developmentalist intervention in Colombia's remote and "savage" regions considered beyond the control of the state.[41] As Margarita Serje underscores, the construction of "context" exercises a profound discursive power over people, events, and possibilities of action, and these latter forms of "diagnosis," based on forms of knowledge that purport to be technical, neutral, and objective, are, in fact, conceptualized in a manner that obscures and legitimates the colonial social order that they represent.[42] A key aspect of social and political diagnosis taking place within the *planes de vida*, by contrast, is that the analysis of context begins with the viewpoints of the people living in a territory. Multiple methodologies have been developed for these processes in different parts of Colombia: community forums, research into political economy, social cartography, local history. But the aim is not simply to understand the present in the context of histories of oppression and struggle. It is to use this as a guide for the transformation of the future.[43]

Another important aspect of the process of diagnosis is a concern with how relations of power and violence are reproduced within the process of forging a would-be alternative. This was reflected in CISCA's decision to avoid visible figureheads and to adopt a rotating leadership structure. One leader commented that, when the process started, it was heavily dominated by men, generating the question of whether women were being excluded because of structural inequalities. "Some people said, 'Oh, women aren't interested in this sort of thing,'" she explained, "but when they started asking women about it, it was clear the problem was actually that women did not have time because of their domestic responsibilities. So we had to change that . . . traditional patriarchal division of labor." Alongside the decision to have a permanent rotation of leadership, CISCA has insisted on—in the words of this female leader—"a respectful inclusion of women and young people, even though this implies some profound cultural transformations." At the start of the two-day forum that brought together groups involved in different *planes de vida* across the country, the first PowerPoint slide bore the slogan "Before Taking Power, We Must Avoid Being Taken by Power," which is associated with the Zapatista Indigenous struggle in Mexico, as well as with various strands of anarchist thought. My friend from Arauca, facilitating the conversation, characterized the demand as moving past "a logic of war, a logic that annuls, marginalizes, that tells the other, 'not you,' that is always negating the other."

The idea that social movements should seek to avoid being taken by power and that they should put into practice the norms of the future society to which they aspire is often described as "prefiguration," an expression that reflects the origins of these ideas in medieval and early modern radical social movements.[44] Unlike the *planes de vida*, these movements held fast to the idea that there was already a direction in which history was going, the "absent promise" of the Kingdom of God in which equality and justice would prevail. Thus, struggles in the present were deemed literally to prefigure this future fulfilment, within the temporal frame of a linear history moving under its own momentum.[45] Within the *planes de vida*, the temporal framing is very distinct from this. Rather than evoking an "absent promise" of the future realization of a better life, the prefigurative aspect of the *planes de vida* reflects the "generative" temporal logic that Uri Gordon identifies in European anarchist thought (framed in opposition to an authoritarian Marxism and, certainly, those Marxists who saw future revolution as preordained).[46] This is the idea of a path dependence between means and ends; that a movement's way of doing and being in the world is inseparable from what it seeks to create. As the CNA put it in its booklet, the *planes de vida* are a way of life in themselves, as well as part of a political struggle for *buen vivir*:[47] "The *planes de vida* are word and action: they have a public manifestation as political action by communities and organizational processes, and they are also a horizon of desire in which our form of life is shown. This aspect is fundamental because what is at stake is . . . the projection of another mode of being, knowing and acting in the world."[48]

It is only in this context, within the everyday practice of building a *plan de vida*—in which "life" remains to be "filled with content"; in which an "unfinished" idea of *buen vivir* is defined and redefined within the open-ended process of struggle—that we can understand the appeal to human rights. Despite the challenge to the ontology of the individual at the heart of dominant human rights narratives, demands for rights are nevertheless central to the *planes de vida*. At one level, they are demands simply for survival: that the state stop killing and stop abandoning the population to the exigencies of wealth extraction. For instance, la Red's visit to Catatumbo in November 2007 was undertaken with the purpose of collecting the evidence that community groups had collated regarding the murders of more than thirty local people by the Colombian Army since February of that year. Shortly before the delegation's visit, Eliécer Ortega was detained in his home by the army and later appeared in the municipal morgue reported as a guerrilla killed in combat. Carlos Daniel Martínez was alone in his house the same morning when the army arrived. He, too, was reported as a guerrilla killed in combat, as were two teenage boys whose bodies were found by the river the following day. As one of the committee's leaders commented at the time, "We can't walk the paths alone anymore because at any moment we could be shot and a report made of a 'guerrilla' killed in combat, when it is a *campesino* who was going to market for their family, who was harvesting crops or just working on their farm."

In this situation, a central part of CISCA's response was the documentation and reporting of human rights abuse in a manner that would be entirely recognizable to the mainstream human rights movement (and that, as I mentioned in the introduction, has been part of la Red's combined activities from the start). The committee also sought to highlight and denounce the high level of militarization in a region inhabited by only 250,000 people. It had been announced that a further army brigade, the 21st, would soon be in operation alongside the 5th Mobile Brigade and the 30th Brigade, who at that time were the state's only presence in Catatumbo. However, CISCA was clear that what it wanted to denounce to the national and international community was a genocidal strategy deployed in the interests of capital. The pretext for the killing may have been counterinsurgency, but as a leader of CISCA summed up to a fellow member of the November 2007 delegation:

> We believe that underneath this military strategy there is an aim to guarantee the extraction of mineral and energy resources and natural resources in general. . . . This military presence provides security for the oil companies, for the transnational corporations who are putting everything into coal extraction, those who are sowing oil palm, those who want to privatize the water. . . . We think that this strategy of terror is being sown by the national army so that we are afraid, so that we leave. In some cases, the army has directly asked the peasants, "Why don't you go? Why don't you leave the region?" Which is to say that there is an interest in emptying the territory by whatever means—by criminalization, by legal cases against us, by detentions, by murders, by the strategy of terror, so that the people leave.[49]

It was in direct opposition not only to this genocidal strategy, but also to the imposition of a political economy threatening an ecological disaster that would "end life in the region" that CISCA mobilized a discourse of human rights.[50] Over subsequent years, the committee has established three "Houses of Rights," designed to build mutual capacity to document abuses and undertake advocacy directed at public institutions and national and international human rights networks. However, these initiatives are presented explicitly as part of a wider struggle to "defend life and a dignified existence in the territory."[51] Human rights—and institutional mechanisms to ensure their urgent protection—are demanded as a guarantee so that people can continue to build their *planes de vida*.[52] Just as, in the hearings of the PPT, law's logic of equity was deployed to critique the tyranny of actually existing legality, people involved in the *planes de vida* have demanded human rights as part of a practice of immanent critique. That is to say that the appeal to human rights, like appeals to "equality, peace, social justice and popular sovereignty," deploys the system's own stated principles against it.[53] Human rights can be demanded, as one of the leaders of the Catatumbo process put it, only as "a party in conflict with the state," to expose these contradictions and call the state to account for its abandonment and repression of the population. As such, the appeal to human rights serves to contest given definitions of lives worth living within international development discourse. It is an implicit condemnation of abstract ethics, of the privatization of human rights as add-ons to an economic model that has brought suffering, death, and the destruction of the land.

Alongside the appeal to rights formally recognized but disregarded in practice, CISCA and other organizations building *planes de vida* have added their voices to those of social movements around the world that demand that international law and national legislative processes recognize the peasantry as a collective subject of territorial and cultural rights. A central focus of the demands of organizations involved in *planes de vida* across Colombia has been the legal recognition of collective rights for peasant populations akin to the Indigenous and Afro-descendant rights already recognized. The point is not to pit the rights of peasants against those of these other populations. On the contrary, the demand is sometimes conceptualized in terms of the construction of "intercultural territories" based on unity, fraternity, and solidarity among these groups. What is key is that these territories are founded autonomously by their populations and rooted in their own processes of food production, care for the natural world, and grassroots politics.[54] The law— and, specifically, the demand for rights—is used here as a terrain of struggle on which the goal is to reshape relationships between humans and nature. Here, too, rights are demanded as a "party in conflict" with the state. The demand for a right to territorial autonomy is conceived as one that can create room for self-government, and for a space in which the population's own code of conduct—in the form of "Manuals for Coexistence for *Buen Vivir*"—can be put in place and followed.[55] Far from limiting struggle to the reference points of law and state sovereignty, the demand for rights is conceptualized within a horizon of *buen vivir*, along "an open path of constant becoming, the dream held by so many of enjoying the rivers and mountains, without the latent threat imposed by the lords of capital who sow war and death in order to appropriate the goods of nature."[56]

Thus, there is no place within the *planes de vida* for human rights as add-ons to the present order of things, any more than there is room for a predefined understanding of the "life" to be protected and defended. On the contrary, the very meaning of "the human" is inseparable from the understanding of life that takes shape in struggle. As the CNA expresses it directly, the *planes de vida* "seek the transformation of the human" through this collective process.[57] The appeal to human rights in these struggles thus occupies a sort of liminal space, a use of available normative and legal vocabularies in pursuit of a yet-to-be-defined alternative. By invoking "human rights" and setting out visions for "life" in opposition to a dehumanizing, life-negating political economy, "humanity," "life," and the understanding of the present to which these ideals are opposed are not given once and for all. Rather, they are defined and redefined in relation to one another. The diagnostic process of developing an understanding of global capitalism as inimical to "life" is emergent from the experience of being routinely treated as if less than human by the architects of law and policy. Yet, crucially, this process of critique and the experiences that drive it are also inseparable from efforts to reach beyond critique to a deeper sense of worth. The commitment remains to the possibility that something good—a better plan for life, an "unfinished" idea of *buen vivir*—can be built in the aftermath of atrocity and amid ongoing repression, holding on to a sense of the good that is always, and indefinitely, something yet to be pinned down.

Hope against Optimism

The open-endedness of the *planes de vida* reflects an affective orientation that is quite at odds with the pernicious optimism that inspires much mainstream human rights advocacy. There is no possibility here of suppression of what is known about the consequences of capitalism or of disavowal of the significance of that knowledge. There is no room for attachment to a fantasy of future revolutionary change emerging from the contradictions of capitalism, or (as I discuss further in the next chapter) for fetishistic invocation of *buen vivir* as an expression of a difference conceived outside of modernity/coloniality. The ethos of the *planes de vida* resists a "logic of war," of "us" versus "them," revolutionary versus reformist, coloniality versus a romantically conceived decolonial alternative. At the heart of this ethos is a reckoning with power: not just the global, national, and regional dynamics of capitalist coloniality, but also how everyday power relations that negate or limit life are reproduced within political organization for an alternative to capitalism. As "word and action" the *planes de vida* embody the recognition that there is no available solution, nothing with its "own name and number plate" to form an object of attachment and desire. Yet the *planes de vida* are nevertheless a challenge to those thinkers, such as Žižek, who advocate despair from the comfort of the academy. For all that Žižek has to say about the "courage of hopelessness," he has little to say about the nature of hope.

The title of Terry Eagleton's 2015 book, *Hope without Optimism*, encapsulates the distance between optimism and hope. Unlike optimism, Eagleton writes, hope "is needed most when the situation is at its starkest, a state of extremity that optimism is generally loath to acknowledge."[58] Hope does not entail the expectation, or even the belief, that things will somehow turn out well. It does not involve the inclination that Berlant identifies "to return to the scene of fantasy that enables you to expect that *this* time, nearness to *this* thing will help you or a world to become better in just the right way."[59] On the contrary, in Eagleton's words, "The most authentic kind of hope is whatever can be salvaged, stripped of guarantees, from a general dissolution. It represents an irreducible residue that refuses to give way, plucking its resilience from an openness to the possibility of unmitigated disaster."[60] This, I think, is what we find within the *planes de vida* as struggles that emerge from the experience of atrocity and oppression. Hope is an avoidance of despair that has nothing to do with optimism. In Jonathan Lear's words, "The commitment is only to the bare possibility that, from this disaster, something good will emerge."[61]

Lear's analysis of the nature of hope is particularly insightful in juxtaposition with the *planes de vida*. His reflections revolve around the story of Plenty Coups, a chief of the Crow Indigenous people in the United States, who saw the transition of his people's nomadic hunting culture into a life confined to reservations. What the Crow faced in that context, for Lear, was a "crisis of intelligibility": the very concepts with which to construct a narrative about life broke down.[62] Yet Plenty Coups persisted and continued to lead his people when their world no longer hung together. He avoided despair at a point when despair might appear inevitable.[63] This is what Lear calls "radical hope." It shows, he says, that "a very peculiar form of commitment is possible and intelligible: namely, that although Plenty Coups can recognise that his understanding of self and world is based on a set of living commitments that are vulnerable, it is nevertheless possible to commit to a goodness which transcends that understanding."[64] Lear, however, evades the context of Plenty Coups's persistence as one of a genocidal settler colonialism. It is also not clear—as Hubert Dreyfus points out—how total the devastation was; whether Lear is really talking about a way of life becoming impossible rather than entirely unintelligible.[65] What Lear himself seeks to highlight by reference to the story of Plenty Coups is a "peculiar form of human vulnerability": an ontological vulnerability to a crisis of intelligibility to which all humans are subject.[66]

It would not, however, be difficult to reread Lear's account through the lens of a more specific ontological vulnerability, faced by those constituted as ontological lack, which is to say rendered insufficiently "human" (in hegemonic terms) to thrive in the face of "development."[67] While Berlant suggests in her discussion of optimism a need to move away from "trauma" as a genre for describing the historical present—at least in the context through which she develops her concepts—trauma does seem a relevant category for characterizing the crisis of intelligibility from which hope (without optimism) can be salvaged. We are all exposed to perpetual instability and fragmentation of the symbolic world that we inhabit. Any of us might be exposed to ordeals that set reality adrift. Yet some are particularly exposed to such ordeals, and it is worth observing that discussions of trauma have tended to overlook quotidian and persistent forms of trauma such as those with their roots in colonialism.[68] Reading the story of Plenty Coups as a story of the trauma of colonialism allows us to identify a parallel form of vulnerability among all of those that Frantz Fanon called *les damnés*, "imperial constructs who can only be understood as the differences outside . . . the *anthropos* in relation to *humanitas* as *humanitas* is defined by those who conceive of themselves as Human."[69] These are people who are not just confined to reservations and kept in place while their way of life is wrest asunder, but who are also massacred and displaced for the sake of extractive projects or allowed to die from hunger, thirst, exhaustion. For Fanon, the trauma of colonialism was such that the cleansing violence of anticolonial struggle was required to introduce "a new language and a new humanity."[70] In the PPT's ruling on Political Genocide, Impunity, and Crimes against Peace in 2021, it was trauma that was identified as the source of the disavowal of a genocide that was ongoing. Yet the *planes de vida* indicate another possible response to trauma: that in the face of the intolerable, when there is no fixed or discernible path ahead, hope is embodied in the capacity to pursue "unfinished," open-ended ideas of *buen vivir*, "life," "humanity," or—in Lear's words—"a future goodness that transcends the ability to understand what it is."[71]

Today, Eagleton suggests, the very idea of hope has been surrendered to the "banality of optimism." So far apart are the two that optimism should be considered as much a form of hopelessness as should despair.[72] Social movement struggles such as the *planes de vida*, however, point us to an alternative way of thinking, to an affective disposition that resists the optimistic attachment to abstract values, idealized theories, or romanticized alternatives (as well as to the fantasies of the "good life" highlighted by Berlant). These struggles point us to a use of human rights that goes beyond the promotion of fetishized values, beyond attempts to "bring to justice" within the framework of dominant legal narratives, beyond even strategic invocations of rights that reveal the violence of legality and the impossibility of justice. When configured as demands that the forces of capital and the state desist from their atrocities against those treated as less than human, in the context of struggles to make the human anew, human rights can be harnessed to the pursuit of an alternative where what is being fought for has yet to be pinned down. There is nothing programmatic or abstract about these initiatives, no optimistic attachment to reified categories of emancipation or expectation that their struggles will ever be complete. There is, however, a commitment to continuing to try to transform the world, a refusal to acquiesce with capitalism, even in the face of atrocity and devastation. In contrast to mainstream international human rights activism, these struggles invoke human rights within a forward-looking conception—with all its open-endedness and uncertainty intact—of what it might mean to be human.

for an insurgent humanism

When Amnesty International urged people to help "protect the human" through easy, everyday gestures of support, there was no space for questioning how admission to the category of the human is regulated. Nevertheless, if the policies of today's global institutions can be understood in Humberto Cárdenas and Álvaro Marín's terms as "defending life by sowing death," then we should remember that it is a very specific understanding of "life" that is defended.[1] It is a "human" whose survival has already meant devastation for the victims of capitalism and colonialism and that, ultimately, implies "unparalleled catastrophe" for our species and for the planet.[2] The solemn humanism of the United Nations Charter feeds itself from this historical subsoil, irrigated by an optimism that quickly gives way to despair for rights promoted at the same time that they are systematically neglected. "If this is European 'humanism,'" Cárdenas and Marín write, "then it is a 'humanism' that still implies damnation for African and Latin American humanity."[3]

The struggles I discuss in this book all emerge, in one way or another, from the contestation of a vision of the human confined within the parameters of "development" into which populations are forced by blood and fire. This being the case, struggles over what it is to be human are far from merely symbolic or epiphenomenal to material struggles for structural change. The sovereign, rational individual is not just an idea out there, having its effects at an ideological or epistemological level. It is a material reality that surrounds and suffocates attempts to be otherwise. It confers on the legal order normative underpinnings, making possible the legal fictions of "free" worker, corporate "person," responsible individual, and party to a contract. It is, as such, a constitutive part of a global political economy premised on exploitation, expropriation, and the degradation of human and nonhuman life. Indeed, one of the key contributions of Sylvia Wynter's genealogy of "overrepresented Man" has been her insistence that the human is never a purely biological description of our species, with everything cultural coming after, but always a hybrid creation of biology and narrative—of *bios* and *mythos* or, in Frantz Fanon's terminology, of skins and masks.[4] In other words, the human is not a noun but a praxis.[5] When those involved in the *planes de vida* insist on thinking the human otherwise, or when social movement lawyers advance counterlegalities that decenter the rational individual, they are not simply engaging in epistemic struggles. They are also, simultaneously, confronting contradictions of capitalist development and legality as they are lived and felt in material conditions.

In this final chapter, I want to consider the implications of this for human rights as an ethical discourse harnessed within struggle. Traditionally, philosophical accounts of human rights have tended to rely on a humanist position, grounding the universalism of rights in the inherent dignity of the human individual. There are various permutations of humanism (from liberal political theory to Marxist humanist accounts of Man's ability to throw off false consciousness and discover "his" essential nature). Nevertheless, the category of the human tends to be circumscribed by reference to attributes of the individual deemed morally valuable, such as reason, judgment, autonomy, and freedom.[6] In other words, this is precisely the sort of "humanism" that Cárdenas and Marín decry as a death sentence for much of humanity. As Nelson Maldonado-Torres comments in his reflections "on the coloniality of human rights," inasmuch as human rights operate within the terms of such a humanism, they "engage in the performative contradiction of denying humanity in the very process of seeking to affirm human rights."[7] Once we unsettle sovereign, rational Man from the place he occupies as the subject of ethics, important questions arise for how we understand the ethical call to defend "life" or to act in solidarity with others. "Interrogating the subject of ethics, as 'Man,' renews the question of ethics," Louiza Odysseos emphasizes.

It "shows us that the modern colonial stabilisation of knowledge about who we are as human cannot function as a foundation for a revisioned humanism or for decolonial ethics."[8] For Odysseos, following Wynter, the task is to construct a decolonial ethics that can retell the story of what it is to be human, drawing on and participating in struggles that seek to rupture the hegemony of the vision of "Man" that has justified expropriation and dehumanization.[9]

While the *planes de vida* can be considered instances of this sort of struggle, the ethnographic lens of this book leads me to highlight two aspects of how normative visions are shaped in struggle that may not otherwise come readily into view. First, at an empirical level, we should not lose sight of how the *planes de vida* are sites of immanent critique in which retelling the story of what it is to be human takes place in the context of a critique of capitalist social relations in the present. They are, furthermore, enmeshed with other struggles: struggles of rural populations for agrarian reform, struggles of trade unions against "the empire behind the multinationals," initiatives such as the Permanent Peoples' Tribunal (PPT), and so on, drawing on an array of tools of critique within which Marxist ideas are prominent. This is not an insight at odds with Wynter's own emphasis on the experience and concrete struggles of those constituted as less than human. Indeed, Wynter herself has emphasized how the need to understand totality emerges from the experience of oppression and dispossession.[10] Nevertheless, this aspect is important to dwell on, given the tendency of some "decolonial" thought to romanticize and reify "other" worlds and knowledges. Retelling the story of what it is to be human, filling the "unfinished" concept of *buen vivir* with content, is a praxis that emerges through this process of structural critique.

Second, and more substantively, I want to suggest that these struggles point us beyond the injunction to decolonize the praxis of being human and back to the question of the grounds of ethical obligation: of the relations between the immanent and the transcendent, between politics and its outside. Without the inherent dignity of sovereign "Man" as a foundation for the ethical obligation to "protect the human," reference to anything transcendent has become unfashionable. In much decolonial scholarship, the question of the normative underpinnings of struggle is superseded by an emphasis on the ontologies rooted in Indigenous cosmologies and the submerged political worlds of those in struggle (often romanticized as ontologically "Other"). Wynter, by contrast, does gesture to something beyond the "masks," orders of consciousness, modes of being through which we experience ourselves as human. Her rejection of the "false humanity" of European humanism does not lead her to abandon humanism or even to disavow the partial breakthroughs at the level of cognition made possible by earlier humanisms. Rather, what she seeks is humanism's "re-enchantment."[11]

Yet Wynter herself does not engage directly with what I think is a real and compelling feature of the struggles I have discussed here. That is, they reach toward a transcendent sense of the good, represented in the *planes de vida* by *buen vivir* as a concept with profoundly spiritual connotations but that is, at the same time, "unfinished," impossible to fully pin down.[12] This leads me on, in the second part of this chapter, to a more philosophical discussion in which I set out the coordinates of what I call an "insurgent humanism" that embodies a dialectical tension between immanent critique and the ineffable transcendence of the ethical call. It is in these terms, I suggest, that we need to understand human rights as ethical discourse and as vocabulary of solidarity with others.

Between *Buen Vivir* and Immanent Critique

The Coordinador Nacional Agrario (CNA) describes *planes de vida* as "the projection of another mode of being, knowing and acting in the world," embodying a sense of what it is to be human radically at odds with the "human" hailed within development discourse.[13] Thus, these struggles can be understood as actively contesting what Wynter calls the "master code of symbolic life and death" on which the dominant conception of humanity is predicated, as *homo economicus*, as sovereign and self-interested subject.[14] At this point, however, I want to underscore a point that is already implicit in the previous chapter: the process of filling "life" and "territory" with content, of giving flesh to the "unfinished" concept of *buen vivir*, is not simply a matter of invoking Indigenous ontologies as a ready-made framework for understanding the world in opposition to modern/colonial ontologies of Man and associated discourses of development. Wynter herself is clear that "unsettling the coloniality of Being/Power/Truth/Freedom" is not a matter of invoking radical alterity but something that takes place in relationship to the modern/colonial sedimentation of knowledge about what it means to be human, through struggle and through the experience of being constituted as "lack," as insufficiently human, as ethically exploitable and available for expropriation.[15] This is important because it runs counter to an increasingly prominent trend of thought that understands decoloniality through the lens of radical ontological difference, where "ontology" is not, as David Graeber emphasized, understood in standard philosophical terms as referring to "a discourse (*logos*) *about* the nature of being (or alternatively about its essence, or about being in itself, or about the basic building blocks of reality)"—humanity, time, nature, the source of morality, and so on—that then invests our modes of being and acting in the world. Rather, ontology has, in this more recent literature, been taken to refer to incommensurable "ways of being," in the sense of multiple worlds or multiple realities.[16]

The recent work of Arturo Escobar is a good example of this line of thinking, particularly given that his earlier genealogy of development discourse has been an important influence on the *planes de vida*.[17] Escobar describes Afro-descendant territorial struggles against extractivism in Colombia as "ontological struggles" at heart, because they involve a fight for Afro-Colombians' own way of "worlding."[18] The account that Escobar presents of ontological difference is not of "one" world that might be viewed, engaged with, acted within through different perspectives. Instead, difference is understood as ontological in a way that sustains "multiple worlds" or "reals."[19] The distinction is a subtle one, but it matters, because there is a risk of subsuming the complexities of political struggle within an understanding of alterity that appears desirable from the perspective of a "decolonial" framework shaped within the academy and then applied to actual struggles (in precisely the manner that Silvia Rivera Cusicanqui criticizes). In reality, Afro-descendant movements in Colombia draw on plural traditions of thought and, indeed, plural ontologies (in the sense of discourses about the nature of being). Alongside the CNA, the Committee for the Social Integration of Catatumbo, and the Social Organizations of Arauca, which I have already discussed in relation to the *planes de vida*, the Proceso de Comunidades Negras (Process of Black Communities [PCN]) is another organization in la Red de Hermandad involved in similar struggles. The PCN is an umbrella organization that brings together more than 140 grassroots groups and community organizations to coordinate territorial struggles against extractive projects in defense of Black populations' way of life and right to remain on the land. There is certainly an important ontological dimension to these struggles. As Naka Mandinga, one of the leaders of the PCN, put it while he was staying with me during a speaking tour of Britain, a key aspect of these struggles is against the state's efforts to "impose one identity and one way of life" in the name of "development." The PCN rejects Eurocentric models of leftist thought that separate the material from the cultural and from the culturally specific understanding of "Man" that underwrites capitalist coloniality.[20] Yet while Escobar is not wrong that Afro-descendant populations seek to preserve their own way of "worlding," this is also combined with deep historical analysis of political economy within a Marxist tradition (clearly on display, for instance, in Gearóid Ó Loingsigh's book researched with and published by the PCN, the title of which translates as *The Reconquest of the Pacific*).[21] Likewise, when those mobilizing via the *planes de vida* seek to develop their own concepts of *buen vivir*, to fill "life" and "territory" with content and, in the process, retell the story of what it is to be human, this is a product of deep critical analysis of the capitalist relations they seek to transcend.

This ontological plurality is not unique to social movement struggles in Colombia. In an article that resonates strongly with Rivera Cusicanqui's critique of the reification and romanticization of Indigenous thought by "decolonial" academics, Ana Carolina Teixera Delgado offers a similar account of Bolivian peasant and Indigenous movements' uses of the Indigenous Aymara concept of *suma qamaña* (which has similar connotations to *buen vivir*: living well together, implying harmonious relations between humans and nature). Delgado points out that these struggles also have long histories of opposing capitalism and structural racism, not just via affirmation of *suma qamaña* as a "new paradigm for humanity," but also through analysis of how the present juncture has been shaped by colonial history, capitalism, racialization, and class—in dialogue with the non-Indigenous world.[22] Thus, Delgado insists, emphasizing the assertion of ontological difference without considering how *suma qamaña* has been developed and deployed strategically within struggles against a racist, colonial political economy is to depoliticize and underestimate these struggles.[23]

In Colombia, even trade unions that rely on Marxist analytical tools also invoke the concept of *buen vivir*. For example, when I was working with the Food Workers Union in Colombia, *buen vivir* was sometimes mentioned in reference to the alternatives for food and agriculture that the union seeks to promote in alliance with other social movement organizations. The union's recent thirty-eighth anniversary statement ends in this spirit by saying, "We will continue to stand up in struggle today and forever, hoping that our dream continues to be built across the years and that, sooner or later, we will attain *buen vivir* with sovereignty, democracy and well-being."[24] It is, by the same token, important to stress that Indigenous cosmovisions are not the only spiritual influence on formulations of *buen vivir* or on the wide network of struggles that finds expression in the *planes de vida*. Significantly, the radical left Christian tradition of liberation theology, or liberationist Christianity—which emphasizes the ideological captivity of Christianity as institutionalized religion and rejects capitalism as a reflection of "structural sin"—has also been a profound influence on these struggles since the 1960s.[25] For liberationist Christianity, too, the orientation is toward a total transformation of society that implies, sometimes explicitly, a remaking of the human.[26] Indeed, it is worth observing that liberationist Christianity has itself been a key influence on what was to become Latin American decolonial thought and, since at least the start of the twenty-first century, on social movement expressions of *buen vivir* across the continent.[27]

I should be clear about what I am not arguing here. I am not trying to suggest that invocation of *buen vivir* and related concepts should be considered *merely* strategic, or that Indigenous, Afro-descendant, or even dissident Christian beliefs should be understood (as they have by some Marxist scholars) as mere "idioms" of resistance, expressions of cultural specificity within a dynamic reality of "extended class struggle" or "combined-oppositional consciousness.[28] Rejecting the idea of multiple "worlds" does not mean that we should try to appropriate ontological dissonance within a single economy of truth or, still less, replicate a model of leftist thought that separates the material from the (merely) cultural. We might better think of this as a constitutive incoherence, akin to that in physics where light can be composed of either wave or particle, depending on how you interact with it, although it cannot be both. As Gaston Bachelard expressed it in his philosophy of science, even scientific statements are "pure fiction": it makes no sense to refer to light as a "thing" that exists outside of how we construct and interact with it, in incompatible ways, as waves or as particles.[29] We must understand photons as particles to make a photovoltaic cell, but if we want to understand the refraction of light in a rainbow, then we must understand them as waves. Yet this does not make the light any less real. Nor does it imply that the light of the rainbow is not the same light that hits the photovoltaic cell and causes it to emit electricity. We can think of the dissonant ontologies at play in struggle in a similar way.[30] Dissonance is a feature of one world, one "real," because of the limitations of our conceptual resources as we interact with the world. This, put at its most basic level, is an invitation to approach struggle as lived thought rather than attempt to interpret it within static frameworks derived from canonical texts ("decolonial," Marxist, or otherwise).

Within the *planes de vida* and the wider network of struggles of which they are part, macro-historical narratives of capitalism and colonialism and political-economic analyses of extraction and exploitation are drawn on alongside understandings of the world that emerge from Indigenous cosmological visions, and that revolve around distinct—indeed, incompatible—ontologies. Linear historical analysis rubs alongside cyclical understandings of time. Likewise, characteristically modern understandings of nature as external object of study might be invoked when social movements commission research on the ecological effects of mining. Yet while it is necessary to have the measure of things in this way—through detailed reports on water levels and pollution levels, for example—these investigations, as one member of the Wayúu Indigenous movement put it during a conversation in Bogotá, can "only tell us why the river is gone, why the river is no more. They cannot tell us about the river or render the relation between the rock and the river a matter also worthy of struggle, whether or not drinking water is provided." Movements shift ontologies, depending on the matter under consideration; dissonant ontological commitments coexist in one political process. When people in Catatumbo set out to construct a *plan de vida* by filling "life" and "territory" with content through a process of collective thought, they drew on understandings of being, time, land, nature, and humanity that cannot be translated within the terms of even the most anticolonial, ecologically minded historical materialism. Yet life, territory, humanity, and *buen vivir* are all categories filled with content in and through a "diagnosis" that draws on thinking tools that have themselves emerged from the contradictions of capitalism, that are immanent to modern/colonial history and to historical relations of struggle. Furthermore, the process of diagnosis emerges from reflection on what leaders of the Catatumbo process described as the contradictions between a material reality that is lived and experienced, and the state's promise of "development" or a Social Rule of Law that would follow the arrival of foreign direct investment in resource extraction. In this spirit, the CNA explicitly draws out the contradictions embodied within an idea of "development"—that is supposed to bring progress and an improved quality of life, but that can never fulfill its promise of a dignified life, because it entails the destruction of nature and the dispossession of populations who occupy territories destined for resource extraction.[31]

One aspect of note here is that these processes of diagnosis, like the counter-legal modes of argument that I discussed in chapter 4 in relation to the PPT and the campaigns accompanying strategic litigation against multinational companies, reflects a mode of critique tied to a logic of contradiction experienced within the materiality of life. The normative expectations that emerge from existing institutional frameworks (development, a Social Rule of Law, and so on) are revealed, persistently, to be contradicted by lived experience. *Immanent* critique is to be contrasted with "internal" critique (critique within discursive parameters of the existing order of things).[32] Yet also, as *critique* it differs from mere assertion of difference; of alterity; of alternative parameters for society, politics, and ethics, or an alternative praxis of being human. The system's own economy of representation is transcended *through the process* of critique of the contradictions of development and legality that have brought death and destruction in the name of promoting life. It is through this process that categories such as "life," "territory," and so on are defined and redefined to enable another mode of being, knowing, and acting to be projected into the world.[33] It is also within this process, as I discussed in chapter 5, that we must understand appeals to human rights. The demand that human rights be respected is tactical, for sure, mobilizing what exists to protect life, however understood. Yet it exceeds the parameters of a legality that recognizes humans only as sovereign, rational individuals. The appeal to human rights serves both to expose the constitutive violence of the existing order of things by holding the system up to its own promises, and to defend a vision of life that is quite at odds with the human as conceived within dominant narratives of law and development.

This, then, is one aspect of what I call an insurgent humanism. Resignification of what it is to be human takes place not by means of attachment to a pregiven "alternative," but in and through immanent critique of the contradictions and real-life effects of legal and policy institutions constructed around a prevailing modern/colonial humanism. There is another aspect, however, that is intimately tied to this. The *planes de vida* are also—as the CNA put it—"a horizon of desire."[34] They reach beyond critique toward a deeper sense of the good that is represented by the "unfinished," and yet profoundly spiritual, concept of *buen vivir*. In the absence of a ready-made proposal for a better life, the shape that *buen vivir* might take is always in the making. Rather than fixing "the human" in terms of a series of morally desirable qualities (whether those qualities derive from the rationality of the sovereign individual or are drawn from a romanticized conception of alterity), it is open-ended, shaped through struggle. It involves the pursuit, in Jonathan Lear's words, of "a future goodness that transcends the ability to understand what it is."[35] As such, it points us back to the question of the grounds of the ethical call beyond that which is merely immanent to struggle. It invites further reflection on the relation between the immanent and the transcendent, on the old question: "Why fight?"

Transcendence, after "Man"

There are two reasons that I think it is important to come back to questions about the grounds of ethical obligation. The first concerns the long-standing debate about human rights as a universal ethical discourse. If the vision of

"Man" traditionally deemed to ground human rights is revealed to be not only contingent and particular, but also historically indissociable from exploitation, expropriation, and other forms of systemic violence, the question arises as to whether all we are left with is relativism. That is to say, can we appeal to anything beyond specific cultural formulations of ethics and associated understandings of humanity and so on that are entirely immanent to the practices or struggles through which those understandings are enacted? Some thinkers in the poststructuralist tradition have approached human rights advocacy and humanitarian intervention as self-grounding, immanent expressions of a commitment to life or to humanity, or a rejection of an intolerable reality as a means of preserving some form of ethical universalism. Yet without an understanding of how systemic violence may be reproduced and occluded within humanistic intervention, and without attention to the struggles of those rendered absent from this economy of representation, attempts to reframe ethical obligation as immanent and self-grounding are entirely compatible with (even philosophical fuel for) the fetishism of abstract values that I criticized in the previous chapter.[36]

This brings me to a further concern. Without a sense of anything beyond the immanent sphere of politics, there is a risk of further romanticization and reification of "Other" ontologies and epistemologies: of fetishizing decolonial alternatives instead of abstract values. The spiritual dimension of concepts such as *buen vivir* is often reduced to what can be seen through an anthropological lens—as a feature of the alterity deemed desirable within a decolonial framework. Wynter, by contrast, seeks a "planetary humanism" that demands we come to understand the processes through which our "genres of being human" are produced. Only then, she suggests, can we revalorize what it is to be human and find "a new mode of experiencing ourselves in which every mode of being human, every form of life that has even been enacted, is a part of us."[37] Yet Wynter does not address the normative underpinnings of the more agonistic humanism to which she reaches, and this is where I think struggles such as the *planes de vida* have something important to add. In these struggles, *buen vivir* is not just an open-ended concept given shape through critique of relations of power and violence. It is also the expression of a sense of goodness that transcends the process of struggle, calling for what the CNA describes as an ethical and spiritual "code of conduct" toward others and toward nonhuman life.[38] What is more, this sense of a transcendent ethical call is a much wider feature of human experience: an observation that is just as pertinent to the other spiritual influences that shape these struggles, such as liberationist Christianity, as it is to the Indigenous cosmologies that inform expressions of *buen vivir*. As Che Guevara once observed, "At the risk of seeming ridiculous . . . , the true revolutionary is guided by great feelings of love."[39]

We do not, Lear underscores, have to say "that there is a transcendent source of goodness—that is, a source of goodness that transcends the world—to think that the goodness *of the world* transcends our finite powers to grasp it." The emphasis is not on some "mysterious source of goodness," but (again) on "the limited nature of our finite conceptual resources."[40] While Lear offers the insight that it may sometimes be in the absence of a path ahead, when even ordinary language breaks down, that a human capacity to work toward an elusive sense of goodness is revealed, the idea that the good is elusive and unrepresentable has been a conclusion of other philosophers who have attempted to read human experience in a holistic manner. Iris Murdoch placed particular emphasis on how dominant Western traditions of philosophy pushed such an understanding aside because of a prevailing account of the subject of ethics as rational individual, whose reason is accompanied by a separate faculty of will that comes into play in the making of value judgments and associated moral decisions, with firm lines drawn between "fact" and "value," between descriptive and normative statements.[41] For Murdoch (whose work can be considered an underacknowledged critique of overrepresented Man as he crops up in moral philosophy), good "partakes of the infinitely elusive character of reality."[42] Moral concepts such as good, love, and so on are the limits of the public rules of discourse. We learn them in depth, she maintained, only through attention, contemplation, and a loving disposition toward the world, including the natural world.[43] Murdoch, too, recognized that suffering, devastation (what she called "the void"), can lead us to something close to Lear's "radical hope."[44] More broadly, however, the idea of good as elusive, yet part of the fabric of the world, is an understanding that Murdoch offered "as a general metaphysical background to morals."[45]

The idea of an insurgent humanism takes us beyond Murdoch, who has been criticized for focusing almost exclusively on the personal dimension of ethical life, even though her ethics emerged from her critique of the present and her historicization of the abstract individual.[46] Despite observing that the prevailing conception of the moral agent lent itself to Marxist critique, Murdoch did not develop her approach to address how experience, or the "often falsifying veil" that our minds fabricate to conceal the world, is shaped by social power relations.[47] Nevertheless, Murdoch's understanding of how we come to grasp the good of the world is utterly at odds with the pernicious optimism that characterizes so much humanistic intervention. The loving attention that Murdoch emphasizes is an ongoing practice, something that can never be perfected or completed but that is always messy and entangled with contradiction. As prefigurative struggles that cultivate attention to how their own practices might exclude or marginalize, the *planes de vida* might be thought of as reaching toward a sense of good in something close to Murdoch's understanding. I say this not to eulogize these struggles, but to underscore their messiness and incompleteness as (deeply human, imperfect, difficult) processes rather than as practices that already embody *buen vivir*. What the lens of an insurgent humanism adds to Murdoch is the insistence on immanent critique of power and violence as part of the construction of an ethical horizon that transcends what is immanent to struggle

The idea of good as a part of the fabric of the world, as a limit to language, is not a fashionable one in Western critical thought. It does, however, provide a path beyond the limitations of what is perhaps the most prominent recent attempt to provide grounds for our ethical obligation while holding fast to the idea that "the human" is a category that is socially and culturally produced: Judith Butler's ethics of vulnerability, which is sometimes referred to as a "new humanism." Butler's approach is of particular note for the discussion here because she and Wynter arguably offer "mostly complementary approaches" to critical intervention in the socio-ontological production of the human.[48] While Butler does not situate the development of a specific hegemonic understanding of the human within the history of modern colonialism and capitalism, she is concerned with a need to unsettle the norms through which humanness is recognized. She has long emphasized the fact that, as embodied and moral beings, we are shaped to the core by the collective historical norms and forms of social and political organization that maximize life chances for some and minimize them for others.[49] In more recent work, however, Butler has argued that this condition—of being formed as selves within a social world shaped by others—is not only constitutive of our being but also the basis of our ethical obligation to one another.[50] It is important to underscore that Butler's "ethical turn" does not initiate a humanism based on the ontological fact of vulnerability (as opposed to the capacity to reason).[51] For Butler, we can only begin within the space of our relations with others and within existing political and economic constellations. The ethical claim inheres not in the ontological condition of precariousness per se but in the unequal political distribution of precarity.[52] It is the universality of our vulnerability, for Butler, that generates an egalitarian demand that we oppose the politically induced conditions that exhaust and destroy life in unequal ways.[53] Thus, "vulnerability becomes a figure that is capable of grounding a humanistic ethic that resists a closed or hermetic understanding of what it means to be human."[54]

Nevertheless, for all the influence of Butler's ethical turn, several philosophers have observed that it seems to be her prior commitments to equality and democracy that shape her critique of the unequal distribution of precarity.[55] As Catherine Mills writes, "Butler's claim that the recognition of precariousness entails a commitment to egalitarianism and the universalization of rights appears to be without justification."[56] Butler does not tell us why there should be anything *outside* the frames shaping our responses to vulnerability that makes an ethical claim on us, and still less why this should involve a commitment to equality in particular.[57] In fact, when Butler does go further, to provide a stronger basis for grounding the ethical call in our shared vulnerability, she does so via Emmanuel Levinas's account of the ethical call of the face of the Other, apparently taking for granted the face's ethical priority as something prior to and outside any political ontology through which faces are allocated different degrees of humanness. Thus, in Moira Lloyd's words, "Butler argues as if the ethical imperative is apolitical (because it is presented as pre-discursive and, thus, not predicated on power relations) and as if ethical encounters in determinate contexts are political (because they operate through power relations and normative violence)."[58] Given everything that Butler has done to displace the theoretical move of establishing foundations, it is telling that she ultimately is unable to avoid gesturing to a transcendent ground beyond the immanent sphere of politics.[59] There is nothing problematic about this in itself. The problem is how Butler makes the links between the immanent and the transcendent. As Sima Kramer puts it, "Without a clear account of a method of rendering foundations contingent, or of rendering ontologies provisional, we tend to repeat the political move to establish an apolitical ground on which we can found a politic."[60]

If the good exceeds our capacity to represent it, however, then the foundations to which we appeal can only ever be contingent. If we take seriously the idea of a good that transcends our capacity to fully grasp it, this implies a call to reach beyond the ideas to which we might otherwise attach ourselves. Furthermore, I would suggest that an insurgent humanism of the sort that I have described points us to a method of rendering foundations contingent because of the tension between the immanent and the transcendent at its heart. Such a humanism is motivated and propelled by a deeper sense of worth that is elusive, known in ways other than through the conventions of language, expressed in an instinctual love toward the world that may persist even when language breaks down. This may be part of what inspires efforts to give life to an alternative vision of what it is to be human, although within the *planes de vida* that vision is filled with content collectively, in struggle, through ongoing critique of the contradictions of the existing order of things, of the violence both concealed and authorized through humanistic narratives of law and "development." A dialectic is at play between immanent critique and a transcendent sense of good that not only gives flesh to the idea of a livable life but also invites a response to the question that has vexed human rights advocates since the "death of Man": the question of the grounds of the ethical call in the absence of stable foundations. From this perspective, grounds are by nature impossible to fully specify, although that does not mean that our obligations to others are baseless. It is within the terms of this insurgent humanism that I propose we approach human rights as a vocabulary of ethical commitment and solidarity with others.

For an Insurgent Humanism

The *planes de vida* express lived thought, the pursuit of another praxis of being human shaped through ongoing critique of the violence encountered within existing political-economic relations, in one specific context. There are, however, wider aspects of the politics of human rights that can be drawn from these struggles, with implications for what it might mean to practice an insurgent humanism more generally.

The first point I want to underscore is that rejection of the "Man" traditionally regarded as grounding human rights does not entail rejecting human rights as a vocabulary of liberatory struggle. Obviously, this is the case at an empirical level: the *planes de vida* do involve mobilization for human rights, despite being sites at which alternative visions of the human are forged. However, what is important to understand is that this goes beyond the merely tactical (using human rights simply as a means of survival). Appealing to human rights as "a party in conflict with the state," to hold the state up to its own promises, reflects a logic of immanent critique that calls the existing legal order into question. A similar logic was at play when peasant organizations in Casanare used human rights to call attention to the contradiction between newly recognized constitutional rights and their systemic exclusion from accessing such rights, as it was when the Colombian Food Workers denounced the violation of human rights to draw attention to "the empire behind the multinationals."[61] This logic of immanent critique comes to the fore in the counterlegal modes of argument that I discussed in chapter 4, where the meanings of harm and responsibility are reworked in ways that demonstrate the contradictions of dominant legal narratives and reveal the violence of the system. Critics might respond that the effectiveness of law as a means of this mode of critique is limited. There is always a risk that human rights and other legal categories will be interpreted from the outside within the confines of a liberal legalism, reinforcing the idea of a neutral and benign rule of law. Of course, some who seek to support these struggles from a position of distance will understand the appeal to human rights in this way. Yet even if counterlegal arguments and uses of human rights to expose the violence of the system are bound to be sometimes translated (or mistranslated) within the terms of dominant legal narratives, the fact that success is only ever likely to be partial does not entail that nothing can be achieved. Indeed, given the extent to which social relations are constituted by law and by the moral economies on which law rests, it is difficult to imagine how those social relations could be transformed without legal change and, crucially, without changes to how legal categories are conceptualized. This is not to suggest that this immanent critique is sufficient for social transformation, but it is, arguably, necessary. What is more, by rejecting human rights and law as "inherently capitalist" or "inherently colonial" rather than attending to social movement praxis, there is also a risk of being drawn into fantasy, fixing our coordinates in advance, and reading politics off a ready-made theory or conceptual framework. The form of liberatory praxis that those coordinates prescribe can easily become a comfortable object of attachment that comes to stand in for existing struggles, inhibiting us from working through our own challenges for political action and forms of solidarity, through which we might contribute to the transformation of the present.

My second point follows from this. To suggest that the ethical call is underpinned by an ineffable goodness is to ascribe a different basis of authority to human rights from those understood in terms of the dignity of the sovereign, rational individual. In her reflections on the source of authority of another mechanism of alternative justice—the World Tribunal on Iraq—Ayça Çubukçu suggests that it is "the love of humanity" that undergirds these unofficial courts.[62] Çubukçu herself does not reflect on the ways in which "humanity" might be understood, but the idea that this pursuit of "justice" is grounded in love resonates with Murdoch's reflections on the need to look lovingly at the world and at the reality of others. The answer to the question "Why fight?" can only be that if you need to ask it, then it is necessary to pay more attention—more loving attention, as Murdoch would have it—to others:

not only to their suffering, but also to their struggles and to the critical understandings of the world shaped within struggle. This, in other words, is a prompt to become attuned to the realities and struggles of others rather than being immersed in our own attachments and fantasies.

My third point relates to a core component of this attunement: the need for any appeal to human rights to be accompanied by critique of the violence authorized and concealed through the law and through the easy, abstract categories through which we might otherwise frame ethics. As Butler emphasizes, ethical deliberation must always find itself embroiled within social theory and critique, because we need to deliberate on normative categories and how they are socially produced.[63] Yet the operation of critique needs to go beyond Butler and the sorts of questions that she raises: "Who counts as human? Whose lives count as lives?" and "What is real? Whose lives are real? How might reality be remade?"[64] These questions are vital, but they need to be embedded within a general understanding of power relations, the nature of violence, and the being of social and political life if we are to talk about what is at stake, what we are up against, what is to be transformed. To act politically, to resist effectively, we need social theory—not only in the pulling-everything-apart, deconstructive, de-reifying sense that Butler so rightly advocates. We need at least provisional theorizations of the power relations we are up against. We need to know how a struggle relates to our contemporary global situation. In the end, we cannot do without assumptions about the nature of social and political life.[65] This is the case even if we recognize that no frame can fully capture the relations of power and violence confronted by any political struggle. We need to ask questions not only about whose humanity is recognized, but also—against the backdrop of a more global understanding—about what counts as violence or as harm. Which harms are misrecognized because of the way in which dominant narratives of law and development frame certain practices as neutral or benign? What about when attempts to protect and support the lives of others actually bolster those forms of harm? How might efforts to defend life serve in practice to disseminate death because of the terms in which they recognize "the human"? Against this background, legal argument, too, can become an important part of a critical reopening of these questions (as we saw in the earlier discussion of counterlegality) because of how it expresses dominant, often taken-for-granted normative frameworks that underpin systemic forms of violence.

The fourth aspect of an insurgent humanism that I want to emphasize is that it attends to struggles that seek to embody a liberatory praxis of being human. Rather than just engaging in relentless criticism of relations of power and oppression or legislating for emancipatory praxis on the basis of that critique, it is important to pay attention to actual struggles, to human possibilities in the face of oppression, even in the absence of a clear path ahead. It is important not to romanticize such struggles and certainly not to attempt to replicate visions of life that are, in any case, malleable, forged in context, in and through ongoing struggle. Rather, what matters is to ask what might be learned from the critical thought and ethical deliberation taking place on the ground so that those who seek to act in solidarity are respectful toward processes that are taking shape in opposition to capitalist coloniality.

This is closely related to my final point, which is to underscore the need to embrace messiness and incompleteness, the tensions in lived thought (our own, as well as that of others). This is not to say that we should demur from making global claims about political economy, law, the coloniality of power or what it might mean to be human. It is vital not to enclose everything within a fixed framework with no way out; rather, we must remember that "there is always more to and of reality."[66] Sometimes a different lens is required, and not everything has the vocation to be translated, recoded, caught directly within the categories of language at all. Embracing messiness also means paying attention to what might be obscured by appealing to abstract values, resisting the temptation to assume, when we encounter expressions of normative categories such as human rights, that people are talking about the same thing. Instead, it is important to understand what vision of life is being defended and what relations of power contested through appeal to human rights. Yes, it will be difficult to convey this into wider lexicons of human rights, although not impossible. Human rights can "travel" to shape global norms (albeit at the risk of co-optation); legal categories more widely can be shifted on the basis of specific counterlegal arguments.[67] To translate, so the well-known saying goes, is to betray. Yet as Eduardo Viveiros de Castro reminds us, it is often that the best translations betray the destination language rather than the language at their source.[68]

conclusion

What Do We Make of
Human Rights? *Ten Points*

What, then, are we to make of human rights as tools of struggle against capitalist extraction and its constitutive violences? What do we make of human rights as an expression of ethical commitment or of solidarity with others? From the discussion in the foregoing chapters, the following points can be drawn:

1 — We should reject the blackmail of the demand that we decide "for" or "against" human rights. Indeed, at a conjuncture in which neoliberal necroeconomics and right-wing populism are converging within so many different sites of struggle, it is vital that we reject this either-or mode of thinking if we are to build bridges that can be traversed in the pursuit of solidarity. The history of human rights is, of course, inseparable from the history of capitalism and colonialism. The human recognized as the subject of rights has largely been understood in terms of the figure of the sovereign, rational individual that has long underpinned exploitation and expropriation. Yet human rights have also been tools of resistance to oppression throughout that history. Appeals to human rights may be easily co-opted, but this is the case with any discourse of resistance to a capitalism that persistently transgresses its own bound-

aries. That which has been co-opted can also be resisted or inserted into alternative frames of reference. Rather than advocating for or against human rights, it is more productive to focus on the discontinuities among ways in which human rights are mobilized: by capital, by mainstream human rights organizations, and within social movement struggles.

2 — Over the past three decades, human rights have been "privatized" in a manner that reduces them to add-ons to a global legal order that generates predictable premature death for much of the world's population (not least, the "stakeholders" in corporate operations and workers in multinationals' commodity chains whose rights are defended in the process). As a neoliberal vision of "rule of law" has been constitutionalized at a global level, an ever more powerful corporate elite has had unprecedented success in shaping global ethics in its image. Interventions configured around "corporate social responsibility" and "decent work" have made human rights contingent on corporate processes of accumulation, with the subjects of rights defined exclusively in relation to those processes. These privatized human rights actively contribute to the consolidation of neoliberalism as a moral and legal project aimed, from its inception, at constructing a legal and institutional order that can encase wealth within the coffers of a few. They are the counterpart—not the antidote—to a global necroeconomy and the armed repression of resistance.

3 — The idea that corporations should promote, or even respect, human rights was never part of the neoliberal project. That this has become received wisdom is illustrative of capitalism's capacity to reshape and absorb opposition. Since the second half of the 1990s, when neoliberalism gained its much touted "human face," ethical discourse not only has become a central component of corporate business as usual. It has become so in a way that collapses the old tension in liberal thought between criteria for moral action and criteria for economic action. The neoliberal thinkers of the mid-twentieth century also sought to collapse the criteria for economic and moral action into each other but in a manner that reduced human rights to rights of property and investment. What is remarkable about the privatization of human rights is that it subtly recasts the very meaning of what it is to hold rights. I am not claiming that this was a conscious extension of the neoliberal

project. Rather, key tenets of neoliberal thought have become so embedded within law and policy discourses that they are perpetuated even unconsciously.

4 — Much of the problem is a particular style of transnational cosmopolitan ethics in which human rights (and other categories of ethics) are approached as abstract values—as if everyone were talking about the same thing. Ethical action on behalf of others has been consolidated as a feel-good exercise premised on disavowing the implications of capitalism for actual human beings. This feel-good ethics embodies a pernicious optimism in which the desire to affirm the ethical potentiality of the present takes the form of a fantasy that inhibits the possibility of addressing the relationship between the promotion of human rights and the harm perpetuated toward those said to be the holders of those rights.

5 — "Anti-impunity" occupies an ambiguous position in this scenario. When understood against the backdrop of a neutral or benign rule of law and within the terms of juridical individualism, "anti-impunity" offers little challenge to systemic violence. Yet law is also an important terrain of struggle. The fictions of the law underpin very real material relations of exploitation and expropriation, meaning that law can—perhaps must—be harnessed to struggles that seek to transform those relations. The law is malleable. It can be shaped in accordance with ethical instincts, although legal struggles must draw on existing legal categories and modes of argument. Social movements also articulate what I have called *counterlegalities* within efforts to tackle impunity, pushing the system beyond what it can contain by, for example, exposing the mutually constitutive nature of capitalist extraction and international crimes such as genocide. Struggles against impunity can be shaped in ways that expose the violence of the law and the fictive nature of the rational individual at its heart.

6 — It is a well-worn claim that appeals to rights can be disruptive; that they can intervene in what is visible or sayable; and that that rights claims can be means through which new subjects of rights come to exist. Yet taken alone, such claims do not take us beyond affirmation of the emancipatory potential of liberal democracy. It is important to consider how disruptive claims to rights are situated in relation to the materiality of

social relations, how they expose violence concealed by dominant legal narratives, and how they challenge received understandings of harm and injury in ways that offer an immanent critique of the law. This may, at a modest level, foment changes to the law that make it more difficult for certain forms of harm to keep happening. What matters, beyond this, is how the disruptive appeal to rights is tied to social movement pedagogies and how it helps strengthen movements to transform material social relations.

7 — Appeals to human rights need not fall back on a conception of the human as sovereign individual. Rejecting the latter does not entail rejection of the former. This is evident both in the expression of counterlegalities that challenge juridical individualism and where social movements harness human rights to struggles that reach toward an alternative praxis of being human. The source of authority of these rights is not the inherent dignity of overrepresented "Man," for the appeal to human rights takes place only in the context of immanent critique of the relations of power that naturalize the sovereign subject. It is only in relation to that critique that normative visions are shaped in struggle, as another vision of life is filled with content. Human rights are deployed in struggle not only to hold the system up to its own promises and expose the contradictions and violent effects of legal and policy institutions constructed around a modern/colonial humanism, but also to defend an alternative vision of life in the making.

8 — If defenders of human rights are to learn from or support such struggles, it is important to avoid attachment to fantasy. This applies not only to the feel-good promotion of abstract values but also other forms of perniciously optimistic attachment characteristic of some leftist politics. Whether in the form of revolutionary teleologies of a future collapse of capitalism or in the form of romanticization of "Other" ontologies, fantasies of another possible world readily become formulas that inhibit possibilities of transformation in the present and blind their adherents to the dynamics and aspirations of actual struggles on the ground.

9 — The question "Why fight?"—the grounds of normative commitment and of solidarity with others—is not superseded by the injunction to decolonize our praxis of being human. To jettison questions of transcendence and the grounds of ethics in their entirety is to fail to attend

to human experience in a holistic manner. This does not mean that grounds must be specified or that we need to identify a transcendent source of goodness. It means simply that good is ineffably part of the fabric of the world; that the ethical and spiritual instincts that often animate struggle are beyond the limits of language. Whether manifest in the radical hope that makes it possible to keep pursuing the good in the wake of devastation or in other expressions of a loving regard for others that animates struggle, even against the odds, resistance and solidarity are very often propelled by a deeper sense of worth. A sensitivity to the relations between the immanent and the transcendent does not imply legislating for politics on the basis of a fixed conception of human dignity. Rather, it inspires and is nourished by a loving attention to the suffering and struggles of others, an attention that itself demands an ongoing praxis of social and political critique.

10 — With all this in mind, it is possible—indeed, necessary—to hold on to some sort of humanism. This is what I have called an insurgent humanism. There is a universalism to an insurgent humanism insofar as it insists that life—and, more substantively, the possibility of a good life—is worth defending. Yet this is animated by a deeper sense of good that does not seek to settle the question of "the human" in advance. An insurgent humanism pays attention to how admission to the category of human is regulated and to how humanistic interventions, in practice, often involve disseminating death. It engages struggles that seek to embody a liberatory praxis of being human without reifying or romanticizing the terms of these struggles. It engages struggles that seek to defend visions of life that are at odds with those of capital, the neoliberal rule of law, and the supervisory benevolence of international development nongovernmental organizations, alongside struggles for conditions of work that are more than merely "decent" while an elite amasses wealth at the expense of human and nonhuman life. An insurgent humanism does not shy away from relentless criticism of relations of power and violence. It attends to critical understandings of the world forged within struggle, to normative visions emergent from struggle, and to human possibilities in the face of oppression—even in the absence of a clear path ahead.

notes

Introduction

1 Cárdenas and Marín, *La biodiversidad es la cabalgadura de la muerte*, 19.
2 Cárdenas and Marín, *La biodiversidad es la cabalgadura de la muerte*, 13.
3 Rodríguez Garavito, *Extractivismo versus derechos humanos*.
4 Klein, *The Shock Doctrine*, 118–21.
5 Hopgood, *The Endtimes of Human Rights*.
6 Cf. Tate, *Counting the Dead*.
7 Khoury and Whyte, *Corporate Human Rights Violations*, 1.
8 See, among others, Baars, "It's Not Me, It's the Corporation"; Coleman at al., *Righting Corporate Wrongs?*; Khoury and Whyte, *Corporate Human Rights Violations*.
9 This reflects anthropological traditions of "global" or "multisited" ethnography: see Burawoy, "The Extended Case Method"; Marcus "Ethnography in/ of the World System."
10 L. Gordon, "Shifting the Geography of Reason in an Age of Disciplinary Decadence," 98.
11 Golder, "Beyond Redemption?"
12 See, e.g., Wenar, "The Nature of Rights."
13 See Sikkink, "Human Rights."
14 Wynter, "Unsettling the Coloniality of Being/Power/Truth/Freedom," 306.
15 For analysis of the genesis of Man from the rational subject of Renaissance humanism to the biological, Darwinian conception that remains predominant, see Wynter, "Unsettling the Coloniality of Being/Power/Truth/Freedom."

16 Dussel, *Filosofía de la liberación*.

17 Mbembe, "Necropolitics," 23–24.

18 Maldonado-Torres, *Against War*, 4.

19 Abello, *Violencias y culturas*, 17–19; Jahn, "One Step Forward, Two Steps Back," 630–31.

20 Suárez-Krabbe, *Race, Rights and Rebels*, 3–4.

21 De Vitoria, "The First Reflection of the Reverend Father," xii.

22 De Vitoria, "The First Reflection of the Reverend Father," xiii–xiv.

23 Mignolo, "Who Speaks for the Human in Human Rights?," 50.

24 Rojas-Páez, "Whose Nature?," 7. See also Vázquez, "Translation as Erasure," 37–38.

25 Shilliam, *Race and the Undeserving Poor*, 6, 32–58.

26 Federici, *Caliban and the Witch*, 186–200.

27 Wynter, "Unsettling the Coloniality of Being/Power/Truth/Freedom," 306–21. See also Mignolo, "Who Speaks for the Human in Human Rights?," 52–54.

28 Suárez-Krabbe, *Race, Rights and Rebels*, 93.

29 Marx, "On the Jewish Question," 62, 64.

30 Marx, "On the Jewish Question," 59–61.

31 Moyn, *Not Enough*, 45–67.

32 Carr, "Rights and Obligations."

33 Rancière, "Who Is the Subject of the Rights of Man?"

34 Moyn, *Not Enough*, 59–61. For discussion of the racialized and colonial nature of postwar welfare states, see Bhambra and Holmwood, "Colonialism, Postcolonialism and the Liberal Welfare State."

35 Moyn, *Not Enough*, 116.

36 Moyn, *Not Enough*, 109–18.

37 See Klein, *The Shock Doctrine*, 118–21.

38 Hopgood, "Reading the Small Print in Global Civil Society."

39 Brown, "The Most We Can Hope For . . ."

40 Moyn, *Not Enough*, chap. 7; Moyn, "A Powerless Companion."

41 J. Whyte, *The Morals of the Market*. See also J. Whyte, "Powerless Companions or Fellow Travellers?"

42 J. Whyte, "Powerless Companions or Fellow Travellers?," 17–20.

43 Slobodian, *Globalists*.

44 J. Whyte, "Powerless Companions or Fellow Travellers?," 24.

45 J. Whyte, *The Morals of the Market*, 226–27.

46 J. Whyte, *The Morals of the Market*, 227. See also Slobodian, *Globalists*, chap. 4.

47 Marx, *Capital*; D. Whyte, "Naked Labour," 59–60.

48 Thompson, *Whigs and Hunters*, 204.

49 Pashukanis, *Law and Marxism*. See also Miéville, *Between Equal Rights*, chap. 3.

50 See, among others, Baars, "It's Not Me, It's the Corporation"; Miéville, *Between Equal Rights*.

51 Lorde, *The Master's Tools Will Never Dismantle the Master's House*, 19.

52 Thompson, *Whigs and Hunters*, 203–4, 208.

53 Shilliam, *Race and the Undeserving Poor*, 13–15.

54 Bhambra and Holmwood, "Colonialism, Postcolonialism and the Liberal Welfare State," 579.

55 Thompson, *Whigs and Hunters*, 206.

56 Thompson, *Whigs and Hunters*, 263.

57 Thompson, *Whigs and Hunters*, 207.

58 Barreto, "Introduction," 21.

59 Baars, "It's Not Me, It's the Corporation."

60 Hopgood, *The Endtimes of Human Rights*, viii.

61 Coulthard, *Red Skin, White Masks*, 3.

62 Santos, "Human Rights as an Emancipatory Script?"

63 Madhok, *Vernacular Rights Cultures*.

64 Dunford, *The Politics of Transnational Peasant Struggle*. See also Dunford and Madhok, "Vernacular Rights Cultures and the 'Right to Have Rights.'"

65 In his well-known discussion of the subject of rights, Rancière emphasizes that there is an inherent openness and disputability to political ideals, and that the very gap between the abstract human and possible subjects of rights makes it possible to interrupt the schemas that define who counts as a subject of rights. Costas Douzinas has coined the term *right-ing* for this disruptive aspect of human rights. *Right-ing* connotes an open-ended process of invention, "like-writing," that occurs within struggles for rights. See Douzinas, *The End of Human Rights*, 215–16; Rancière, "Who Is the Subject of the Rights of Man?," 304.

66 Christodoulidis, "Strategies of Rupture," 7.

67 Wynter, "Unsettling the Coloniality of Being/Power/Truth/Freedom," 263. See also Odysseos, "Prolegomena to Any Future Decolonial Ethics"; Tsantsoulas, "Sylvia Wynter's Decolonial Rejoinder to Judith Butler's Ethics of Vulnerability," 168–77.

68 J. Butler, *Frames of War*, 29.

69 *Unarmed Bodyguards* is the title of the handbook of the London-based NGO Peace Brigades International.

70 See Escobar, "Development, Violence and the New Imperial Order." Escobar's seminal work on the genealogy of "development" is *Encountering Development*, translated in Spanish as *La invención del tercer mundo*.

71 See Mignolo, *Local Histories/Global Designs*.

72 See, among others, Delgado, "*Suma Qamaña* as a Strategy of Power"; Rivera Cusicanqui, "*Ch'ixinakax utiwa*," 95–97.

73 Rivera Cusicanqui, "*Ch'ixinakax utiwa*," 101–4.

74 Rivera Cusicanqui's emphasis on a "political economy" of knowledge is a counter to Mignolo's notion of a "geopolitics of knowledge." This is not only because such a "geopolitics" is contradicted by the colonialism of much "decolonial" intellectual practice but also because "it is necessary to leave

the sphere of the superstructures to analyze the economic strategies and material mechanisms that operate behind discourses": Rivera Cusicanqui, "Ch'ixinakax utiwa," 102; cf. Mignolo, "The Geopolitics of Knowledge and the Colonial Difference."

75 Nair, "Sociability in International Politics," 197.

76 Motta, *Liminal Subjects*, 46–50.

77 D. Taylor, *¡Presente!*, 2.

78 Foucault, "For an Ethic of Discomfort," 448.

79 On the need to step back in this sense from struggle as part of a praxis of engaged scholarship while thinking beyond Foucault's ethos of critique, see Coleman, "Ethnography, Commitment and Critique," 267–69, 275–78.

80 The discussion in the workshops is summarized in Coleman et al., *Cómo reparar las injusticias cometidas por los empresarios*, previously published in English translation as *Righting Corporate Wrongs?* See also my reflections on this project in chapter 4 in this volume.

81 Cf. Foucault, "Polemics, Politics, and Problematizations," 385.

82 Cf. J. Butler, "What Is Critique?," 3.

83 Cárdenas and Marín, *La biodiversidad es la cabalgadura de la muerte*, 11.

Chapter One. Necroeconomics

1 Amnesty International USA, "Impunity."

2 Cárdenas and Marín, *La biodiversidad es la cabalgadura de la muerte*, 11.

3 Vega Cantor, *¡Sindicalicidio!*

4 See, e.g., Escobar, "Displacement, Development and Modernity in the Colombian Pacific," 161. The most detailed, fieldwork-based study of paramilitary strategy available is Ó Loingsigh, *La estrategia integral de los paramilitares en el Magdalena Medio*.

5 Brodzinsky, 'Terrorism and Bananas in Colombia"; Kovalik, "Lawyer for Chiquita in Colombia Death Squad Case May Be Next US Attorney General."

6 Amnesty International, *A Laboratory of War*, 6.

7 See, e.g., Gillard et al., "BP Hands Tarred in Pipeline Dirty War."

8 See Carson et al., "Gilberto Torres Survived Colombia's Death Squads."

9 See Giraldo and Laverde, *Casanare*, 13.

10 Sindicato Nacional de Trabajadores de la Industria de Alimentos (SINALTRAINAL)—literally, the National Union of Food Industry Workers but abbreviated in this book as the Colombian Food Workers Union.

11 SINALTRAINAL, "Genocidio en Carepa"; SINALTRAINAL, "La transnacional Coca-Cola y el paramilitarismo en Colombia"; conversations with displaced members of the union, April 2006.

12 Conversations with union leaders in Barranquilla, September 2006. See also Collingsworth et al., *Complaint Submitted to the US District Court*.

13 SINALTRAINAL, *Report to UN Special Rapporteur on the Rights to Freedom of Peaceful Assembly and of Association and to UN Special Rapporteur on Extrajudicial, Summary or Arbitrary Executions.*

14 Zwehl, "Nestle Worker and Union Activist Killed by Paramilitary."

15 SINALTRAINAL, "Martires."

16 Conversations with leaders of the Food Workers Union in Bogotá, April and September 2006; Barranquilla, September 2006; and Bucaramanga, December 2007.

17 SINALTRAINAL, "El hambre."

18 Policante, "Of Cameras and Balaclavas," 460.

19 Marx, *Capital*, 342, 367, 915.

20 Rojas-Páez, "Understanding Environmental Harm and Justice Claims in the Global South," 59–85.

21 See also the short documentary by the José Alvear Restrepo Lawyer's Collective, "El Mal Vecino" (https://www.colectivodeabogados.org/documental-el -mal-vecino/).

22 The Associación Nacional de Trabajadores Hospitalarios y de Clínicas was subsequently renamed the Associación Nacional Sindical de Trabajadores y Servidores Públicos de la Salud y Seguridad Social Integral y Servicios Complementarios de Colombia (National Trade Union Association of Workers and Public Servants in Health and Social Security and Supplementary Services).

23 Forster, "NHS Cuts Blamed for 30,000 Deaths in New Study." On NHS privatization, see El-Gingihy, *How to Dismantle the NHS in 10 Easy Steps*; Pollock, *NHS Plc.*

24 See Lawrence et al., "COVID-19 Investigation."

25 Cooper and Whyte, "Introduction," 3.

26 Cooper and Whyte, "Introduction," 18–19.

27 Patients4NHS, "The Health and Social Care Act 2012"; Rose, "The Firm That Hijacked the NHS."

28 P. Butler, "Destitution Is Back"; Campbell et al., "NHS Faces 'Humanitarian Crisis' as Demand Rises"; Pring, "Welfare Reform and the Attack on Disabled People," 5.

29 The role of the real estate multinational Savills in the Housing and Planning Act of 2016 was exposed in Paul Sng's documentary *Dispossession: The Great Social Housing Swindle* (2017). See also Beswick et al., "Speculating on London's Housing Future"; Perraudin, "Tories Reject Move to Ensure Rented Homes Fit for Human Habitation."

30 Radical Housing Network, "Justice for Grenfell Tower."

31 Osborne, "Two Women Feared Dead in Grenfell Tower Were 'Threatened with Legal Action' for Questioning Fire Safety."

32 Sommerlad and Bagot, "Deathtrap Towers as 87 Blocks Face Enforcement Orders over Fire Safety Rules."

33 Tapsfield, "John McDonnell Says Grenfell Deaths Were 'Social Murder' as He Uses Marxist Phrase Describing How Rich Oppress Proletariat."

34 Engels, *The Condition of the Working Class in England in 1844*, 95–96, 109.

35 For such sentiments, see, for example, Aditya Chakrabortty, "Over 170 Years after Engels, Britain Is Still a Country That Murders Its Poor," *Guardian*, June 20, 2017, https://www.theguardian.com/commentisfree/2017/jun/20/engels-britain-murders-poor-grenfell-tower; James Masters, "London Fire: Mourning, Anger and Questions over Lives Lost in Inferno," CNN, June 15, 2017, https://edition.cnn.com/2017/06/15/europe/london-fire-grenfell-tower/index.html; Jackie Long, "'Heartbroken' MP David Lammy Becomes Tearful Remembering Friend Who Died in Grenfell Tower Fire," *Channel 4 News*, June 16, 2017, https://www.channel4.com/news/david-lammy-mp-remembers-friend-grenville-tower-fire-london; Natalie Evans, "'My Brother's in the Flat but He's Dead': Five-Year-Old Grenfell Fire Survivor's Harrowing Words to Firefighter," *Mirror*, June 17, 2017, https://www.mirror.co.uk/news/uk-news/grenfell-tower-fire-brother-dead-10637608; Alessandra Rizzo, "Grenfell Victims 'May Not Be Identified until Year-End,'" *Sky News*, July 4, 2017, https://news.sky.com/story/javid-says-councils-face-crisis-of-trust-after-grenfell-fire-10937107; Melissa Fielding, "From the Fire: Grenfell, Activism and Government Accountability," *King's Review*, June 10, 2020, https://www.kingsreview.co.uk/essays/from-the-fire; and Owen Jones, "All of Us Now Have to Question How This Country Is Run," video, LBC Facebook page, September 24, 2017, https://www.facebook.com/watch/?v=10155453587496558.

36 See, among others, Canning, "The Multiple Forms of Violence in the Asylum System"; Cooper and Whyte, "Introduction," 11–15; Emejulu and Bassel, "Women of Colour's Anti-austerity Activism"; Pring, "Welfare Reform and the Attack on Disabled People," 51–58; Tepe-Belfrage, "The Intersectional Consequences of Austerity."

37 Chakrabortty, "Over 170 Years after Engels."

38 Cf. Koram, *Uncommon Wealth*, 3–7.

39 See Moyn, *Not Enough*, and my discussion in the introduction.

40 J. Whyte, "Powerless Companions or Fellow Travellers?," 24.

41 Žižek, *Violence*, 1, 31.

42 Mattei and Nader, *Plunder*, 10.

43 T. Bingham, *The Rule of Law*.

44 Magna Carta, chap. 39, quoted in T. Bingham, *The Rule of Law*, 10.

45 Mattei and Nader, *Plunder*, 12.

46 Federici, *Caliban and the Witch*, 205.

47 Thompson, *Whigs and Hunters*, 1–2.

48 Thompson, *Whigs and Hunters*, 1.

49 Thompson, *Whigs and Hunters*, 206.

50 Bhandar, *Colonial Lives of Property*, 4.

51 Abello, *Violencias y culturas*, 21.

52 Abello, *Violencias y culturas*, 21–23; Hylton, "An Evil Hour," 53–58.

53 Quoted in Rojas-Páez, "Understanding Environmental Harm and Justice Claims in the Global South," 53.

54 Sanders, *Contentious Republicans*, 20.

55 Cf. Thompson, *Whigs and Hunters*, 206.

56 Sanders, *Contentious Republicans*, 4, 17.

57 Sanders, *Contentious Republicans*, 6, 17.

58 Mattei and Nader, *Plunder*, 14.

59 Mattei and Nader, *Plunder*, 14.

60 Mattei and Nader, *Plunder*, 14.

61 Mattei and Nader, *Plunder*, 43.

62 Kochi, *Global Justice and Social Conflict*, 8.

63 Mattei and Nader, *Plunder*, 14–15.

64 Bhandar, *Colonial Lives of Property*.

65 Mattei and Nader, *Plunder*, 14–15.

66 Slobodian, *Globalists*, 260.

67 See Marx, "The Jewish Question," and my discussion in the introduction.

68 See, e.g., Hirshman, *The Passions and the Interests*; Hume, *A Treatise of Human Nature*, vol. 2, book 2, pt. 1, sec. 1; Myers, *The Soul of Modern Economic Man*; Smith, *The Theory of Moral Sentiments*.

69 Montag, "Necro-economics."

70 For a comparison of Smith's position on slavery with the similar position of David Hume (although the latter, unlike Smith, actively elided the depth of the connection between eighteenth-century society and the uncivil practice of slavery), see Ince, "Between Commerce and Empire."

71 See Brown, "Neoliberalism and the End of Liberal Democracy," 46.

72 The institutionalist political economy that underpinned the welfare state was strongly influenced by the arguments of the economic historian Karl Polanyi on the dangers of the market becoming "disembedded" and thereby turning everything—from land to labor, bodies to seeds—into commodities, until capitalism eliminates the basis of social life and destroys its own capacities for reproduction: Polanyi, *The Great Transformation*.

73 Bhambra and Holmwood, "Colonialism, Postcolonialism and the Liberal Welfare State."

74 Shilliam, *Race and the Undeserving Poor*, 72–73.

75 Bhambra, "Relations of Extraction, Relations of Redistribution," 8–12.

76 Bhambra, "Relations of Extraction, Relations of Redistribution," 12.

77 J. Whyte, *The Morals of the Market*, 14. See also Slobodian, *Globalists*, esp. chap. 4.

78 J. Whyte, *The Morals of the Market*, 36.

79 J. Whyte, *The Morals of the Market*, 21.

80 J. Whyte, *The Morals of the Market*, 23.

81 J. Whyte, *The Morals of the Market*, 12.

82 J. Whyte, *The Morals of the Market*, chap. 1.

83 J. Whyte, *The Morals of the Market*, 101–9.

84 Montag, "War and the Market," 127.

85 Montag, "War and the Market," 126.

86 Montag, "War and the Market," 135–37.

87 Montag, "War and the Market," 127.

88 Slobodian, *Globalists*, 45.

89 Montag, "War and the Market," 138.

90 Montag, "War and the Market," 133. For a discussion in relation to neoliberal thought more widely, see J. Whyte, *The Morals of the Market*, chap. 3.

91 Slobodian, *Globalists*.

92 J. Whyte, *The Morals of the Market*, 134.

93 For von Mises, what distinguished races was not only an inequality of intelligence and willpower but an unequal ability to form societies based on an extensive division of labor. The "better races" were those with a special aptitude for cooperation through the market. Where it was lacking, this aptitude had to be actively inculcated—through measures to create adequate attitudes among the population and, if necessary, by force: see J. Whyte, *The Morals of the Market*, 58.

94 Cornelissen, "Neoliberalism and the Racialized Critique of Democracy," 351.

95 Slobodian, *Globalists*, 240–60. See also Petersmann, "How To."

96 Shilliam, "Enoch Powell," 246.

97 Serje, *El revés de la nación*.

98 See Coleman, "The Gendered Violence of Development."

99 Montag, "War and the Market," 134–36.

100 D. Whyte, "Naked Labour." On cuts to the HSE budget, see Palmer and Whyte, "Health and Safety at the Frontline of Austerity." On deregulation more widely, see Tombs, "Undoing Social Protection."

101 Corredor, "El problema del desarrollo," 73–74, my translation. See also Ortiz, "La política energética en Colombia durante los años noventa," 232. The term *Estado Social de Derecho* cannot be rendered fully in English. *Derecho* in Spanish translates literally as *droit* in French and connotes both law and right(s). *Estado*, meanwhile, is rooted in the concept of the state—in the same way that the German concept of *Rechtstaat* is. I am grateful to Lars Cornelissen for pointing out to me that it is a particular problem of English that it translates those concepts solely as "rule of law," thus failing to convey the central role played by the state in generating and enforcing the law. The underpinning of the idea in contractualist theories is thus far more obvious in Spanish than in the English translation. Likewise, the translation "rule of law" fails to make it easier to occlude how neoliberals saw the state as central to the maintenance of the market.

102 Constitución Nacional de Colombia, 1991, arts. 39, 53, 55.

103 International Labour Organization conventions 87 and 98, both ratified by Colombia in 1974.

104 Ó Loingsigh, *La estrategia integral de los paramilitares en el Magdalena Medio*, 96; Ó Loingsigh, "Peace Laboratories," 4.

105 In 1990, under the rationale of needing to foster flexible labor markets, Law 50 created the service-provision contract. This legislation has generated extensive subcontracting of labor. Law 50 further limited the right to stable work by facilitating mass sackings of permanent employees. Then in 2002, Law 189 further dispossessed workers of the right to adequate rest by lengthening the working day and cutting remuneration for night work. The same law made apprenticeships a form of non-labor contract, meaning that apprentices were stripped of labor rights—including the right to a salary—and companies were motivated to sack more employees in favor of a trainee workforce who could be paid just a nominal "economic compensation." I am grateful to Alejandro García for his detailed exposition of Colombian labor law.

106 Asociación de Abogados Laboralistas de Trabajadores, "Aniquilamiento sindical y precarización de los derechos de los trabajadores."

107 SINALTRAINAL, *Complaint to the International Labour Organization against the Colombian Government for Violating SINALTRAINAL's Rights of Trade Union Freedom*, 10; interview with labor lawyer, May 2008.

108 This strategy of forcing resignations through mass detention and threats had been used on other occasions over the previous two years. For example, SINALTRAINAL has reported to the ILO that on January 23, 2001, bottling plant managers in Medellín locked up workers, refused to allow them to leave, and pressured them to resign their contracts or else be sacked: SINALTRAINAL, *Complaint to the International Labour Organization against the Colombian Government for Violating SINALTRAINAL's Rights of Trade Union Freedom*, 6, 8, 13.

109 The government draws a line between "prior consultation" and the right of communities to veto projects on their lands: see Ó Loingsigh, *La reconquista del pacífico*.

110 Hale, *"Resistencia para que?"*

111 García Villegas and Rodríguez, "La acción de tutela."

112 Conversations with Lúz Ángela Uriana, London, October 2016. See also Quinn, "Air of Discontent around Cerrejón Mine Deepens as Colombians Cry Foul."

113 Agamben, *Homo Sacer*, 171.

114 Agamben, *State of Exception*, 28.

115 Veltmeyer et al., *Neoliberalism and Class Conflict in Latin America*, chap. 3.

116 Franco, *Cruel Modernity*, 7–8.

117 García Villegas, "Constitucionalismo perverso," 306.

118 Hylton, "An Evil Hour," 67.

119 Escobar, *Encountering Development*, 24.

120 Franco, *Cruel Modernity*, 2.

121 Hylton, "An Evil Hour," 57.

122 Human Rights Watch, *Colombia's Killer Networks*.

123 García Villegas, "Constitucionalismo perverso," 221–22.

124 Human rights groups documented 12,859 political killings in the 1980s, compared with 1,053 in the 1970s: see Human Rights Watch, *Colombia's Killer Networks*. During the second half of the decade, paramilitaries murdered between three thousand and five thousand members of a leftist electoral coalition, the Unión Patriótica, which had been formed to represent both demobilized guerrillas and people not affiliated to traditional political parties: Hylton, "An Evil Hour," 82.

125 García Villegas, "Constitutionalismo perverso," 323.

126 Law 48 remained in force until 1989, when the Supreme Court declared the arming of civilians unconstitutional. As we have seen, however, paramilitary groups were not thereby dismantled.

127 Giraldo, *Colombia*, 62–66; Santos and García Villegas, "Colombia," 73–74.

128 Order 200-05/91 (written by the Colombian military with a US Defense Department and CIA team). See Human Rights Watch, *Colombia's Killer Networks*; Human Rights Watch, *The "Sixth Division."*

129 The figure of the *estado de sitio* (state of siege) was replaced with that of the state of internal commotion, which was limited, in the first instance, to a duration of ninety days. Santos and García Villegas, "Colombia," 329. The 1991 National Constitution was drawn up by a Constituent Assembly, in which opposition groups participated alongside traditional political parties. This was part of a peace deal with guerrilla groups, although the process itself was a government initiative.

130 Giraldo, *Colombia*, 61–62; Human Rights Watch, *A Wrong Turn*; Santos and García Villegas, "Colombia," 334–35, 349.

131 Giraldo, *Colombia*, 61–62, 48.

132 García Villegas, "Constitutionalismo perverso," 360; Santos and García Villegas, "Colombia," 79.

133 Thompson, *Whigs and Hunters*, 1–2.

134 Riot Act, 1714, para. 1.

135 For discussion of the evolution of repressive legality through the nineteenth century British Empire, see Roberts, "From the Evolution of the State of Emergency to the Rule of Law."

136 Mattei and Nader, *Plunder*, 44–45.

137 Coleman and Blanchard, *Terrorismo de estado en la universidad*, 24–30.

138 Coleman and Blanchard, *Terrorismo de estado en la universidad*, 28.

139 Olarte, "Depoliticization and Criminalization of Social Protest through Economic Decisionism."

140 Coleman and Blanchard, *Terrorismo de estado en la universidad*, 26.

141 Coleman and Tucker, "Between Discipline and Dissent," 407.

142 Taylor, "Alfie Meadows Calls on IPCC to Re-open Investigation into Student Protest."

143 Cf. Veltmeyer et al., *Neoliberalism and Class Conflict in Latin America*, 57. On the importance of the "shock" of disaster or dictatorship for the imposition of neoliberal economics, see Klein, *The Shock Doctrine*.

144 Bruff, "Neoliberalism and Authoritarianism," 109–10.

145 Atiles-Osoria and Whyte, "State of Exception, Law and Economy," 816. See also D. Whyte, "The Neo-Liberal State of Exception in Occupied Iraq," 135.

146 Mattei and Nader, *Plunder*, 47.

147 J. Whyte, *The Morals of the Market*, 160–78.

148 Parra Dussan, "La regla fiscal configura una política económica del Estado," my translation.

149 These constitutional reforms were given legal status by Law 1471 of 2011. Prior to the constitutionalization of budget control, a series of laws had incrementally imposed restrictions on public borrowing. Law 358 of 1997 restricted regional government borrowing, while Law 617 of 2000 placed further restrictions on region public spending. Law 819 of 2003 imposed strict fiscal monitoring and projection on both local and national governments.

150 See Knox, "Legalising the Violence of Austerity," 182; Mattei and Nader, *Plunder*, 14–15, chap. 3; J. Whyte, *The Morals of the Market*, 25.

151 Bruff, "Neoliberalism and Authoritarianism," 107.

152 Bruff, "Neoliberalism and Authoritarianism," 108, 112.

153 Bickerton, *European Integration*, 125–30.

154 Bruff, "Neoliberalism and Authoritarianism," 112–13.

155 Knox, "Legalising the Violence of Austerity," 183.

156 Knox, "Legalising the Violence of Austerity," 183.

157 European Commission, quoted in Bruff, "Neoliberalism and Authoritarianism," 112–13.

158 Quoted in Hewitt, "Greece."

159 Knox, "Legalising the Violence of Austerity," 181; Bickerton, *European Integration*, 137.

160 Known respectively as the "golden rule" and the "sustainable investment rule." The following year, the Finance Act reinforced these austerity measures by making it incumbent upon the Treasury to produce a code for fiscal stability and mandating the production of a Debt Management Report: Knox, "Legalising the Violence of Austerity," 184.

161 Knox, "Legalising the Violence of Austerity," 184.

162 Knox, "Legalising the Violence of Austerity," 185.

163 See, e.g., Centre for Welfare Reform, "UK in Breach of International Human Rights"; J. Bingham et al., "Bedroom Tax 'Breaches Human Rights of Vulnerable People.'"

164 Santos, *Towards a New Legal Common Sense*, 456ff.

165 Santos, *Towards a New Legal Common Sense*, 451.

166 Santos and García Villegas, "Colombia."

167 Santos and García Villegas, "Colombia," 30.

168 For a prescient discussion, see S. Gill, "New Constitutionalism, Democratisation and Global Political Economy," 23.

169 Santos, *Towards a New Legal Common Sense*, 456ff.

170 On liberal democratic values as "window dressing," see Brown, "Neoliberalism and the End of Liberal Democracy."

171 Bruff, "Neoliberalism and Authoritarianism," 115.

172 Wade, "Showdown at the World Bank."

173 Cammack, "Attacking the Poor"; Cammack, "What the World Bank Means by 'Poverty Reduction' and Why It Matters"; Suárez-Krabbe, *Race, Rights and Rebels*, 100–101.

174 Bruff, "Neoliberalism and Authoritarianism," 108.

175 Bruff, "Neoliberalism and Authoritarianism," 111–12.

176 See Blair and Schroeder, *Europe*.

177 It should be noted that the Labour government's commitment to public-private partnerships in the health service was "as much a foreign policy as a domestic one," as the General Agreement on Trade in Services demanded an opening up of all countries' public services to private sector provision: Pollock, *NHS Plc*, 50, 53–54.

178 Chand, "A Moment of Honesty Is Required." See also El-Gingihy, *How to Dismantle the NHS in 10 Easy Steps*.

179 Rudqvist and van Sluys, *Informe final de evaluación de medio término Laboratorio de Paz del Magdalena Medio*, 5.

180 Rudqvist and van Sluys, *Informe final de evaluación de medio término Laboratorio de Paz del Magdalena Medio*, 8.

181 Coleman, "The Gendered Violence of Development," 215; Ó Loingsigh, "Peace Laboratories," 4, 20.

182 Quoted in Ó Loingsigh, *La estrategia integral de los paramilitares en el Magdalena Medio*, 98. For a longer discussion, see Coleman, "The Gendered Violence of Development," 215–16.

183 Ó Loingsigh highlights how paramilitaries have even set up their own NGOs to channel international development funding: Ó Loingsigh, *La estrategia integral de los paramilitares en el Magdalena Medio*, 84–85.

184 Cárdenas and Marín, *La biodiversidad es la cabalgadura de la muerte*, 11.

185 See Coleman, "The Violence of the Peace."

Chapter Two. Deadly Colonial Ethics

An earlier version of part of this chapter was published under a Creative Commons license as "Rights in a State of Exception: The Deadly Colonial Ethics of Voluntary Corporate Responsibility for Human Rights," *Oñati*

Socio-Legal Series 6, no. 8 (2018): 874–900. Some of the empirical research for this chapter was the basis of a chapter in COSPACC's book *Por dentro e'soga: Una mirada social al boom petrolero y al fenómeno transnacional en Casanare* (Bogotá: Desde Abajo, 2010). This was misattributed to Josep Montesinos, but authorship had been previously registered under my name with Colombia's National Directorate for the Rights of the Author on April 30, 2008, certificate no. 10-183-75.

1 Chandler, "Business and Human Rights," 2.
2 Klein, *No Logo*, 327–29.
3 Chandler, "Business and Human Rights," 2.
4 See Rajak, *In Good Company*, 49–61.
5 Friedman, "The Social Responsibility of Business Is to Increase Its Profits."
6 Khoury and Whyte, *Corporate Human Rights Violations*, 25–26.
7 Friedman, "The Social Responsibility of Business Is to Increase Its Profits," 173.
8 J. Whyte, *The Morals of the Market*, 120.
9 See J. Whyte, *The Morals of the Market*, 160–75.
10 Friedman, "The Social Responsibility of Business Is to Increase Its Profits," 173–74.
11 See Shamir, "Between Self-Regulation and the Alien Tort Claims Act"; Shamir, "The De-radicalization of Corporate Social Responsibility," 676. This was not the first time that business had acted collectively to generate a specific understanding of responsibility. By the 1970s, in the face of a fractious international consensus that some action to establish an international standard for multinational corporations was necessary, business lobbyists and Western governments forestalled binding UN regulations on multinational corporations in favor of the (voluntary) Organization for Economic Cooperation and Development (OECD) Guidelines on Multinational Corporations: see Khoury and White, *Corporate Human Rights Violations*, chap. 1; Rowe, "Corporate Social Responsibility as Business Strategy."
12 Christian Aid, *Behind the Mask*; Doane, "The Myth of CSR"; Frynas, "The False Developmental Promise of Corporate Social Responsibility"; Madeley, *Big Business, Poor Peoples*.
13 Rodríguez Garavito, *Extractivismo versus derechos humanos*.
14 United Nations Office of the High Commissioner for Human Rights, *Guiding Principles on Business and Human Rights*, 28–35. More recently, moves have been made toward a binding human rights mechanism for transnational corporations, as I discuss in chapter 5.
15 Rajak, *In Good Company*, 12.
16 On the definitions of *respect* and *protect* and the wider "respect, protect, and fulfil" framework with regard to international human rights obligations, see Karp, "Fixing Meanings in Global Governance."
17 See, among others, Coleman, "Struggles, over Rights"; Rojas-Páez, "Understanding Environmental Harm and Justice Claims in the Global South."

18 For discussion of the concept of "extractivism" in Latin American political-economic thought, see Grigera and Álvarez, "Extractivismo y acumulación por desposesión."

19 See Giraldo and Laverde, *Casanare*, 13.

20 Procuraduría General de la Nación et al., *Informe de la Comisión Interinstitucional sobre la situación de derechos humanos en los departamentos de Casanare y Arauca*, 16.

21 See Giraldo and Laverde, *Casanare*.

22 Escobar, "Development, Violence and the New Imperial Order," 16.

23 For discussions of development as fantasy and myth, see Rist, *The History of Development*, 25–46; Sachs, "Introduction."

24 Associación Nacional de Usarios Campesinos is loosely translatable as National Association of Peasant Smallholders.

25 Colombian Constitution, 1991, arts. 48–49, 53, 79–80.

26 See Suárez-Krabbe, *Race, Rights and Rebels*, 100–102.

27 See Gillard, "BP Links with Colombian Military Intelligence Revealed," 16; Procuraduría General de la Nación et al., *Informe de la Comisión Interinstitucional sobre la situación de derechos humanos en los departamentos de Casanare y Arauca*, 17.

28 The evidence of the commander of military intelligence was recorded in a Colombian inter-institutional report: see Procuraduría General de la Nación et al., *Informe de la Comisión Interinstitucional sobre la situación de derechos humanos en los departamentos de Casanare y Arauca*, 13. See also Gillard, "BP Links with Colombian Military Intelligence Revealed."

29 This was in addition to a compulsory security payment of $1.25 per barrel: Harrison and Jones, "Black Gold Fuels Colombia Killing Machine."

30 Gillard and Jones, "BP's Secret Military Advisers."

31 Ejército de Liberación Nacional (National Liberation Army): see Pearce, "Beyond the Perimeter Fence," 6.

32 Translated from the transcript of Gearóid Ó Loingsigh's interview with Carlos Guzman Daza (alias Salomón), November 2007, 11. A printout of the transcript, supplied by Ó Loingsigh, is in the author's possession.

33 Santos and García Villegas, "Colombia," 45, my translation. See also Giraldo, *Colombia*, 57–58.

34 García Villegas, "Constitucionalismo perverso," 359–61.

35 Coleman, "The Gendered Violence of Development," 216.

36 See Serje, *El revés de la nación*, 18–19.

37 See Serje, *El revés de la nación*, 271.

38 Gillard, "BP Links with Colombian Military Intelligence Revealed," 2.

39 See, e.g., Phil Mead, quoted in Harrison, "Oilmen Dread Columbian [*sic*] 'Kiss'"; John Browne, quoted in Ghazi and Hargreaves, "BP's Chief Executive Is Making the Running on Green Strategy"; Newton, "Business and Human

Rights." See also the letter to the editor by BP's managing director Russell Seal, *Guardian*, May 13, 1997.

40 Christiansen, *Beyond Petroleum*, 5–6, 14. See also Browne, "The Case for Social Responsibility"; Browne, "International Relations."

41 United Nations Human Rights Council, *Report of the Special Representative of the Secretary-General (SRSG) on the Issue of Human Rights and Transnational Corporations and Other Business Enterprises*, 17.

42 David Rice, "RE: Human Rigths [*sic*]. Oxfam, NGOs meeting," email dated September 18, 1997, 10:40 a.m., to John O'Reilly, Howard J. Chase, Rita P. Barrera, Javier A. Torres, Mauricio Jimenez, Philip Mead, Alonso Ortiz, Fanny Umana, and Andres M. Penate [*sic*], with copies to Doug Webb (Colombia), Ines Shuk, and Alfonso Cuellar.

43 John Ruggie, UN Special Representative on Business and Human Rights, "Video Message to VP's Plenary," transcript, Oslo, March 16, 2009, http://business-humanrights.org/sites/default/files/media/bhr/files/Text-of-Ruggie-video-message-to-VPs-plenary-16-Mar-2009.pdf, 2.

44 Giraldo and Laverde, *Casanare*, 53.

45 Pearce, "Oil and Armed Conflict in Casanare," 261.

46 See also Aeberhard et al., *Informe de la misión internacional de solidaridad Roque Julio Torres*, 10–11.

47 Comments attributed to Jorge Guzmán, February 2003, cited in COSPACC, "Caso contra la empresa transnacional British Petroleum."

48 Pearce, personal email 23 April 2016.

49 Pearce, "The Case of Casanare," 36–37.

50 IAG, "Good Intentions Are Not Enough," 1, 4.

51 British Petroleum changed its name to BP Amoco in 1998, following a merger. In 2001, as part of its rebranding, the company became simply BP.

52 IAG, "Good Intentions Are Not Enough," 1.

53 Duffield, *Global Governance and the New Wars*, esp. chap. 5.

54 See, among others, Cramer, *Civil War Is Not a Stupid Thing*.

55 Baudrillard, *Simulacra and Simulation*, 1.

56 Cf. MacGinty and Richmond, "The Local Turn in Peace Building"; Pugh, "The Political Economy of Peace-Building."

57 MacGinty and Williams, *Conflict and Development*, 28.

58 Interview, Palo Gordo Prison, December 11, 2007.

59 Escobar, *Encountering Development*, 162.

60 IAG, "Good Intentions Are Not Enough," 2, 4–7.

61 See Escobar, *Encountering Development*, esp. chap. 2.

62 Duffield, *Development, Security and Unending War*, 8.

63 IAG, "Good Intentions Are Not Enough," 3–4.

64 Interview with senior representative of the Fundación Amanecer, Casanare, October 2007.

65 This term can also be used to refer to business partners but normally connotes the English *stakeholder* in NGO usage.

66 See also BP, "Developing Business, Improving Income"; Fundación Amanecer, *Informe Social 1994-2004*.

67 Harrison, "Oilmen Dread Columbian [*sic*] 'Kiss,'" 6.

68 Interviews with victims' family members and other local residents, Recetor, Colombia, July 30, 2007.

69 Interviews with IAG representatives via Skype from Bogotá to London, November 2007–January 2008.

70 Chandler, "Business and Human Rights," 2.

71 Spivak, "Righting Wrongs," 190.

72 These were the words of BP's senior spokesperson in London, quoted in Harrison and Jones, "BP Accused of Funding Colombian Death Squads." BP's spokesman acknowledged he had not seen a copy.

73 See, e.g., "Están 'Pillaos'"; Fidler, "Oil Giant in Troubled Waters"; "Human Rights and Wrongs," Raynor, "A Lethal Brew of Oil and Blood"; Raynor, "Shadowy Trail That Leads to London"; Raynor and Halstead, "Colombia's 'Dirty War' Embroils BP."

74 "Están 'Pillaos'"; Raynor, "Shadowy Trail That Leads to London."

75 Manuel Vega, COSPACC, interview with Asdrúbal Jiménez, June 30, 2007, transcript in the author's possession. Jiménez had represented a different guerrilla group—the Maoist Popular Liberation Army—in peace negotiations with the Colombian government.

76 "Están 'Pillaos.'"

77 Rajak, *In Good Company*, 40, 57–58.

78 Chandler, "Business and Human Rights," 5.

79 Rice, "Human Rights Strategies for Corporations," 135.

80 Rajak, *In Good Company*, 35, 62.

81 See Browne, "International Relations."

82 Browne, "The Case for Social Responsibility"; Balch, "Interview with John O'Reilly"; Rice, "Human Rights Strategies for Corporations," 135.

83 Muppidi, *The Colonial Signs of International Relations*, 40.

84 See Coleman, "The Making of Docile Dissent," 182.

85 See, among others, Lefort, *The Political Forms of Modern Society*; Rancière, "Does 'Democracy' Mean Something?"; Rancière, "Who Is the Subject of the Rights of Man?"

86 D'Souza, *What's Wrong with Rights?*, 10.

87 D'Souza, *What's Wrong with Rights?*, 15–17.

88 United Nations Office of the High Commissioner on Human Rights, *Guiding Principles on Business and Human Rights*, 23. While the *Guiding Principles* underscore the importance of effective state-based judicial mechanisms and highlight a need to reduce legal, practical, and other barriers that may inhibit access to justice, much of the emphasis is on private grievance mechanisms

(which may be incorporated into codes of conduct as means of showing that a company is monitoring how effectively it is paying "due diligence" to human rights): see United Nations Office of the High Commissioner on Human Rights, *Guiding Principles on Business and Human Rights*, 2–35.

89 Agamben, *Homo Sacer*, 139.

Chapter Three. Privatizing Workers' Rights

1 Friedrich Hayek, quoted in J. Whyte, *The Morals of the Market*, 95.
2 J. Whyte, *The Morals of the Market*, 95–96.
3 Selwyn, "Social Upgrading and Labour in Global Production Networks," 81.
4 See Bhambra and Holmwood, "Colonialism, Postcolonialism and the Liberal Welfare State," 74–75, 82, 90–92.
5 Bhambra and Holmwood, "Colonialism, Postcolonialism and the Liberal Welfare State"; Fishman, "The Phoney Cold War in British Trade Unions," 83–104. For a discussion of related dynamics in US trade unionism, see Gallin, "Labour as a Global Social Force," 236–37; F. Romero, *The United States and the European Trade Union Movement*; Waterman, "A Trade Union Internationalism for the 21st Century," 252; Weiler, "The United States, International Labor, and the Cold War."
6 See, among others, Davis, "Labour, Race and Empire"; Kelemen, "Planning for Africa"; Shilliam, *Race and the Undeserving Poor*, 72–73.
7 International Trade Secretariats emerged from the Socialist International in the 1890s but aimed to gain distance from international socialism and unite unions of different political persuasions—normally under the control of powerful European unions. International Trade Secretariats were renamed Global Union Federations in 2006 and, over recent years, the term *global unions* increasingly has been used.
8 Waterman, "A Trade Union Internationalism for the 21st Century," 252–54.
9 ILO, *Decent Work*.
10 Bieler et al., "The Future of the Global Working Class," 21; Bieler et al., "What Future Strategy for the Global Working Class?," 268; ILO, *Decent Work*.
11 Bieler et al., "What Future Strategy for the Global Working Class?," 97. See also Prentis, "Sharing the Benefits of Globalisation," 27–28; Simpson, "Globalisation," 35; Waterman, "A Trade Union Internationalism for the 21st Century," 252. On more recent trends toward the inclusion of preexisting human rights instruments, see Hadwiger, "Global Framework Agreements," 78, 80–82.
12 Justice, "The International Trade Union Movement and the New Codes of Conduct," 97.
13 Justice, "The International Trade Union Movement and the New Codes of Conduct," 97–98; Rütters and Zimmermann, *On the History and Policy of the IUF*, 27–28.

14 Fichter and McCallum, "Implementing Global Framework Agreements";
Hadwiger, "Global Framework Agreements."

15 Bieler, "Workers of the World, Unite?," 372.

16 Bieler, "Workers of the World, Unite?," 372; Selwyn, "Social Upgrading and
Labour in Global Production Networks," 76, 80–82.

17 Fichter and McCallum, "Implementing Global Framework Agreements,"
s65, s80–81. On the limitations of global framework agreements, see also
Croucher and Cotton, *Global Unions, Global Business*; Cumbers and Rout-
ledge, "The Entangled Geographies of Trans-national Labour Solidarity";
Fichter et al., *Globalising Labour Relations*; Herrnstadt, "Are International
Framework Agreements a Path to Corporate Social Responsibility?";
Herrnstadt, "Corporate Social Responsibility, International Framework
Agreements and Changing Corporate Behavior in the Global Workplace";
McCallum, *Global Unions, Local Power*.

18 Moody, *Workers in a Lean World*; Waterman, *Social Movements, Globalization
and the New Internationalisms*; Waterman, "Social Movement Unionism."

19 See, among others, F. Cooper, *Decolonization and African Society*; Tilley,
"A Strange Industrial Order."

20 Acciari's specific concern is with how domestic workers have challenged
the legacies of slavery that meant that domestic work was not recognized
as proper work. By means of a subaltern "epistemology of rights," domestic
workers have shifted the mainstream discourse of "decent work" at a global
level to challenge the separation between productive and reproductive labor
and garner recognition of a "human right to labour rights": Acciari, "Decolonising Labour, Reclaiming Subaltern Epistemologies," 43, 52.

21 The Sindicato de la Industria de Gaseosas de Colombia (Colombian Union
of the Fizzy Drinks Industry) fused with the Food Workers Union in 1993.

22 SINALTRAINAL, *Complaint to the International Labour Organization against
the Colombian Government for Violating SINALTRAINAL's Rights of Trade Union
Freedom*, 4–9.

23 Rancière, "Who Is the Subject of the Rights of Man?," 304. See also my discussion in the introduction to this volume.

24 SINALTRAINAL, *Complaint to the International Labour Organization against
the Colombian Government for Violating SINALTRAINAL's Rights of Trade Union
Freedom*, 5.

25 Audiencia Pública Popular and SINALTRAINAL, "Reparación integral de las
víctimas."

26 IUF, email circular, July 15, 2003. Forwarded to the author by the Colombia
Solidarity Campaign.

27 IUF, email circular, July 15, 2003. In particular, the call referred to "the assassination, imprisonment, displacement, kidnapping, threatening, and firing
of union leaders . . . in Iran," where Coca-Cola did not operate. General-
Secretary Ron Oswald of the IUF said, "The absence of any Coca-Cola opera-

tions in Iran and the fact that it was one of only two countries where you could not buy a Coke (North Korea being the other) made the claim appear absurd and lacking any credibility": Ron Oswald, email, November 4, 2020.

28 IUF, email circular, July 15, 2003.

29 In a letter to General-Secretary David Begg of the Irish Congress of Trade Unions, dated February 29, 2004 (ref. ro/pg/0205), the IUF's general-secretary stated that, in the case of the murder of Isidro Gil and the subsequent elimination of the Food Workers Union from the Carepa bottling plant, it was "clear that, at the very least, local plant management did little or nothing to protect a local union leader who was killed by paramilitaries inside the plant"; that "specific allegations around this atrocity appear to have substance"; and that the IUF had raised the matter with Coca-Cola.

30 Ron Oswald, comments at a meeting held on February 17, 2006. I attended the meeting as an adviser to the campaign group UK Students against Coke.

31 IUF, email circular, July 15, 2003.

32 IUF, email circular, July 15, 2003.

33 Ron Oswald, conversation via Skype, June 2020; IUF, "Statement on ILRF/USWA Lawsuit Filed against the Coca-Cola Company."

34 IUF, email circular, July 15, 2003. This position was repeated in subsequent correspondence with unions: IUF, email circular to British trade unions, December 2005 (received by email January 15, 2006); IUF Italy, email to Luigi Nieri, December 2005 (forwarded by Comitato Carlos Fonseca, March 15, 2006).

35 See, e.g., Amicus, "Amicus and Coca-Cola Statement"; Colombia Solidarity Campaign, transcript of meeting between Juan Carlos Galvis and Brian Revell, London, July 4, 2005.

36 Barber, "Building Partnerships across the Globe."

37 Justice for Colombia was set up in 2002 by the Trades Union Congress and thirty-five other unions as a vehicle for solidarity with Colombian trade unionists.

38 Over the following years, NUS Services issued and updated a number of communications defending its position: see, e.g., NUS Services Ltd., "Accusations of Human Rights Violations against Coca-Cola Workers in Colombia"; NUS Services Ltd., "Coca-Cola Enterprises Ltd."; NUS Services Ltd., "Coca-Cola"; NUS Services Ltd. "Summary of the Ongoing Constructive Engagement with Coca-Cola in Relation to the Accusations Relating to Colombia and India."

39 Coca-Cola Company and the IUF, "Joint Coca-Cola and IUF Statement."

40 IUF, email circular to British trade unions, December 2005. The IUF went on to complement this ongoing dialogue with the building of a Global Coca-Cola Workers' Alliance among its affiliates, which focused on promoting a charter of demands against job destruction and casual contracts: see IUF, "Charter of Demands against Job Destruction."

41 See Caccio, "Garbatella, Rifondazione vieta la Coca-Cola"; Capponi, "Olim-
    piade e Coca-Cola"; Occhipinti, "Tensione e proteste anti-sponsor all' arrivo
    della fiaccola olímpica"; Offeddu, "Empoli boicotta la Coca-Cola."

42 Nicola Raffa, quoted in Comuni di Roma, press release, November 7, 2005;
    Rete Boicottaggio Coca-Cola, press release, November 8, 2005, received by
    email from Comitato Carlos Fonseca, March 15, 2006.

43 IUF, "IUF and Coca-Cola Agreement to Request United Nations' ILO to
    Conduct Independent Investigation of Coca-Cola Labour Practices in
    Colombia." This was despite opposition from Italian activists and their
    ongoing insistence that the mayor of Rome should honor his commitment to
    organizing a truth commission. Rete Boicottaggio Coca-Cola, Letter to Luigi
    Nieri, Massimiliano Smeriglio, and Sandro Medici, March 9, 2006; open let-
    ter to Walter Veltoni, June 30, 2006.

44 See NUS, "Motion on Coke Passed at NSU Conference in March 2006."
    Between 1982 and 1985, GMB was a widely used abbreviation for the General,
    Municipal, Boilermakers' and Allied Trade Union (GMBATU). In 1987, the
    union officially changed its name to the acronym GMB.

45 UK Students against Coke, "Informe de la votación en la conferencia annual
    del Sindicato Nacional de Estudiantes, Reino Unido sobre el boicot a Coca
    Cola—30 Marzo 2006," report on the vote at the NUS Annual Conference on
    the Boycott of Coca-Cola, received by email April 2, 2006.

46 Federación Nacional Sindical Unitaria Agropecuaria (FENSUAGRO) to
    Colombia Solidarity Campaign, letter, May 24, 2006. Letter in possession of
    the author.

47 UK Students against Coke, "Informe de la votación en la conferencia annual
    del Sindicato Nacional de Estudiantes."

48 Conversation with one of the Food Workers' US-based lawyers, March 2015.

49 Ron Oswald, conversation via Skype, June 2020.

50 Ron Oswald, conversation via Skype, June 2020

51 IUF, "Coca-Cola Is Becoming a Serial Human Rights Offender."

52 Ron Oswald, conversation via Skype, June 2020.

53 Fichter and McCallum, "Implementing Global Framework Agreements,"
    S80–81.

54 Ron Oswald, conversation via Skype, June 2020.

55 Barber et al., "Solidarity with Colombia"; IUF, email circular, Decem-
    ber 2005; Fletcher, "Something to Be Proud Of"; NUS Services Ltd., "Coca-
    Cola." There were in fact four other unions: Sindicato de Trabajadores de la
    Industria de Gaseosas (Union of Workers in the Fizzy Drinks Industry [SIN-
    TRAINDEGA]); Asociación de Trabajadores de la Industria de Gaseosas (As-
    sociation of Workers in the Fizzy Drinks Industry [ASONTRAGASEOSAS]),
    Sindicato Nacional de Trabajadores de la Industria de Bebidas (National
    Union of Workers in the Drinks Industry [SINALTRAINBEC]), and Sindi-

cato Nacional de Trabajadores de la Industria de los Alimentos y Bebidas (National Union of Workers in the Food and Drinks Industry of Colombia [SICO]). More than half of the frequently mentioned "twelve other unions" in Coca-Cola existed only on paper. The president of SINTRAINDEGA confirmed in an interview in June 2008 that he had set them up to protect workers from sacking by taking advantage of a legal loophole. Moreover, the presidents of ASONTRAGASEOSAS and SINTRAINDEGA stated that they respected the Food Workers' boycott when I spoke to them that same month. This leaves the two unions who opposed the campaign: SICO and SINALTRAINBEC. SINALTRAINBEC was set up with the support of management in the Atlantic coast region as a direct counter to the Food Workers. In a June 2008 interview, SINALTRAINBEC's national president underscored the two unions' political differences, contextualizing his union's opposition to the boycott on the basis that SINALTRAINBEC wanted to maintain good relations with management. I discuss the more nefarious origins of SICO later.

56 Carlos Rodríguez, president of the CUT, had actually appeared in support of the Food Workers at the press conference launching the boycott before changing his position. According to the CUT's general-secretary Boris Montes de Oca, this change of position was influenced by the IUF's position. Rodríguez and Montes de Oca went on to make statements against the boycott without the CUT's endorsement, prompting almost half of the CUT's national executive to sign an open letter in complaint: see Rodríguez and Montes de Oca, *La CUT y las empresas multinacionales*; Carlos Rodríguez, email to Giuseppe Iuliano, Confederazione Italiana Sindacati Lavoratori, 2005. In response, see Miguel Antonio Caro, Gloria Inés Ramírez, Luis Alfonso Velásquez, Domingo Tovar Arrieta, Tarsicio Rivera Muñoz, Orlando Ospina, José Diógenes Orjuela, Gustavo Rubén Triana and Alvaro Morales Sánchez, "Open Letter to Carlos Rodríguez Díaz, Boris Montes de Oca, Hernán Correa, Fabio Arias, Tarsicio Mora, María Del Carmen Trujillo, Fernando Morales, Manuel Márquez, Benjamín Rizzo, Jorge Albín Anaya, Ligio Inés Alzate and Ramón Támara," June 22, 2006. Email in the author's possession.

57 Justice for Colombia, "Trade Union Delegation to Colombia," 20. International Union of Food, email circular, December 2005; NUS Services Ltd., "Accusations of Human Rights Violations against Coca-Cola Workers in Colombia," 3; IUF, email to NUS Services Limited Environment and Ethics Committee in run-up to meeting with UK Student against Coke, January 2006.

58 Barber et al., "Solidarity with Colombia." Trade unions in Colombia had links with a number of solidarity organizations, including the Colombia Solidarity Campaign, which was promoting the Food Workers' campaign.

59 Justice for Colombia, "Trade Union Delegation to Colombia," 20–22.

60 Drainville, *Contesting Globalization*, 10; Eco, *Travels in Hyperreality*.

61 Conversation with Domingo Tovar, Director of Human Rights, CUT, Bogotá, April 2006.

62 See "A juicio ex alcalde de Apartadó"; "Condenan a ex alcalde de Apartadó"; M. Romero, "Los trabajadores bananeros de Urabá"; "Sindicalismo de derecho."

63 "A juicio ex alcalde de Apartadó"; "Condenan a ex alcalde de Apartadó"; M. Romero, "Los trabajadores bananeros de Urabá"; "Sindicalismo de derecha."

64 Ron Oswald, comments at a meeting held on January 17, 2006, at which the author was present.

65 Ron Oswald, interview via Skype, May 2020.

66 Ó Loingsigh, *La estrategia integral de los paramilitares en el Magdalena Medio*, 84–85.

67 Sarmiento, *El Magdalena Medio*, 33. For discussion, see Ó Loingsigh, *La estrategia integral de los paramilitares en el Magdalena Medio*, 11–24.

68 Cárdenas and Marín, *La biodiversidad es la cabalgadura de la muerte*, 11.

69 IUF, "Gains for Colombian Beverage Workers"; IUF, "Coca-Cola Union Wins Improved Collective Bargaining Agreement in Colombia"; IUF, "Colombia."

70 See J. Whyte, *The Morals of the Market*, chap. 4.

71 Santos and García Villegas, "Colombia," 45.

72 Ron Oswald, comments by email, November 2020.

73 Ron Oswald, comments by email, November 2020.

74 When in 2006 the British antipoverty NGO War on Want published its own report setting out the allegations against Coca-Cola and calling for a "global framework of corporate regulation" to curb the power of multinationals, the IUF published a statement welcoming the report. "While unions today can and do force global companies to recognize and negotiate, including negotiations at the global level, this process can never substitute for the kind of regulatory framework that War on Want's report calls for," Oswald stated. "Voluntary but enforceable agreements may currently represent unions' best concrete mechanisms to control worker rights abuses by global corporations, but they can never be allowed to substitute for the long-term goal of enforceable global regulations governing the behaviour of such companies. This is particularly true given the real danger at present that the protection of global investor rights threatens to supersede the protection of human rights": IUF, "Time to Regulate TNCs."

75 Collins et al., *Labour Law*, 76.

76 ILO, *Evaluation Mission*, 45–47.

77 Ron Oswald, copy of email to Terry Collingsworth, n.d. I thank Bob Perillo for additional background information on the case: Bob Perillo, conversation via Skype, December 2020.

78 *Aldana v. Fresh Del Monte Produce*, US Court of Appeals, 11th Circuit, no. 12-16143, decided February 6, 2014. The court agreed with an early ruling that the plaintiffs should have appealed the Guatemalan court's refusal to hear their case, effectively leaving the plaintiffs without a forum in which their case could be heard.

79 The court had ordered reinstatement, but the company refused: US Labor Education in the Americas Project to Incasa, letter, September 2, 2005; Bob Perillo, open letter to the board of US/LEAP, February 2010.

80 Ron Oswald, email to Bob Perillo, January 29, 2006.

81 Bob Perillo, open letter to the board of US/LEAP, February 2010.

82 Ron Oswald, email to Bob Perillo, February 2, 2006.

83 Perillo, open letter to the board of US/LEAP, February 2010.

84 Bruff, "The Rise of Authoritarian Neoliberalism," 115.

85 Slobodian, *Globalists*, 2.

86 ILO, *Decent Work*.

87 Selwyn, 'Social Upgrading and Labour in Global Production Networks," 81.

88 For a critique of the "social upgrading" concept, see Selwyn, "Social Upgrading and Labour in Global Production Networks."

89 Selwyn, "Social Upgrading and Labour in Global Production Networks," 81.

90 Cammack, "Attacking the Poor," 129.

91 See Polanyi, *The Great Transformation*, and my discussion in chapter 1 of this volume.

92 ILO, *Decent Work*.

93 Migone, "Embedded Markets," 367; Slobodian, *Globalists*, 16.

94 IUF, "Charter of Demands against Job Destruction."

95 Drainville, *A History of World Order and Resistance*, 137.

96 Drainville, *Contesting Globalization*; Drainville, "The Fetishism of Global Civil Society."

97 See Bhambra and Holmwood, "Colonialism, Postcolonialism and the Liberal Welfare State," 579.

98 Shilliam, *Race and the Undeserving Poor*, 32–58.

99 Davis, "Labour, Race and Empire"; Kelemen, "Planning for Africa."

100 See, among others, Davis, "Labour, Race and Empire"; Shilliam, *Race and the Undeserving Poor*, 72–73; J. Whyte, *The Morals of the Market*, 120–26.

101 Gill, "The Limits of Solidarity."

102 Representative of NUS Services Ethical and Environmental Committee, comments in meeting, February 17, 2006. While NUS Services did ask Coca-Cola for a response to various specific allegations during its period of dialogue with the company, Coca-Cola continued to dismiss the Food Workers' claims as "malicious and offensive." The NUS Services summary of the dialogue suggests that it did not press the matter of the allegations to any significant extent and that the benefit of the doubt was routinely given to Coca-Cola. Indeed, NUS Services went on to hail numerous "positive initiatives" on the company's part and even to propose that Coca-Cola contribute to a generic development fund for Colombia in place of remedy for any human rights abuses that may (or may not) have occurred: see NUS Services Ltd., "Accusations of Human Rights Violations against Coca-Cola Workers in Colombia"; NUS Services Ltd., "Summary of the Ongoing Constructive

Engagement with Coca-Cola in Relation to the Accusations Relating to Colombia and India."
103 Fisher, *Capitalist Realism*, 42–43.
104 D'Souza, *What's Wrong with Rights?*, 18.

Chapter Four. Elusive Justice

1 Engle, "Anti-impunity and the Turn to Criminal Law in Human Rights," 1071.
2 Schwöbel-Patel, *Marketing Global Justice*, 123.
3 For in-depth discussion, see Khoury and Whyte, *Corporate Human Rights Violations*, chaps. 2, 6. With regard to the Ruggie agenda, it is worth noting that even the United Nations' special rapporteur on business and human rights had openly recognized that voluntary corporate responsibility can detract from abuses. In the United Nations' *Guiding Principles on Business and Human Rights*, Ruggie emphasized the need for measures to compensate victims— including judicial remedy—where "due diligence" for human rights fails and urged states to "address obstacles to access to justice." This, however, was not a significant departure from the emphasis on voluntary mechanisms. While *Guiding Principles* underscores the importance of effective state-based judicial mechanisms and highlights a need to reduce legal, practical, and other barriers that may inhibit access to justice, much of the emphasis is on private grievance mechanisms (which may be incorporated into codes of conduct as means of showing that a company is monitoring how effectively it is according due diligence to human rights): see United Nations Office of the High Commissioner on Human Rights, *Guiding Principles*, 2–35.
4 Baars, "It's Not Me, It's the Corporation," 154–55.
5 Schwöbel-Patel, *Marketing Global Justice*, 87. See also Engle, "Anti-impunity and the Turn to Criminal Law in Human Rights."
6 The quote is from Petersmann, "How to Promote the International Rule of Law?," 31. See also Petersmann, "The WTO Constitution and Human Rights," and, for discussion, Tzouvala, "Neoliberalism as Legalism."
7 Schwöbel-Patel, *Marketing Global Justice*, 85–89, 184–85.
8 Schwöbel-Patel, *Marketing Global Justice*, 181–83.
9 Schwöbel-Patel, *Marketing Global Justice*, chap. 7.
10 Krever, "Dispensing Global Justice," 97. See also Schwöbel-Patel, *Marketing Global Justice*.
11 Krever, "Dispensing Global Justice," 68–69.
12 Veitch, *Law and Irresponsibility*, 29, 32.
13 Veitch, *Law and Irresponsibility*, 24, 32.
14 Veitch, *Law and Irresponsibility*, 2.
15 Veitch, *Law and Irresponsibility*, 22.

16 Tombs and Whyte, *The Corporate Criminal*, 82.

17 Norrie, *Crime, Reason and History*, 38–39.

18 Thomas, "Blind to Complicity?," 167.

19 Cited in Norrie, *Crime, Reason and History*, 38.

20 Thomas, "Blind to Complicity?," 167.

21 See Norrie, *Crime, Reason and History*, 11, 35–36.

22 Norrie, *Crime, Reason and History*, 24–26; Tombs and Whyte, *The Corporate Criminal*, 78–82.

23 Thomas, "Blind to Complicity?," 168.

24 Thomas, "Blind to Complicity?," 168.

25 Thomas, "Blind to Complicity?," 173. See also Thomas, "Good Faith and (Dis)honest Mistakes?," 371–85.

26 Norrie, "Simulacra of Morality?," 104.

27 Veitch, *Law and Irresponsibility*, 86–87.

28 Inter-American Human Rights Commission, *Precautionary Measures 51/15*.

29 Rojas-Páez, "Understanding Environmental Harm and Justice Claims in the Global South," 71.

30 Rojas-Páez, "Understanding Environmental Harm and Justice Claims in the Global South," 73–75.

31 Rojas-Páez, "Understanding Environmental Harm and Justice Claims in the Global South," 73.

32 Rojas-Páez, "Understanding Environmental Harm and Justice Claims in the Global South," 72.

33 Rojas-Páez, "Understanding Environmental Harm and Justice Claims in the Global South," 61.

34 Ireland, "Finance and the Origins of Modern Company Law."

35 D. Whyte, "The Autonomous Corporation," 99.

36 Tombs and Whyte, *The Corporate Criminal*, 85, 89.

37 Baars, "It's Not Me, It's the Corporation," 162–63.

38 D. Whyte, "The Autonomous Corporation," 101, discussing W. G. Carson, "The Conventionalization of Early Factory Crime."

39 D. Whyte, "The Autonomous Corporation," 101.

40 Meeran, "Tort Litigation against Multinational Corporations for Violations of Human Rights," 3. In many jurisdictions it is not possible to obtain civil redress for human rights violations per se directly against corporations, although this depends to some extent on the governing law. For instance, the constitutions of Colombia and South Africa are "horizontally" applicable, meaning that corporations can be held liable for breaches of fundamental constitutional rights, including the possibility of compensation awards. I thank Paul Dowling of Leigh Day and Company for this clarification.

41 A good example of this is the landmark judgment won by Indigenous and peasant communities when Chevron was found guilty by three layers of

courts in Ecuador of having dumped billions of gallons of toxic waste in the Amazon rainforest, causing an epidemic of cancer likened to an "Amazon Chernobyl." Chevron had initially spent significant resources arguing that the case should be heard in Ecuador rather than the United States and then unsuccessfully attempted to convince the Ecuadorian Justice Ministry to step in and stop the proceedings. After years of litigation, Chevron refused to accept the Ecuadorian court's ruling and pay the compensation ordered, instead filing civil proceedings against the victims' lawyers for "a fraudulent litigation and [public relations] campaign": see Coleman et al., *Righting Corporate Wrongs?*, 10; Wheyler, "Chevron's Amazon Chernobyl Case Moves to Canada."

42 Baars, "It's Not Me, It's the Corporation," 157.

43 Coleman et al., *Righting Corporate Wrongs?*, 15.

44 Baars, "It's Not Me, It's the Corporation," 152; D. Whyte, "The Autonomous Corporation," 102–3.

45 Baars, "It's Not Me, It's the Corporation."

46 Demonstrating "attributability" of the acts to the corporation requires that a seamless chain of causation be established between company personnel and the individuals who carried out these acts, opening up the corporation as singular entity in a way that further shields "the company" from being held liable for the acts: Coleman et al., *Righting Corporate Wrongs?*, 14.

47 Likewise, when victims attempt to use the courts of the country where a multinational corporation is domiciled to address allegations against operating subsidiaries, subsidiaries can challenge the court's jurisdiction. For more in-depth discussion, see Coleman et al., *Righting Corporate Wrongs?*, 11–12.

48 Dowling, "Limited Liability and Separate Corporate Personality in Multinational Corporate Groups," 15–16.

49 Dowling, "Limited Liability and Separate Corporate Personality in Multinational Corporate Groups," 18.

50 Meeran, "The 'Zero Draft.'"

51 Coleman et al., *Righting Corporate Wrongs?*, 21–23; Global Campaign to Dismantle Corporate Power and Stop Impunity, "Global Campaign Statement on the Third Draft of the Binding Treaty."

52 Dowling, "Limited Liability and Separate Corporate Personality in Multinational Corporate Groups," 18–21.

53 This is the idea of corporate mens rea, developed over the twentieth century. In particular, Lord Denning's 1975 judgment in *H. I. Bolton (Engineering) Co. Ltd. v. T. J. Graham and Sons* tried to set out how a corporation could be understood in law to have the "guilty mind," or mens rea, necessary to establish criminal conduct by likening the corporation to a human body with "a brain and a nerve centre which controls what it does" (i.e., directors and managers; others are no more than hands that do the work): Tombs and Whyte, *The Corporate Criminal*, 90.

54 Tombs and Whyte, *The Corporate Criminal*, 91, 101–7.

55 There is an implicit recognition here of the fictional nature of corporate personhood, and some legislation has even included provision for the cancellation of legal personhood where the company is found liable for certain kinds of crime (a cost that could not be easily accommodated within normal risk-benefit calculations): Coleman et al., *Righting Corporate Wrongs?*, 25–26.

56 Baars, "It's Not Me, It's the Corporation," 150–52; Gray, "The Regulation of Corporate Violations," 875–92.

57 Baars, "It's Not Me, It's the Corporation," 151–52.

58 Baars, "It's Not Me, It's the Corporation," 150.

59 Knox, "Strategy and Tactics," 195.

60 Knox, "Strategy and Tactics," 215.

61 Thomson, "Was *Kiobel* Detrimental to Corporate Social Responsibility?"

62 Gill, "The Limits of Solidarity," 674.

63 Gill, "The Limits of Solidarity," 674.

64 Sebastian Ordoñez, conversation with the author, London, January 2020.

65 Knox, "Strategy and Tactics," 199.

66 The reflections of project participants are summarized in the conclusion to a part of a short coproduced book, published in English and Spanish, that came out of the project: Coleman et al., *Righting Corporate Wrongs?*, 53–56.

67 See Coleman et al., *Righting Corporate Wrongs?*, 55–56.

68 Marx, *Capital*, 181–82, cited in Knox, "Strategy and Tactics," 217–18.

69 An overview of the "Peoples Treaty" and the process behind it is available online at https://www.stopcorporateimpunity.org/request-solidarity-actions (accessed December 12, 2018).

70 Coleman et al., *Righting Corporate Wrongs?*, 54.

71 Rojas-Páez, "Understanding Environmental Harm and Justice Claims in the Global South," 81.

72 Rojas-Páez, "Understanding Environmental Harm and Justice Claims in the Global South," 78.

73 Tribunal Permanente de los Pueblos, "Empresas transnacionales y derechos de los pueblos en Colombia," 37, 39.

74 Tribunal Permanente de los Pueblos, "Empresas transnacionales y derechos de los pueblos en Colombia," 37, 39. On the exclusion of political genocide from the 1948 convention to appease powerful political interests, see, among others, Nersessian, *Genocide and Political Groups*; Van Schaack, "The Crime of Political Genocide." Unlike the Genocide Convention, the Colombian Criminal Code does recognize "political genocide."

75 Greenawalt, "Rethinking Genocidal Intent," 2259.

76 Tribunal Permanente de los Pueblos, "Empresas transnacionales y derechos de los pueblos en Colombia," 32.

77 Greenawalt, "Rethinking Genocidal Intent," 2265.

78 Tribunal Permanente de los Pueblos, "Empresas transnacionales y derechos de los pueblos en Colombia," 39.

79 For a summary, see United Nations Office on Genocide Prevention and the Responsibility to Protect, "Crimes against Humanity."

80 Tribunal Permanente de los Pueblos, "Empresas transnacionales y derechos de los pueblos en Colombia," 40, 44.

81 Schwöbel-Patel, *Marketing Global Justice*, 181–83.

82 Tribunal Permanente de los Pueblos, "Empresas transnacionales y derechos de los pueblos en Colombia," 41.

83 Tribunal Permanente de los Pueblos, "Empresas transnacionales y derechos de los pueblos en Colombia," 41, 44.

84 Tribunal Permanente de los Pueblos, "Empresas transnacionales y derechos de los pueblos en Colombia," 11, 37.

85 With regard to how mens rea might be established for crime of "social murder," see Norrie, "Legal and Social Murder."

86 See van de Sandt and Moor, *Peace: Everyone's Business!*, 46–50.

87 This ongoing activism, alongside the opening generated by the left-leaning Kirchner governments from 2003, led to various pioneering initiatives, including the Truth Commission on Economic Complicity established in 2015, which led to representatives of many companies facing criminal proceedings: see Coleman et al., *Righting Corporate Wrongs?*, 30–31.

88 Interestingly, Ayça Çubukçu suggests this latter interpretation was precisely how some of the organizers of another alternative justice mechanism—the World Tribunal on Iraq—saw the process, with the tribunal's 2004 inaugural session featuring a video interview with Jacques Derrida entitled "A Justice to Come": see Çubukçu, *For the Love of Humanity*, 127.

89 Christodoulidis, "Strategies of Rupture," 21.

90 Christodoulidis, "Strategies of Rupture," 4–5.

91 Christodoulidis, "Strategies of Rupture," 3–4; Schwöbel-Patel, *Marketing Global Justice*, 261–62.

92 Christodoulidis, "Strategies of Rupture," 5.

93 Christodoulidis, "Strategies of Rupture," 5.

94 Bhandar, "Strategies of Legal Rupture," 60.

95 Christodoulidis, "Strategies of Rupture," 8.

96 Christodoulidis makes these comments in relation to Vergès's strategy in defense of Barbie: Christodoulidis, "Strategies of Rupture," 7–8.

97 Audiencia Pública Popular and SINALTRAINAL, "Reparación integral de las víctimas."

98 In his book *After Evil*, Robert Meister argues that the narrative of "transitional justice" not only works to draw a line between past wrongs and the present state of affairs. It also, simultaneously, holds the promise of a justice to come, narrating past evils as behind us but deferring redress to a future moment: Meister, *After Evil*, 10–13.

99 Tribunal Permanente de los Pueblos, "Genocidio político, impunidad y los crímenes contra la paz en Colombia." Marcelo Ferreira, one of the judges in the 2006–8 session and professor of human rights at the University of Buenos Aires, published a book chapter on the TPP Colombia Session in 2009 arguing for the application to the Colombian case of Daniel Feierstein's concept of "reorganization genocide." In Feierstein's well-known analysis of the crimes of the dictatorship in Argentina, *reorganization genocide* refers to the partial destruction of the national group with the aim of transforming social relations away from those of reciprocity, solidarity, and resistance: see Feierstein, *El genocidio como práctica social*; Ferreira, "Genocidio reorganizador en Colombia." Feierstein himself was one of the judges in the 2021 session, although the ruling offers its own legal argumentation and does not cite his work.

100 Tribunal Permanente de los Pueblos, "Genocidio político, impunidad y los crímenes contra la paz en Colombia," 78–93.

101 Tribunal Permanente de los Pueblos, "Genocidio político, impunidad y los crímenes contra la paz en Colombia," 96.

102 Indeed, when the PPT subsequently set out its own definition of "crime against humanity" in its 2018 statute, it kept close to the text of the Rome Statute of the ICC and actually ruled out any such expansive interpretation by removing the final clause, which allows for "other inhumane acts of a similar character" to be included within the scope of the crime: see Tribunal Permanente de los Pueblos, "Genocidio político, impunidad y los crímenes contra la paz en Colombia," 72–73.

103 See Winter, "Violence and Visibility."

104 See Thompson, *Whigs and Hunters*, 206, and my discussion in the introduction in this volume.

Chapter Five. From Pernicious Optimism to Radical Hope

1 Povinelli, *Economies of Abandonment*, 4.

2 Povinelli, *Economies of Abandonment*, 2.

3 Povinelli, *Economies of Abandonment*, 12.

4 Montag, "War and the Market," 126–27.

5 Meister, *After Evil*, 10–13.

6 Fisher, *Capitalist Realism*, 8.

7 Fisher, *Capitalist Realism*, 13.

8 Fisher, *Capitalist Realism*, 13.

9 Fisher, *Capitalist Realism*, 14.

10 Meeting between British union leaders and UK Students against Coke, January 2006, at which author was present.

11 NUS Services Ltd., "Accusations of Human Rights Violations against Coca-Cola Workers in Colombia"; NUS Services Ltd., "'Summary of the Ongoing

Constructive Engagement with Coca-Cola in Relation to the Accusations Relating to Colombia and India."

12 National Union of Students, "The Importance of Ethics to Students."

13 Fisher, *Capitalist Realism*, 74.

14 For insightful reflections on the permutations of "the man" of mainstream moral philosophy, see Murdoch, *The Sovereignty of Good*, 4–10.

15 Amnesty International UK, Amnesty International Launches Protect the Human."

16 Schwöbel-Patel, *Marketing Global Justice*, 65.

17 Schwöbel-Patel, *Marketing Global Justice*, 76.

18 Schwöbel-Patel, *Marketing Global Justice*, 32.

19 See, among others, Latimer, *The Campaigning Handbook*; Amnesty International, *Amnesty International Campaigning Manual*, 20–21, 89, 114, 130, 148–49; Christian Aid, "Inviting Others to Campaign," 5, 7; Oxfam, *Influencing for Impact Guide*, 27, 49–50, 60. For a discussion of marketing and branding tactics in relation to Amnesty International, see Schwöbel-Patel, *Marketing Global Justice*, 87.

20 Interviews with IAG representatives via Skype from Bogotá to London, November 2007–January 2008. The distinction between strategy and tactics in the previous chapter is pertinent here. Knox's point, that "strategic" uses of law tend to focus only on short-term tactical matters rather than the strategic matter of whether and on what terms it might be possible to use the law *without* fatally undermining longer term structural considerations, also relates to wider processes of campaigning. Our partner in the Righting Corporate Wrongs project, the British NGO War on Want, is an example of an organization that seeks to work within the parameters established by its charitable status and long-term links to the British trade union movement to address "the structures of inequality and justice" at a global level. Despite using the language of human rights, War on Want has an explicit commitment to solidarity with social movements and workers' organizations fighting for their rights. It has not been reticent to identify a "new colonialism" within contemporary capitalist extraction. Rather than seeking to replicate the prevailing ideology, War on Want is explicit about the importance of language and the need to frame things in terms that reflect the struggles of social movements rather than the abstract categories of policy-speak. This is not to say that War on Want is unhampered by institutional constraints. Indeed, dependence on the support of British trade union affiliates made it very difficult for War on Want to openly support the Colombian Food Workers in their call for a boycott of Coca-Cola. Without seeking to suggest that War on Want deploys its strategic approach perfectly or completely, what we see through this example is a very different attitude from that at play within the interventions of NGOs, trade unions, and student groups that have served to neutralize social movement struggles in the name of human

rights: see, among others, War on Want, "The Importance of Language"; War on Want, *The New Colonialism*. See also the organization's description at War on Want, "About War on Want," accessed September 20, 2021, https://waronwant.org/about.

21 Pearce, "The Case of Casanare," 36.

22 On the problematic opened up by the concept of *Verleugnung*—normally translated as "disavowal" or "denial"—in Freud's work, see Cohen, *States of Denial*, 25–37; Mannoni, "I Know Well, but All the Same."

23 Cohen, *States of Denial*, 25, 28.

24 Berlant, *Cruel Optimism*, 1.

25 Berlant, *Cruel Optimism*, 2.

26 Berlant, *Cruel Optimism*, 2–3.

27 Berlant, *Cruel Optimism*, 2.

28 George Orwell, cited in Žižek, *The Courage of Hopelessness*, x.

29 Žižek, *The Courage of Hopelessness*, x.

30 Rivera Cusicanqui, "*Ch'ixinakax Utxiwa*," 12.

31 Žižek, *The Courage of Hopelessness*, xi.

32 Žižek, *The Courage of Hopelessness*, x.

33 William Mendoza was a leader of the Food Workers Union in the city of Barrancabermeja when paramilitaries attempted to kidnap his four-year-old daughter in June 2002. Afterward, the family was sent a note assuring them that the would-be kidnappers had not intended to keep the child but would return her body parts in plastic bags. In September 2003, the fifteen-year-old son of a leader of the Barranquilla branch of the union, Limberto Carranza, was abducted and tortured while paramilitaries called Carranza's home and threatened him for his trade union activities: SINALTRAINAL, "La transnacional Coca-Cola y el paramilitarismo en Colombia," 15–16.

34 Quotes and other information on the *plan de vida* in Catatumbo are drawn from conversations with members of CISCA between November 2007 and June 2008, unless otherwise stated. I do not use names at the request of those involved, as it is part of the collective ethos of the *planes de vida* not to have visible figureheads.

35 Ó Loingsigh, *Catatumbo*, 14.

36 Coordinación Colombia Europa Estados Unidos, "Informe preliminar de la misión internacional de observación sobre ejecuciones extrajudiciales," February 2008, received by email, February 5, 2008.

37 On the ways in which grassroots *planes de vida* are distinct from development, as promoted by the state institutions and mainstream NGOs, see CNA, *Construyendo nuestros planes de vida*, 21. Nevertheless it should also be pointed out that, outside of social movement struggle, state institutions have adopted the idea of the *plan de vida*, more specifically as an alternative to traditional notions of development that recognizes the autonomy of Indigenous populations under the 1991 constitution, although this is sometimes referred to as

ethnodesarollo (ethnodevelopment): see, e.g., Monje Carvajal, *Los planes de vida de los pueblos indígenas en Colombia*. Discussion of these institutionally backed *planes de vida* is beyond the scope of this book, except to emphasize that they should be distinguished from the grassroots social movement *planes de vida* that I discuss here.

38 CNA, *Construyendo nuestros planes de vida*, 15.

39 CNA, *Construyendo nuestros planes de vida*, 15.

40 CNA, *Construyendo nuestros planes de vida*, 12, 15.

41 For discussion, see Serje, *El revés de la nación*, 38–40, 47–73. On the distinctions between these two different understandings of *diagnosis*, see CNA, *Construyendo nuestros planes de vida*, 21.

42 Serje, *El revés de la nación*, 48, 60, 72–73.

43 CNA, *Construyendo nuestros planes de vida*, 17.

44 U. Gordon, "Prefigurative Politics between Ethical Practice and Absent Promise," 525–26.

45 U. Gordon, "Prefigurative Politics between Ethical Practice and Absent Promise," 526–27.

46 U. Gordon, "Prefigurative Politics between Ethical Practice and Absent Promise," 528–31.

47 CNA, *Construyendo nuestros planes de vida*, 31–32.

48 CNA, *Construyendo nuestros planes de vida*, 32.

49 CISCA leader, interview by member of la Red, Catatumbo, November 19, 2007. Transcript in author's possession.

50 CISCA leader, interview.

51 CISCA et al., *Catatumbo*, 1.

52 CISCA et al., *Catatumbo*, 3.

53 CNA, *Construyendo nuestros planes de vida*, 4.

54 Conversations with members of CISCA, CNA, and la Red, 2008–present. On CISCA's work in particular, see Cifuentes Tarazona, *Buen vivir en Colombia*, 105–17.

55 Cifuentes Tarazona, *Buen vivir en Colombia*, 106.

56 Cifuentes Tarazona, *Buen vivir en Colombia*, 107.

57 CNA, *Construyendo nuestros planes de vida*, 21.

58 Eagleton, *Hope without Optimism*, 4.

59 Berlant, *Cruel Optimism*, 2.

60 Eagleton, *Hope without Optimism*, 114.

61 Lear, *Radical Hope*, 97.

62 Lear, *Radical Hope*, 34.

63 Lear, *Radical Hope*, 100.

64 Lear, *Radical Hope*, 95.

65 Dreyfus, "Comments on Jonathan Lear's *Radical Hope*."

66 Lear, *Radical Hope*, 6.

67 See Maldonado-Torres, "On the Coloniality of Being"; Wynter, "Unsettling the Coloniality of Being/Power/Truth/Freedom."

68 In the early 1990s, the joining of psychoanalytic and deconstructive critique in studies of Holocaust literature spawned the field of trauma studies. However, although the aim was to bear witness to human suffering and formulate an ethical response, postcolonial critics have decried a tendency in the literature to privilege the suffering of white Europeans: see Andermahr, *Decolonizing Trauma Studies*; Craps, *Postcolonial Witnessing*.

69 Mignolo, "Sylvia Wynter," 108.

70 Fanon, *The Wretched of the Earth*, 28.

71 Lear, *Radical Hope*, 103.

72 Eagleton, *Hope without Optimism*, chap. 1.

Chapter Six. For an Insurgent Humanism

1 Cf. Cárdenas and Marín, *La biodiversidad es la cabalgadura de la muerte*, 11.

2 Wynter, in McKittrick and Wynter, "Unparalleled Catastrophe for Our Species?," 18.

3 Cárdenas and Marín, *La biodiversidad es la cabalgadura de la muerte*, 16.

4 That is to say, according to this account the emergence of a sociocultural conception of humanity based on Western bourgeois tenets shapes us even at the levels of neurochemistry and epigenetics. Biology, genes, and so on provide us with what Wynter calls a first "set of instructions," but even at the most basic neurochemical level, human modes of consciousness are informed by a "second set of instructions" that consist of narrative and myth. No form of knowledge stands outside of this narrativization, the myths or symbolic codes of life and death: McKittrick and Wynter, "Unparalleled Catastrophe for Our Species?," 25-37.

5 McKittrick and Wynter, "Unparalleled Catastrophe for Our Species?," 23.

6 For contemporary discussion, see, among others, Gilabert, *Human Dignity and Human Rights*; Tasioulas, "On the Foundations of Human Rights"; Waldron, "Is Dignity the Foundation of Human Rights?"

7 Maldonado-Torres, "On the Coloniality of Human Rights," 132.

8 Odysseos, "Prolegomena to Any Future Decolonial Ethics," 458.

9 Odysseos, "Prolegomena to Any Future Decolonial Ethics," 459. See also Wynter, "Ethno or Socio Poetics," 83.

10 In Scott, "The Re-enchantment of Humanism," 188.

11 Scott, "The Re-enchantment of Humanism," 195.

12 See Coordinador Nacional Agrario, *Construyendo nuestros planes de vida*, 15, and my discussion in chapter 5.

13 Coordinador Nacional Agrario, *Construyendo nuestros planes de vida*, 32.

14 Wynter, "Unsettling the Coloniality of Being/Power/Truth/Freedom," 263.

15 Tsantsoulas, "Sylvia Wynter's Decolonial Rejoinder to Judith Butler's Ethics of Vulnerability," 167–69; Wynter, "Unsettling the Coloniality of Being/Power/Truth/Freedom," 260–64.

16 Graeber, "Radical Alterity Is Just Another Word for Saying 'Reality,'" 15.

17 See Coordinador Nacional Agrario, *Construyendo nuestros planes de vida*, 10.

18 Escobar, "Thinking-Feeling with the Earth," 13, 17.

19 Escobar, "Thinking-Feeling with the Earth," 15.

20 This observation is drawn from numerous conversations with PCN leaders between 2006 and 2017. See also Proceso de Comunidades Negras, "Entrevista con José Santos Caicedo."

21 Ó Loingsigh, *La reconquista del pacífico*.

22 Delgado, "*Suma Qamaña* as a Strategy of Power," 240–45.

23 Delgado, "*Suma Qamaña* as a Strategy of Power," 242.

24 SINALTRAINAL, "SINALTRAINAL 38 años de lucha."

25 I use the term *liberationist Christianity* here, following Michael Löwy's use of the expression, to emphasize that this current of grassroots Christianity was already a social movement prior to being formulated in theological texts: see Löwy, *War of Gods*, 2, 32–39. The best-known expression of this tradition in Colombia is Camilo Torres, the priest who in the 1960s organized a radical popular movement and then joined the guerrillas of the Ejército de Liberación Nacional (National Liberation Army), and whose killing by the army in 1966 had a deep emotional and political impact on the Colombian left. For a book-length account of Torres's life and influence, see Broderick, *Camilo, el cura guerrillero*. I am grateful to Mirian Ruíz and other members of the Christian Base Communities for long conversations about the influence of liberationist Christianity within social movement struggles in Colombia while I was staying with Mirian and learning about the work of the Christian Base Communities in Cali between 2005 and 2007.

26 For example, the first continent-wide gathering of the ecumenical Christians for Socialism movement, held in Santiago de Chile in 1972, set out a "dialectic of faith and revolution" in which "the Christian faith becomes a critical and dynamic leaven for revolution. Faith intensifies the demand that the class struggle move decisively toward the liberation of all men—in particular, those who suffer the most acute forms of oppression. It also stresses our orientation towards a total transformation of society, rather than merely a transformation of economic structures. Thus . . . faith makes its own contribution to the construction of a society that is qualitatively distinct from the present one, and to the appearance of a New Man": quoted in Löwy, *War of Gods*, 47.

27 For in-depth analysis of the intellectual sources of diverse formulations of *buen vivir* in Latin America, see Hidalgo-Capitán and Cubillo-Guevara, "Deconstrución y genealogía del 'buen vivir' latinoamericano."

28 See, among others, Bieler and Morton, *Global Capitalism, Global War, Global Crisis*, 144–50; McNally, "The Dialectics of Unity and Difference in the

Constitution of Wage-Labour"; Webber, *Red October*, 16–30, 260–99. See also, for discussion, Coleman, "Marxism, Coloniality and Ontological Assumptions."

29 Chimisso, "From Phenomenology to Phenomenotechnique," 387–88. See also Bachelard, "Corrationalism and the Problematic"; Maniglier, "What Is a Problematic?"

30 For discussion, see Coleman, "Ethnography, Commitment and Critique," 276–78.

31 Coordinador Nacional Agrario, *Construyendo nuestros planes de vida*, 7, 10–11.

32 As Emilios Christodoulidis summarizes it, immanent critique is tied to the logic of contradiction where contradiction, as "practical" rather than logical, informs a crisis that is experienced by social agents in the materiality of their life. Social reality is experienced by actors in terms of normative expectations that are constitutive (rather than "epiphenomena") of that reality. Normative expectations are part of institutional frameworks that inform actors' perception of social reality. Immanent critique aims to generate *within* these institutional frameworks contradictions that are *inevitable* (they can neither be displaced nor ignored), *compelling* (they necessitate action), and *transformative* in that (unlike internal critique) the overcoming of the contradiction does not restore, but transcends, the "disturbed" framework within which it arose. It pushes it to go beyond its confines and in the process, famously in Marx's words, "enables the world to clarify its consciousness in waking it from its dream about itself": Christodoulidis, "Strategies of Rupture," 6.

33 Coordinador Nacional Agrario, *Construyendo nuestros planes de vida*, 32.

34 Coordinador Nacional Agrario, *Construyendo nuestros planes de vida*, 15.

35 Lear, *Radical Hope*, 103.

36 For a discussion of how this sort of argument has been made in relation to human rights and a critique along these lines, see Coleman, "Struggles, over Rights."

37 Wynter, in Scott, "The Re-enchantment of Humanism," 197.

38 Coordinador Nacional Agrario, *Construyendo nuestros planes de vida*, 15.

39 Guevara, "Man and Socialism in Cuba."

40 Lear, *Radical Hope*, 121–22.

41 Murdoch, *The Sovereignty of Good*, 2–16, 46–47. Murdoch saw the same basic tendency at play in the Anglo-American and Continental traditions. She likened Jean-Paul Sartre's notion of freedom in particular to that of Anglo-American philosophers for its preoccupation with the will and freedom of choice as means of determining value. In subsequent work: Murdoch, *Metaphysics as a Guide to Morals*, 185–216. She also argued that the postmodern turn, as embodied in the work of Jacques Derrida and Jean-François Lyotard had similar implications, rendering value susceptible to being reduced to the effect of mutable and contingent forms of desire. For discussion, see Browning, *Why Iris Murdoch Matters*, 17, 31, 85–98.

42 Murdoch, *The Sovereignty of Good*, 42.

43 Murdoch, *The Sovereignty of Good*, 42, 40. See also Oulton, "Loving by Instinct."

44 On the experience of the "void," see Murdoch, *Metaphysics as a Guide to Morals*, 498–503.

45 Murdoch, *Metaphysics as a Guide to Morals*; Murdoch, *The Sovereignty of Good*, 42. It is worth underscoring that Murdoch's metaphysics is not—as Gary Browning emphasizes—"a world-denying neo-Platonism in which the ideal is divorced from the apparently real" or one derived from first-order principles within a standard tradition of Western philosophy. On the contrary, it is a more modest metaphysics that seeks to read experience in a holistic manner, with all of its awkwardness, dissonance, and contingency, but that is "sensitive to the magnetism of good within experience": Browning, *Why Iris Murdoch Matters*, 11–12, 28. For further discussion of Murdoch's metaphysics, see Browning, *Why Iris Murdoch Matters*, 27–54.

46 Browning, *Why Iris Murdoch Matters*, 86–88.

47 Murdoch, *The Sovereignty of Good*, 8. See also Bagnoli, "The Exploration of Moral Life"; Browning, *Why Iris Murdoch Matters*, 115–44; Lovibond, *Iris Murdoch, Gender and Philosophy*, 15, 26–27, 39–41.

48 Tsantsoulas, "Sylvia Wynter's Decolonial Rejoinder to Judith Butler's Ethics of Vulnerability," 177.

49 This is not to obscure important differences between Judith Butler's understanding of the uneven allocation of humanness and that of Wynter. As Tiffany Tsantsoulas emphasizes in a comparative discussion of the two thinkers, Butler is concerned with the production of subjects and the impossibility of any subject preceding the norms through which the self is shaped. For Butler, those lives excluded from recognition exist in a space that is spectral and liminal, a sort of inassimilable margin forever dislocating existing normative schemas, rather than in a space of symbolic death constituted through modern/colonial history. Butler's account of criticality invokes "an imagined, radically democratic, coalitional space" of people bound in solidarity by a shared susceptibility to suffering. Wynter, by contrast, sees resistant potential in the forms of life persisting despite *homo economicus*'s "hegemonic grip on the human." Far from being based in a shared vulnerability, Wynter's ethical reflections emphasize different vulnerabilities, rooted in historical and material conditions: Tsantsoulas, "Sylvia Wynter's Decolonial Rejoinder to Judith Butler's Ethics of Vulnerability," 175. See also Oliviero, "Vulnerability's Ambivalent Political Life," 6.

50 See, among others, Butler, *Frames of War*, 1–32; Butler, *Precarious Life*, 19–49.

51 Compare Bonnie Honig's interpretation in "Antigone's Two Laws." Butler herself has insisted that she is not trying to posit corporeal vulnerability as the basis for a revisioned humanism, so that all we need to do is recognize the vulnerability of those hitherto excluded and ask what we should do to

ensure their protection. Recognition (in the Hegelian sense in which Butler understands it) can never be of a preexisting vulnerability, because recognition is an ethical encounter that can transform what it is that is recognized: see Butler, *Precarious Life*, 43–44.

52 Kramer, "Judith Butler's 'New Humanism,'" 32.

53 Butler, *Frames of War*, 22–25.

54 Murphy, "Corporeal Vulnerability and the New Humanism," 578.

55 Tsantsoulas, "Sylvia Wynter's Decolonial Rejoinder to Judith Butler's Ethics of Vulnerability," 162. See also Gilson, *The Ethics of Vulnerability*. Scholars of international relations have highlighted some of the political implications of these prior commitments in Butler's work. Ida Danewid emphasizes the risks attendant on an analytic of shared vulnerability by showing how Butler's approach has been mobilized by pro-refugee activists in Europe in a manner that obscures colonialism and its ongoing effects in the present, generating a politics of hospitality and generosity that sidesteps questions of responsibility, reparation, and structural reform. Ritu Vij, meanwhile, suggests that the very lens of precarity/vulnerability is shaped by a characteristically liberal analytic, gaining traction only in relation to the sovereign subject and the expectational horizon of an invulnerability to insecurity: see Danewid, "White Innocence in the Black Mediterranean"; Vij, "The Global Subject of Precarity."

56 Mills, "Undoing Ethics," 48.

57 Kramer, "Judith Butler's 'New Humanism,'" 33.

58 Lloyd, "Toward a Cultural Politics of Vulnerability," 103–4.

59 Kramer, "Judith Butler's 'New Humanism,'" 35.

60 Kramer, "Judith Butler's 'New Humanism,'" 25.

61 See my discussion in chapters 2–3.

62 Çubukçu, *For the Love of Humanity*.

63 Butler, *Giving an Account of Oneself*, 8.

64 Butler, *Precarious Life*, 20, 33.

65 Butler is no exception here. The very way she approaches her questions is, arguably, underpinned by a conceptualization of violence with its origins in liberal political thought—although this is never acknowledged. Violence, particularly when she introduces her ethics of vulnerability in texts such as *Frames of War* and *Precarious Life*, is conceived within a framework of the state, citizenship, inside versus outside.

66 L. Gordon, "Shifting the Geography of Reason in an Age of Disciplinary Decadence," 98.

67 On how human rights "travel," see Dunford, *The Politics of Transnational Peasant Struggle*.

68 Viveiros de Castro, "Perspectival Anthropology and the Method of Controlled Equivocation," 5.

bibliography

Abello, Ignacio. *Violencias y culturas: Seguido de dos studios sobre Nietzsche y Foucault, a propósito del mismo tema*. Bogotá: Alfomega/Uniandes, 2002.

Acciari, Louisa. "Decolonising Labour, Reclaiming Subaltern Epistemologies: Brazilian Domestic Workers and the International Struggle for Labour Rights." *Contexto Internacional* 4, no. 1 (2019): 39–63. https://doi.org/10.1590/S0102-8529.2019410100003.

Aeberhard, Marianne, Lara Montesinos Coleman, and Josep Montesinos. *Informe de la misión internacional de solidaridad Roque Julio Torres, Casanare, Colombia, 29 de julio–1 de agosto 2007*. Bogotá: COSPACC, 2007.

Agamben, Giorgio. *Homo Sacer: Sovereign Power and Bare Life*. Stanford, CA: Stanford University Press, 1998.

Agamben, Giorgio. *State of Exception*. Stanford, CA: Stanford University Press, 2005.

"A juicio ex alcalde de Apartadó." *El Colombiano*, September 30, 2000.

Amicus. "Amicus and Coca-Cola Statement." April 28, 2006. Photocopy.

Amnesty International. *A Laboratory of War: Repression and Violence in Arauca*. London: Amnesty International Secretariat, 2004.

Amnesty International. *Amnesty International Campaigning Manual*. London: Amnesty International Publications, 2001.

Amnesty International UK. "Amnesty International Launches Protect the Human." Press release, October 14, 2005. https://www.amnesty.org.uk/press-releases/amnesty-international-launches-protect-human.

Amnesty International USA. "Impunity." Accessed March 20, 2016. http://www.amnestyusa.org/our-work/countries/americas/colombia/impunity.

Andermahr, Sonya, ed. *Decolonizing Trauma Studies: Trauma and Postcolonialism.* Basel: MDPI, 2016.

Asociación de Abogados Laboralistas de Trabajadores. "Aniquilamiento sindical y precarización de los derechos de los trabajadores." Submission to the Food and Agriculture Hearing of the Permanent Peoples' Tribunal, Colombia sess., Bogotá, April 2006.

Atiles-Osoria, José, and David Whyte. "State of Exception, Law and Economy: A Socio-legal Approach to the Economy of Exception in an Era of Crisis." *Oñati Socio-Legal Series* 8, no. 4 (2018): 808–18. https://papers.ssrn.com/sol3/papers.cfm?abstract_id=3248981.

Audiencia Pública Popular and SINALTRAINAL. "Reparación integral de las víctimas." Proposal for holistic reparation of victims on the part of the Colombian state and the Coca-Cola Company, December 5, 2002.

Baars, Grietje. "'It's Not Me, It's the Corporation': The Value of Corporate Accountability in the Global Political Economy." *London Review of International Law* 4, no. 1 (2016): 127–63. https://doi.org/10.1093/lril/lrw008.

Bachelard, Gaston. "Corrationalism and the Problematic." *Radical Philosophy* 173 (May–June 2012). https://www.radicalphilosophy.com/article/corrationalism-and-the-problematic.

Bagnoli, Carla. "The Exploration of Moral Life." In *Iris Murdoch, Philosopher*, edited by Justin Broakes, 197–226. Oxford: Oxford University Press, 2012.

Balch, Oliver. "Interview with John O'Reilly, Former Senior Vice President for External Affairs, BP Indonesia." Ethical Corporation website, March 11, 2004. http://www.ethicalcorp.com/content.asp?ContentID=1768.

Barber, Brendan. "Building Partnerships across the Globe." In *Trades Unions and Globalisation*, edited by Tony Pilch, 18–25. London: Smith Institute, 2007.

Barber, Brendan, Roger Lyons, Mick Rix, Angela Roger, and Barry Camfield. "Solidarity with Colombia." *New Statesman*, April 12, 2004, 37.

Barreto, José-Manuel. "Introduction." In *Human Rights from a Third World Perspective*, edited by José-Manuel Barreto, 1–42. Cambridge: Cambridge Scholars, 2012.

Baudrillard, Jean. *Simulacra and Simulation.* Translated by Sheila Faria Glaser. Ann Arbor: University of Michigan Press, 1994 (1981).

Berlant, Lauren. *Cruel Optimism.* Durham, NC: Duke University Press, 2011.

Beswick, Joe, Georgia Alexandri, Michael Byrne, Sònia Vives-Miró, Desiree Fields, Stuart Hodkinson, and Michael Janoschka. "Speculating on London's Housing Future: The Rise of Global Corporate Landlords in 'Post-crisis' Urban Landscapes." *City* 20, no. 2 (2016): 321–41. https://doi.org/10.1080/13604813.2016.1145946.

Bhambra, Gurminder K. "Relations of Extraction, Relations of Redistribution: Empire, Nation and the Construction of the British Welfare State." *British Journal of Sociology* 73, no. 1 (2022): 4–15. https://doi.org/10.1111/1468-4446.12896.

Bhambra, Gurminder K., and John Holmwood. "Colonialism, Postcolonialism and the Liberal Welfare State." *New Political Economy* 23, no. 5 (2018): 574–87. https://doi.org/10.1080/13563467.2017.1417369.

Bhandar, Brenna. *Colonial Lives of Property: Law, Land and Racial Regimes of Ownership*. Durham, NC: Duke University Press, 2018.

Bhandar, Brenna. "Strategies of Legal Rupture: The Politics of Judgement." *Windsor Yearbook of Access to Justice* 30 (2012): 59–78.

Bickerton, Chris J. *European Integration: From Nation-States to Member States*. Oxford: Oxford University Press, 2012.

Bieler, Andreas. "Workers of the World, Unite? Globalisation and the Quest for Transnational Solidarity." *Globalizations* 9, no. 3 (2012): 365–78. https://doi .org/10.1080/14747731.2012.680730.

Bieler, Andreas, Ingemar Lindberg, and Devan Pillay. "The Future of the Global Working Class: An Introduction." In *Labour and the Challenges of Globalisation*, edited by Andreas Bieler, Ingemar Lindberg, and Devan Pillay, 1–22. London: Pluto, 2008.

Bieler, Andreas, Ingemar Lindberg, and Devan Pillay. "What Future Strategy for the Global Working Class? The Need for a New Historical Subject." In *Labour and the Challenges of Globalisation*, edited by Andreas Bieler, Ingemar Lindberg, and Devan Pillay, 264–86. London: Pluto, 2008.

Bieler, Andreas, and Adam Morton. *Global Capitalism, Global War, Global Crisis*. Cambridge: Cambridge University Press, 2018.

Bingham, John, Steven Swinford, and Kate McCann. "Bedroom Tax 'Breaches Human Rights of Vulnerable People'—Top Judge." *Telegraph*, January 27, 2016.

Bingham, Tom. *The Rule of Law*. London: Penguin, 2010.

Blair, Tony, and Gerhard Schroeder. *Europe: The Third Way/Die Neue Mitte*. London: Labour Party, and Berlin: Sozialdemokratische Partei Deutschlands, 1999.

BP. "Developing Business, Improving Income: The Yopal Carwash Grew with Fundación Amanecer Support." Accessed April 4, 2011. http://www.bp.com /sectiongenericarticle.do?categoryId=9028641&contentId=7052186.

Broderick, Walter Joe. *Camilo, el cura guerrillero*. Bogotá: Icono, 2013.

Brodzinsky, Sibylla. "Terrorism and Bananas in Colombia." *Time Magazine*, May 2, 2007. http://content.time.com/time/world/article/0,8599,1616991,00.html.

Brown, Wendy. "'The Most We Can Hope For ...': Human Rights and the Politics of Fatalism." *South Atlantic Quarterly* 103, nos. 2–3 (2004): 451–63. https:// muse.jhu.edu/article/169139.

Brown, Wendy. "Neoliberalism and the End of Liberal Democracy." In *Edgework: Critical Essays on Knowledge and Politics*, by Wendy Brown, 37–59. Princeton, NJ: Princeton University Press, 2005.

Browne, John. "The Case for Social Responsibility." Speech delivered at the Annual Conference of Business for Social Responsibility, Boston, November 10, 1998. http://www.bp.com/genericarticle.do?categoryId=98&contentId =2000334.

Browne, John. "International Relations: The New Agenda for Business." Elliot lecture delivered at St. Anthony's College, Oxford, June 4, 1998. http://www. bp.com/genericarticle.do?categoryId=98&contentId=2000274.

Browning, Gary. *Why Iris Murdoch Matters*. London: Bloomsbury, 2018.

Bruff, Ian. "The Rise of Authoritarian Neoliberalism." *Rethinking Marxism* 26, no. 1 (2014): 113–29. https://doi.org/10.1080/08935696.2013.843250.

Bruff, Ian. "Neoliberalism and Authoritarianism." In *Handbook of Neoliberalism*, edited by Simon Springer, Kean Birch, and Julie MacLeavy, 107–17. New York: Routledge, 2016.

Burawoy, Michael. "The Extended Case Method." *Sociological Theory* 16, no. 1 (1998): 4–33. https://doi.org/10.1111/0735-2751.00040.

Butler, Judith. *Frames of War: When Is Life Grievable?* London: Verso, 2009.

Butler, Judith. *Giving an Account of Oneself*. New York: Fordham University Press, 2005.

Butler, Judith. *Precarious Life: The Powers of Mourning and Violence*. London: Verso, 2004.

Butler, Judith. "What Is Critique? An Essay on Foucault's Virtue," 2002. Accessed February 2, 2014. http://eipcp.net/transversal/0806/butler/en.

Butler, Patrick. "Destitution Is Back. And We Can't Just Ignore It." *Guardian*, July 3, 2017.

Caccio, Fabrizio. "Garbatella, Rifondazione vieta la Coca-Cola: Il Municipio XI di Roma ha eliminato per protesta la bevanda dai distributori." *Corriere della Serra*, October 23, 2004, 11.

Cammack, Paul. "Attacking the Poor." *New Left Review* 13 (January–February 2002): 125–34.

Cammack, Paul. "What the World Bank Means by 'Poverty Reduction' and Why It Matters." *New Political Economy* 9, no. 2 (2004): 189–211. https://doi.org/10.1080/1356346042000218069.

Campbell, Denis, Steven Morris, and Sarah Marsh. "NHS Faces 'Humanitarian Crisis' as Demand Rises, British Red Cross Warns." *Guardian*, January 6, 2017.

Canning, Victoria. "The Multiple Forms of Violence in the Asylum System." In *The Violence of Austerity*, edited by Vickie Cooper and David Whyte, 67–74. London: Pluto, 2017.

Capponi, Alesandro. "Olimpiade e Coca-Cola: Una battaglia a sinistra." *Corriere della Sera*, November 7, 2005, 21.

Cárdenas, Humberto, and Álvaro Marín. *La biodiversidad es la cabalgadura de la muerte*. Bogotá: Traviesa, 2006.

Carr, Edward Hallett. "Rights and Obligations." *Times Literary Supplement*, vol. 11, November 1949.

Carson, Mary, Adrian Gatton, Rodrigo Vázquez, and Maggie O'Kane. "Gilberto Torres Survived Colombia's Death Squads. Now He Wants Justice." *Guardian*, May 22, 2015.

Carson, W. G. "The Conventionalization of Early Factory Crime." *International Journal of the Sociology of Law* 7 (1979): 37–60.

Centre for Welfare Reform. "UK in Breach of International Human Rights." June 28, 2016. http://www.centreforwelfarereform.org/news/uk-in-breachhuman-rights/00287.html.

Chakrabortty, Aditya. "Over 170 Years after Engels, Britain Is Still a Country That Murders Its Poor." *Guardian*, June 20, 2017.

Chand, Kailash. "A Moment of Honesty Is Required—New Labour Began the Dismantling of Our N[ational] H[ealth] S[ervice]." *Open Democracy*, April 23, 2014. https://www.opendemocracy.net/en/ournhs/moment-of-honesty-is -required-new-labour-began-dismantling-of-our-nhs.

Chandler, Geoffrey. "Business and Human Rights: Reflections on Progress Made and Challenges Ahead." Talk delivered at Business and Human Rights Resource Centre, December 4, 2007. http://business-humanrights.org/en/doc -business-human-rights-reflections-on-progress-made-and-challenges-ahead.

Chimisso, Cristina. "From Phenomenology to Phenomenotechnique: The Role of Early Twentieth-Century Physics in Gaston Bachelard's Philosophy." *Studies in History and Philosophy of Science Part A* 39, no. 3 (2008): 384–92. https://doi .org/10.1016/j.shpsa.2008.06.010.

Christian Aid. *Behind the Mask: The Real Face of Corporate Social Responsibility*. London: Christian Aid, 2004.

Christian Aid. "Inviting Others to Campaign." May 2019. https://www.christianaid .org.uk/sites/default/files/2022-06/inviting-others-to-campaign-guide -campaigns-may2019.pdf.

Christiansen, Atle Christer. *Beyond Petroleum: Can BP Deliver?* Report no. 6. Fridtjof Nansens Institute, Lysaker, Norway, 2002. Accessed February 18, 2023. https://www.fni.no/getfile.php/131816-1469869156/Filer/Publikasjoner/FNI -R0602.pdf.

Christodoulidis, Emilios. "Strategies of Rupture." *Law and Critique* 20 (2009): 3–26.

Cifuentes Tarazona, Sonia Fernanda. *Buen vivir en Colombia, una apuesta de vida desde el campesinado catatumbero*. Bogotá: Universidad de Santo Tomas de Aquino, 2018. Accessed March 27, 2020. https://repository.usta.edu.co /bitstream/handle/11634/14474/2018soniacifuentes.pdf.

CISCA (Comité de Integración Social del Catatumbo), Asociación para la Promoción Social Alternativa MINGA, and Corporación Servicios Profesionales Sembrar. *Catatumbo: Una mirada a la situacíon de derechos humanos*. Report, 2016. Accessed March 27, 2020. http://asociacionminga.co/wp-content /uploads/2020/08/informe-derechos-humanos-interactivo-2p.pdf.

CNA (Coordinador Nacional Agrario). *Construyendo nuestros planes de vida*. Bogotá: Corporación para la Educación, el Desarrollo y la Investigación Popular, Instituto Nacional Sindical (CEDINS) and Fundación Rosa Luxemburg, 2011.

Coca-Cola Company and the IUF. "Joint Coca-Cola and IUF Statement." IUF website. March 15, 2005. https://web.archive.org/web/20050930225055 /http://www.iufdocuments.org/www/documents/coca-cola/jtstate-e.pdf.

Cohen, Stanley. *States of Denial: Knowing about Atrocities and Suffering*. Cambridge: Polity, 2001.

Coleman, Lara Montesinos. "Ethnography, Commitment and Critique: Departing from Activist Scholarship." *International Political Sociology* 9, no. 2 (2015): 263–80. https://doi.org/10.1111/ips.12096.

Coleman, Lara Montesinos. "The Gendered Violence of Development: Imaginative Geographies of Exclusion in the Imposition of Neoliberal Capitalism." *British Journal of Politics and International Relations* 9, no. 2 (2007): 204–19. https://doi.org/10.1111/j.1467-856x.2007.00288.x.

Coleman, Lara Montesinos. "The Making of Docile Dissent: Neoliberalization and Resistance in Colombia and Beyond." *International Political Sociology* 7, no. 2 (2013): 170–87. https://doi.org/10.1111/ips.12016.

Coleman, Lara Montesinos. "Marxism, Coloniality and Ontological Assumptions." *International Relations* 35, no. 1 (2021): 166–72. https://doi.org/10.1177/0047117821991611.

Coleman, Lara Montesinos. "Struggles, over Rights: Humanism, Ethical Dispossession and Resistance." *Third World Quarterly* 36, no. 6 (2015): 1060–75. https://doi.org/10.1080/01436597.2015.1047193.

Coleman, Lara Montesinos. "The Violence of the Peace." *Alborada Magazine*, August 29, 2017. https://alborada.net/the-violence-of-the-peace.

Coleman, Lara Montesinos, and Olivia Blanchard. *Terrorismo de estado en la universidad: La reestructuración de la educación superior y los derechos humanos en Colombia.* Bogotá: Red de Hermandad, 2007.

Coleman, Lara Montesinos, Gustavo Rojas-Páez, Owen Thomas, Gearóid Ó Loingsigh, and Piergiuseppe Parisi. *Cómo reparar las injusticias cometidas por los empresarios: Extractivismo, impunidad empresarial y uso estratégico del derecho.* Bogotá: Palma Arismendi Colección Académica, 2021.

Coleman, Lara Montesinos, Gustavo Rojas-Páez, Owen Thomas, Gearóid Ó Loingsigh, and Piergiuseppe Parisi. *Righting Corporate Wrongs? Extractivism, Impunity and Strategic Use of Law,* London: War on Want, 2019.

Coleman, Lara Montesinos, and Karen Tucker. "Between Discipline and Dissent: Situated Resistance and Global Order." *Globalizations* 8, no. 4 (2011): 397–410. https://doi.org/10.1080/14747731.2011.585823.

Collingsworth, Terry, William J. Wichmann, and Daniel M. Kovalik. *Complaint Submitted to the US District Court, Southern District of Florida, on Behalf of Gladys Cecilia Rincón de Múnera, on Behalf of Herself Individually and as Representative of the Estate of Adolfo Jesus de Múnera López, and SINALTRAINAL.* Miami, June 2, 2006.

Collins, Hugh, K. D. Ewing, and Aileen McColgan. *Labour Law.* Cambridge: Cambridge University Press, 2012.

Comuni di Roma. Press release, November 7, 2005.

"Condenan a ex alcalde de Apartadó." *El Colombiano,* March 28, 2003.

Cooper, Frederick. *Decolonization and African Society: The Labor Question in French and British Africa.* Cambridge: Cambridge University Press, 1996.

Cooper, Vickie, and David Whyte. "Introduction." In *The Violence of Austerity,* edited by Vickie Cooper and David Whyte, 1–32. London: Pluto, 2017.

Cornelissen, Lars. "Neoliberalism and the Racialized Critique of Democracy." *Constellations* 27, no. 3 (2020): 348–60. https://doi.org/10.1111/1467-8675.12518.

Corredor Martinez, Consuelo. "El problema del desarrollo." In *La falacia neoliberal: Crítica y alternativas,* edited by Dario I. Restrepo Botero, 63–84. Bogotá: Universidad Nacional de Colombia, 2003.

COSPACC (Corporación Social para la Asesoría y Capacitación Comunitaria). "Caso contra la empresa transnacional British Petroleum." Submission to the Peoples' Tribunal, Colombia Session on Transnational Corporations and Crimes against Humanity, Oil Sector Hearing, Bogotá, July 2007.

Coulthard, Glen. *Red Skin, White Masks: Rejecting the Colonial Politics of Recognition.* Minneapolis: University of Minnesota Press, 2014.

Cramer, Christopher. *Civil War Is Not a Stupid Thing: Accounting for Violence in Developing Countries.* London: Hurst, 2006.

Craps, Stef. *Postcolonial Witnessing: Trauma out of Bounds.* Basingstoke, UK: Palgrave Macmillan, 2013.

Croucher, Richard, and Elizabeth Cotton. *Global Unions, Global Business: Global Union Federations and International Business.* Middlesex, UK: Middlesex University Press, 2009.

Çubukçu, Ayça. *For the Love of Humanity: The World Tribunal on Iraq.* Philadelphia: University of Pennsylvania Press, 2018.

Cumbers, Andrew, and Paul Routledge. "The Entangled Geographies of Transnational Labour Solidarity." In *Missing Links in Labour Geography,* edited by Ann Cecilie Bergene and Sylvie Endresen, 43–56. Farnham, UK: Ashgate, 2010.

Danewid, Ida. "White Innocence in the Black Mediterranean: Hospitality and the Erasure of History." *Third World Quarterly* 38, no. 7 (2017): 1697–89. https://doi:10.1080/01436597.2017.1331123.

Davis, Mary. "Labour, Race and Empire: The Trades Union Congress and Colonial Policy, 1945–51." In *The British Labour Movement and Imperialism,* edited by Billy Frank, Craig Horner, and David Stewart, 89–106. Newcastle-upon-Tyne: Cambridge Scholars, 2010.

Delgado, Ana Carolina Teixera. "*Suma Qamaña* as a Strategy of Power: Politicizing the Pluriverse." *Carta Internacional* 13, no. 3 (2018): 236–61.

de Vitoria, Francisco. "The First Reflection of the Reverend Father, Brother Franciscus de Victoria on the Indians Lately Discovered," translated by John Pawley Bate. In *The Spanish Origin of International Law: Francisco de Vitoria and His Law of Nations,* by James Brown Scott, app. A. Union, NJ: Lawbook Exchange, 2009.

Doane, Deborah. "The Myth of CSR." *Stanford Social Innovation Review* (Fall 2005): 23–29. https://ssir.org/articles/entry/the_myth_of_csr#.

Douzinas, Costas. *The End of Human Rights.* Oxford: Hart, 2000.

Dowling, Paul. "Limited Liability and Separate Corporate Personality in Multinational Corporate Groups: Conceptual Flaws, Accountability Gaps and the Case for Profit-Risk Liability." In *Accountability, International Business Operations and the Law: Providing Justice for Corporate Human Rights Violations in Global Value Chains,* edited by Liesbeth Enneking, Ivo Giesen, Anne-Jetske Schaap, Cedric Ryngaert, François Kristen, and Lucas Roorda, chap. 11. Abingdon, UK: Routledge, 2019.

Drainville, André C. *Contesting Globalization: Space and Place in the World Economy.* London: Routledge, 2004.

Drainville, André C. "The Fetishism of Global Civil Society: Global Governance, Transnational Urbanism and Sustainable Capitalism in the World Economy." In *Transnationalism from Below*, edited by M. P. Smith and L. E. Guarnizo, 35-63. London: Transaction, 1998.

Drainville, André C. *A History of World Order and Resistance: The Making and Unmaking of Global Subjects*. London: Routledge, 2012.

Dreyfus, Hubert L. "Comments on Jonathan Lear's *Radical Hope*." *Philosophical Studies* 144 (2009): 63-70.

D'Souza, Radha. *What's Wrong with Rights? Social Movements, Law and Liberal Imaginations*. London: Pluto, 2018.

Duffield, Mark. *Development, Security and Unending War: Governing the World of Peoples*. Cambridge: Polity, 2007.

Duffield, Mark. *Global Governance and the New Wars*. London: Zed, 2001.

Dunford, Robin. *The Politics of Transnational Peasant Struggle*. London: Rowman and Littlefield, 2016.

Dunford, Robin, and Sumi Madhok. "Vernacular Rights Cultures and the 'Right to Have Rights.'" *Citizenship Studies* 19, nos. 6-7 (2015): 605-19. https://doi.org/10.1080/13621025.2015.1053791.

Dussel, Enrique. *Filosofía de la liberación*. Mexico City: Fondo de Cultura Económica, 2011 (1977).

Eagleton, Terry. *Hope without Optimism*. New Haven, CT: Yale University Press, 2015.

Eco, Umberto. *Travels in Hyperreality: Essays*. London: Picador, 1986.

El-Gingihy, Youssef. *How to Dismantle the NHS in 10 Easy Steps*. London: Zero, 2015.

Emejulu, Akwugo, and Leah Bassel. "Women of Colour's Anti-austerity Activism." In *The Violence of Austerity*, edited by Vickie Cooper and David Whyte, 117-22. London: Pluto, 2017.

Engels, Friedrich. *The Condition of the Working Class in England in 1844*. Translated by Florence Kelley Wischnewetzky. New York: Cosimo, 2008.

Engle, Karen. "Anti-impunity and the Turn to Criminal Law in Human Rights." *Cornell Law Review* 100, no. 5 (2015): 1069-128.

Escobar, Arturo. "Development, Violence and the New Imperial Order." *Development* 47, no. 1 (2004): 15-21. https://doi.org/10.1057/palgrave.development.1100014.

Escobar, Arturo. "Displacement, Development and Modernity in the Colombian Pacific." *International Social Science Journal* 55, no. 175 (2003): 157-67. https://doi.org/10.1111/1468-2451.5501015.

Escobar, Arturo. *Encountering Development: The Making and Unmaking of the Third World*. Princeton, NJ: Princeton University Press, 1995.

Escobar, Arturo. "Thinking-Feeling with the Earth: Territorial Struggles and the Ontological Dimension of the Epistemologies of the South." *Revista de Antropologia Iberoamericana* 11, no. 1 (2016): 11-32. https://doi.org/10.11156/aibr.110102e.

"Están 'Pillaos.'" *Semana*, September 8-15, 1997, 52-53.

Fanon, Frantz. *The Wretched of the Earth*. Translated by Richard Philcox. New York: Grove, 1963.

Federici, Silvia. *Caliban and the Witch: Women, the Body and Primitive Accumulation*. Brooklyn, NY: Autonomedia, 2003.

Feierstein, Daniel. *El genocidio como práctica social: Entre el nazismo y la experiencia argentina*. Buenos Aires: Fondo de Cultura Económica, 2007.

Ferreira, Marcelo. "Genocidio reorganizador en Colombia (a propósito de una Sentencia del Tribunal Permanente de los Pueblos)." In *Terrorismo de estado y genocidio en América Latina*, edited by Daniel Feierstein, 101–39. Buenos Aires: Prometeo, 2009.

Fichter, Michael, and Jamie K. McCallum. "Implementing Global Framework Agreements: The Limits of Social Partnership." *Global Networks* 15 (supp.) (2015): S65–85.

Fichter, Michael, Jörg Sydow, Markus Helfen, Lilian Arruda, Özge Agtas, Indira Gartenberg, Jamie McCallum, Kadire Sayim, and Dimitris Stevis. *Globalising Labour Relations: On Track with Framework Agreements?* Berlin: Friedrich-Ebert-Stiftung, 2012.

Fidler, Stephen. "Oil Giant in Troubled Waters." *Financial Times*, November 8, 1996.

Fisher, Mark. *Capitalist Realism: Is There No Alternative?* London: Zero, 2009.

Fishman, Nina. "The Phoney Cold War in British Trade Unions." *Contemporary British History* 15, no. 3 (2001): 83–104.

Fletcher, Kat. "Something to Be Proud Of." *Guardian*, April 26, 2006.

Forster, Katie. "N[ational H[ealth] S[ervice] Cuts Blamed for 30,000 Deaths in New Study." *Independent*, February 17, 2017.

Foucault, Michel. "For an Ethic of Discomfort." In *Power: Essential Works of Foucault, 1954–1984*, edited by James D. Faubion, 443–48. London: Penguin, 1994.

Foucault, Michel. "Polemics, Politics, and Problematizations: An Interview with Michel Foucault." In *The Foucault Reader: An Introduction to Foucault's Thought*, edited by Paul Rabinow, translated by Lydia Davis, 381–90. London: Penguin, 1984.

Franco, Jean. *Cruel Modernity*. Durham, NC: Duke University Press, 2013.

Friedman, Milton. "The Social Responsibility of Business Is to Increase Its Profits." In *Corporate Ethics and Corporate Governance*, edited by Walther Ch. Zimmerli, Markus Holzinger, and Klaus Richter, 173–78. Berlin: Springer, 2007.

Frynas, Jedrzej George. "The False Developmental Promise of Corporate Social Responsibility: Evidence from Multinational Oil Companies." *International Affairs* 81, no. 3 (2005): 581–98. https://doi.org/10.1111/j.1468-2346.2005.00470.x.

Fundación Amanecer. *Informe Social 1994–2004*. Yopal, Colombia: Fundación Amanecer, 2004.

Gallin, Dan. "Labour as a Global Social Force: Past Divisions and New Tasks." In *Global Unions? Theory and Strategies of Organized Labour in the Global Political Economy*, edited by Jeffrey Harrod and Robert O'Brien, 235–50. London: Routledge, 2002.

García Villegas, Mauricio. "Constitucionalismo perverso: Normalidad y anormalidad constitucional en Colombia: 1957–1997." In *El caleidoscopio de las justicias en Colombia*, vol. 1, edited by Boaventura de Sousa Santos and Mauricio García Villegas, 317–70. Bogotá: Siglo de Hombres, 2001.

García Villegas, Mauricio, and César Rodríguez. "La acción de tutela." In *El caleidoscopio de las justicias en Colombia*, vol. 1, edited by Boaventura de Sousa Santos and Mauricio García Villegas, 423–54. Bogotá: Siglo de Hombres, 2001.

Ghazi, Polly, and Ian Hargreaves. "BP's Chief Executive Is Making the Running on Green Strategy." *New Statesman*, vol. 126, no. 4341, July 4, 1997.

Gilabert, Pablo. *Human Dignity and Human Rights*. Oxford: Oxford University Press, 2018.

Gill, Lesley. "The Limits of Solidarity: Labor and Transnational Organizing in Coca-Cola." *American Ethnologist* 36, no. 4 (2009): 667–80. https://doi.org/10.1111/j.1548-1425.2009.01202.x.

Gill, Stephen. "New Constitutionalism, Democratisation and Global Political Economy." *Pacifica Review* 10, no. 1 (1998): 23–38. https://doi.org/10.1080/14781159808412845.

Gillard, Michael. "BP Links with Colombian Military Intelligence Revealed." *Scotland on Sunday*, June 9, 1996, 2, 16.

Gillard, Michael, Ignacio Gómez, and Melissa Jones. "BP Hands Tarred in Pipeline Dirty War." *Guardian*, October 17, 1997.

Gillard, Michael, and Melissa Jones. "BP's Secret Military Advisers." *Guardian*, June 30, 1997.

Gilson, Erin C. *The Ethics of Vulnerability: A Feminist Analysis of Social Life and Practice*. London: Routledge, 2014.

Giraldo Moreno, Javier. *Colombia: The Genocidal Democracy*. Monroe, ME: Common Courage, 1996.

Giraldo Moreno, Javier, and Fabian Laverde. *Casanare: Exhumando el genocidio*. Bogotá: Centro de Investigación y Educación Popular Programa por la Paz and Corporación Social para la Asesoría y Capacitación Comunitaria, 2009.

Global Campaign to Dismantle Corporate Power and Stop Impunity. "Global Campaign Statement on the Third Draft of the Binding Treaty." Media release, September 7, 2021. https://www.stopcorporateimpunity.org/comunicadotercerborradordeltratadovinculante/#.

Golder, Ben. "Beyond Redemption? Problematising the Critique of Human Rights in Contemporary International Legal Thought." *London Review of International Law* 2, no. 1 (2014): 77–114. https://doi.org/10.1093/lril/lru001.

Gordon, Lewis R. "Shifting the Geography of Reason in an Age of Disciplinary Decadence." *Transmodernity* 1, no. 2 (2011): 95–103. https://doi.org/10.5070/T412011810.

Gordon, Uri. "Prefigurative Politics between Ethical Practice and Absent Promise." *Political Studies* 66, no. 2 (2017): 521–37. https://doi.org/10.1177/0032321717722363.

Graeber, David. "Radical Alterity Is Just Another Word for Saying 'Reality': A Reply to Eduardo Viveiros de Castro." *HAU: Journal of Ethnographic Theory* 5, no. 2 (2015): 1–42. https://doi.org/10.14318/hau5.2.003.

Gray, Garry C. "The Regulation of Corporate Violations: Punishment, Compliance and the Blurring of Responsibility." *British Journal of Criminology* 46, no. 5 (2006): 875–92. https://www.jstor.org/stable/23639637.

Greenawalt, Alexander K. A. "Rethinking Genocidal Intent: The Case for a Knowledge-Based Interpretation." *Columbia Law Review* 99, no. 8 (1999): 2259–94. https://doi.org/10.2307/1123611.

Grigera, Juan, and Laura Álvarez. "Extractivismo y acumulación por desposesión: Un análisis de las explicaciones sobre agronegocios, megaminería y territorio en la Argentina de posconvertabilidad." *Revista Theomai* 27–28 (2013): 80–97. http://revista-theomai.unq.edu.ar/NUMERO_27-28/contenido_27-28.htm.

Guevara, Ernesto Che. "Man and Socialism in Cuba." In *Venceremos! The Speeches and Writings of Ernesto Che Guevara*, edited by John Gerassi, 398. New York: Macmillan, 1968.

Hadwiger, Felix. "Global Framework Agreements: Achieving Decent Work in Global Supply Chains?" *International Journal of Labour Research* 7, nos. 1–2 (2015): 75–94.

Hale, Charles R. "*Resistencia para que?* Territory, Autonomy and Neoliberal Entanglements in the 'Empty Spaces' of Central America." *Economy and Society* 40, no. 2 (2011): 184–210. https://doi.org/10.1080/03085147.2011.548947.

Harrison, David. "Oilmen Dread Columbian [*sic*] 'Kiss.'" *Observer*, November 3, 1996.

Harrison, David, and Melissa Jones. "Black Gold Fuels Colombia Killing Machine." *Observer*, October 20, 1996.

Harrison, David, and Melissa Jones. "BP Accused of Funding Colombian Death Squads." *Observer*, October 20, 1996.

Herrnstadt, Owen E. "Are International Framework Agreements a Path to Corporate Social Responsibility?" *Journal of Business and Employment Law* 10, no. 1 (2007): 187–224.

Herrnstadt, Owen E. "Corporate Social Responsibility, International Framework Agreements and Changing Corporate Behavior in the Global Workplace." *Labor and Employment Law Forum* 3, no. 2 (2013): 263–77.

Hewitt, Gavin. "Greece: The Dangerous Game." BBC News, February 1, 2015. http://www.bbc.co.uk/news/world-europe-31082656.

Hidalgo-Capitán, Antonio Luis, and Ana Patricia Cubillo-Guevara. "Deconstrucción y genealogía del 'buen vivir' latinoamericano: El 'buen vivir' y sus diverso manantiales intelectuales." *International Development Policy|Revue Internationale de Politique de Développement* 9 (2017). https://doi.org/10.4000/poldev.2517.

Hirshman, Albert O. *The Passions and the Interests*. Princeton, NJ: Princeton University Press, 1977.

Honig, Bonnie. "Antigone's Two Laws: Greek Tragedy and the Politics of Humanism." *New Literary History* 41, no. 1 (2010): 1–33. https://www.jstor.org/stable/40666482.

Hopgood, Stephen. *The Endtimes of Human Rights*. Ithaca, NY: Cornell University Press, 2013.

Hopgood, Stephen. "Reading the Small Print in Global Civil Society: The Inexorable Hegemony of the Liberal Self." *Millennium* 29, no. 1 (2000): 1–25. https://doi.org/10.1177/03058298000290010601.

"Human Rights and Wrongs." *Economist*, November 30, 1997, 71–72.

Human Rights Watch. *Colombia's Killer Networks: The Military-Paramilitary Partnership and the United States.* New York: Human Rights Watch, 1996.

Human Rights Watch. *The "Sixth Division": Military-Paramilitary Ties and US Policy in Colombia.* New York, Washington, DC: Human Rights Watch, 2001.

Human Rights Watch. *A Wrong Turn: The Record of the Colombian Attorney General's Office.* New York: Human Rights Watch, 2002.

Hume, David. *A Treatise of Human Nature.* Darmstadt, Germany: Scientia Verlag Aalen, 1964.

Hylton, Forrest. "An Evil Hour: Uribe's Colombia in Historical Perspective." *New Left Review* 23 (2003): 53–58.

IAG (Inter-Agency Group). "Good Intentions Are Not Enough: Recommendations and Conclusions of the Inter-Agency Group (CAFOD, Christian Aid, CIIR, Oxfam GB and SCF UK) to BP Amoco on its role in Casanare, Colombia." Report, July 1999.

ILO (International Labour Organization). *Decent Work: Report of the Director General, 87th Session, June 1999.* Geneva: ILO, 1999. Accessed August 15, 2018. http://www.ilo.org/public/english/standards/relm/ilc/ilc87/rep-i.htm.

ILO (International Labour Organization). *Evaluation Mission: Coca-Cola Bottling Plants in Colombia.* Report, Geneva, June 30–July 11, 2008.

Ince, Onur Ulas. "Between Commerce and Empire: David Hume, Colonial Slavery and Commercial Incivility." *History of Political Thought* 39, no. 1 (2018): 107–34.

Inter-American Human Rights Commission. *Precautionary Measures 51/15.* Resolution no. 60/2015. Accessed February 22, 2022. https://www.oas.org/en/iachr/decisions/precautionary.asp?Year=2015&Country=COL#1.

Ireland, Paddy. "Finance and the Origins of Modern Company Law." In *The Corporation: A Critical, Multi-disciplinary Handbook*, edited by Grietje Baars and André Spicer, 238–46. Cambridge: Cambridge University Press, 2017.

IUF (International Union of Food, Agricultural, Hotel, Restaurant, Catering, Tobacco and Allied Workers' Associations). "Charter of Demands against Job Destruction." Accessed September 6, 2009. http://www.iuf.org/drupal/files/Alliance_Charterofdemands_final_en.pdf.

IUF (International Union of Food, Agricultural, Hotel, Restaurant, Catering, Tobacco and Allied Workers' Associations). "Coca-Cola Is Becoming a Serial Human Rights Offender—in Haiti, Indonesia, Ireland, the Philippines and the United States." Campaign statement, June 11, 2018. https://www.iufcampaigns.org/campaigns/show_campaign.cgi?c=1112.

IUF (International Union of Food, Agricultural, Hotel, Restaurant, Catering, Tobacco and Allied Workers' Associations). "Coca-Cola Union Wins Improved Collective Bargaining Agreement in Colombia/Temporary Work Contracts Made Permanent Jobs." Press release, April 3, 2006. http://pre2010.iuf.org/cgi

-bin/dbman/db.cgi?db=default&ww=1&uid=default&ID=3322&view_records
=1&en=1.

IUF (International Union of Food, Agricultural, Hotel, Restaurant, Catering,
Tobacco and Allied Workers' Associations). "Colombia: SICO and Coca-Cola
Franchise Sign New CBA in Urabá." Press release, March 28, 2002. http://
pre2010.iuf.org/cgi-bin/dbman/db.cgi?db=default&ww=1&uid=default&ID
=257&view_records=1&en=1.

IUF (International Union of Food, Agricultural, Hotel, Restaurant, Catering,
Tobacco and Allied Workers' Associations). "Gains for Colombian Beverage Workers/Strike Threat at Coca-Cola Plant." Press release, February 27,
2002. http://pre2010.iuf.org/cgi-bin/dbman/db.cgi?db=default&ww=1&uid
=default&ID=182&view_records=1&en=1.

IUF (International Union of Food, Agricultural, Hotel, Restaurant, Catering,
Tobacco and Allied Workers' Associations). "IUF and Coca-Cola Agreement to Request United Nations' ILO to Conduct Independent Investigation of Coca-Cola Labour Practices in Colombia." Press release, March 2,
2006. https://www.business-humanrights.org/en/latest-news/iuf-and-coca
-cola-agreement-to-request-united-nations-ilo-to-conduct-independent
-investigation-of-coca-cola-labour-practices-in-colombia.

IUF (International Union of Food, Agricultural, Hotel, Restaurant, Catering,
Tobacco and Allied Workers' Associations). "Time to Regulate TNCs: IUF
Welcomes War on Want's Coca-Cola Report." Press release, March 20,
2006. http://pre2010.iuf.org/cgi-bin/dbman/db.cgi?db=default&uid
=default&Private=No&view_records=1&ID=&nh=93.

Jahn, Beate. "One Step Forward, Two Steps Back: Critical Theory as the Latest
Edition of Liberal Idealism." *Millennium* 27, no. 3 (1998): 613–41. https://doi
.org/10.1177/03058298980270030201.

Justice, Dwight W. "The International Trade Union Movement and the New
Codes of Conduct." In *Corporate Responsibility and Labour Rights: Codes of
Conduct in the Global Economy*, edited by Rhys Jenkins, Ruth Pearson, and Gill
Seyfang, 90–100. London: Earthscan, 2002.

Justice for Colombia. "Trade Union Delegation to Colombia." Internal report,
November 2004. Photocopy in author's possession.

Karp, David Jason. "Fixing Meanings in Global Governance: 'Respect' and 'Protect' in the UN Guiding Principles on Business and Human Rights." *Global
Governance: A Review of Multilateralism and International Organizations* 26, no. 4
(2020): 628–49. https://doi.org/10.1163/19426720-02604002.

Kelemen, Paul. "Planning for Africa: The British Labour Party's Colonial Development Policy, 1920–1964." *Journal of Agrarian Change* 7, no. 1 (2007): 76–98.
https://doi.org/10.1111/j.1471-0366.2007.00140.x.

Khoury, Stéfanie, and David Whyte. *Corporate Human Rights Violations: Global
Prospects for Legal Action*. Abingdon, UK: Routledge, 2017.

Klein, Naomi. *No Logo: Taking Aim at the Brand Bullies*. London: Flamingo,
2000.

Klein, Naomi. *The Shock Doctrine: The Rise of Disaster Capitalism*. London: Penguin, 2007.

Knox, Robert. "Legalising the Violence of Austerity." In *The Violence of Austerity*, edited by Vickie Cooper and David Whyte, 181–87. London: Pluto, 2017.

Knox, Robert. "Strategy and Tactics." *Finnish Yearbook of International Law* 21 (2010): 193–229. https://ssrn.com/abstract=1921759.

Kochi, Tarik. *Global Justice and Social Conflict: The Foundations of Liberal Order and International Law*. Abingdon, UK: Glasshouse/Routledge, 2020.

Koram, Kojo, *Uncommon Wealth: Britain and the Aftermath of Empire*. London: John Murray, 2022.

Kovalik, Daniel. "Lawyer for Chiquita in Colombia Death Squad Case May Be Next US Attorney General." *Huffington Post*, November 6, 2008. http://www.huffingtonpost.com/dan-kovalik/lawyer-for-chiquita-in-co_b_141919.html.

Kramer, Sina. "Judith Butler's 'New Humanism': A Thing or Not a Thing and So What?" *philoSOPHIA* 5, no. 1 (2015), 25–40. https://muse.jhu.edu/article/583403.

Krever, Tor. "Dispensing Global Justice." *New Left Review* 85 (2014): 67–97.

Latimer, Mark. *The Campaigning Handbook*. London: Directory of Social Change, 2000.

Lawrence, Felicity, Juliette Garside, David Pegg, David Conn, Severin Carrell, and Harry Davies. "COVID-19 Investigation: How a Decade of Privatisation and Cuts Exposed England to Coronavirus." *Guardian*, May 31, 2020.

Lear, Jonathan. *Radical Hope: Ethics in the Face of Cultural Devastation*. Cambridge, MA: Harvard University Press, 2008.

Lefort, Claude. *The Political Forms of Modern Society*. Translated by John Thompson. Cambridge: Polity, 1986.

Lloyd, Moira. "Toward a Cultural Politics of Vulnerability: Precarious Lives and Ungrievable Deaths." In *Judith Butler's Precarious Politics: Critical Encounters*, edited by Terrell Carver and Sam Chambers, 92–106. London, Routledge, 2008.

Lorde, Audre. *The Master's Tools Will Never Dismantle the Master's House*. London: Penguin, 2018.

Lovibond, Sabina. *Iris Murdoch, Gender and Philosophy*. Abingdon, UK: Routledge, 2011.

Löwy, Michael. *War of Gods: Religion and Politics in Latin America*. London: Verso, 1996.

MacGinty, Roger, and Oliver Richmond. "The Local Turn in Peace Building: Toward a Critical Agenda for Peace." *Third World Quarterly* 34, no. 5 (2013): 763–83. https://doi.org/10.1080/01436597.2013.800750.

MacGinty, Roger, and Andrew Williams. *Conflict and Development*. London: Routledge, 2009.

Madeley, John. *Big Business, Poor Peoples: The Impact of Transnational Corporations*. London: Zed, 1999.

Madhok, Sumi. *Vernacular Rights Cultures: The Politics of Origins, Human Rights and Gendered Struggles for Justice*. Cambridge: Cambridge University Press, 2021.

Maldonado-Torres, Nelson. *Against War: Views from the Underside of Modernity*. Durham, NC: Duke University Press, 2008.

Maldonado-Torres, Nelson. "On the Coloniality of Being: Contributions to the Development of a Concept." *Cultural Studies* 21, nos. 2–3 (2007): 240–70. https://doi.org1/o.1080/09502380601162548.

Maldonado-Torres, Nelson. "On the Coloniality of Human Rights." *Revista Crítica de Ciências Sociais* 114 (2007): 117–36. https://doi.org/10.4000/rccs.6793.

Maniglier, Patrice. "What Is a Problematic?" *Radical Philosophy* 173 (2012): 21–23. https://www.radicalphilosophy.com/article/what-is-a-problematic#:~:text=A%20'problematic'%20in%20this%20pedagogical,certain%20number%20of%20precise%20problems.

Mannoni, Octave. "I Know Well, but All the Same . . ." Translated by G. M. Goshgarian. In *Perversion and the Social Relation: Sic 4*, edited by Molly Anne Rothenburg, Dennis A. Foster, and Slavoj Žižek, 68–92. Durham, NC: Duke University Press, 2003.

Marcus, George E. "Ethnography in/of the World System: The Emergence of Multi-sited Ethnography." *Annual Review of Anthropology* 24 (1995): 95–117. https://doi.org/10.1146/annurev.an.24.100195.000523.

Marx, Karl. *Capital, Volume 1: A Critique of Political Economy*. London: Penguin, 1990.

Marx, Karl. "On the Jewish Question." In *Karl Marx: Selected Writings*, 2nd ed., edited by David McLellan, 46–64. Oxford: Oxford University Press, 2000.

Mattei, Ugo, and Laura Nader. *Plunder: When the Rule of Law Is Illegal*, Oxford: Basil Blackwell, 2008.

Mbembe, Achille. "Necropolitics." *Public Culture* 15, no. 1 (2003): 11–40. https://muse.jhu.edu/article/39984.

McCallum, Jamie K. *Global Unions, Local Power: The New Spirit of Transnational Labor Organizing*. Ithaca, NY: Cornell University Press, 2013.

McKittrick, Katherine, and Sylvia Wynter. "Unparalleled Catastrophe for Our Species? Or, to Give Humanness a Different Future: Conversations." In *Sylvia Wynter: On Being Human as Praxis*, edited by Katherine McKittrick, 9–89. Durham, NC: Duke University Press, 2015.

McNally, David. "The Dialectics of Unity and Difference in the Constitution of Wage-Labour: On Internal Relations and Working Class Formation." *Capital and Class* 39, no. 1 (2015): 131–46. https://doi.org/10.1177/0309816814564819.

Meeran, Richard. "Tort Litigation against Multinational Corporations for Violations of Human Rights: An Overview of the Position outside the United States." *City University Hong Kong Law Review* 3, no. 1 (2011): 1–41.

Meeran, Richard. "The 'Zero Draft': Access to Judicial Remedy for Victims of Multinationals' ('MNCs') Abuse." Business and Human Rights Resource Centre, 2018. Accessed April 15, 2019. https://www.business-humanrights.org/en/the-%E2%80%9Czero-draft%E2%80%9D-access-to-judicial-remedy-for-victims-of-multinationals%E2%80%99-%E2%80%9Cmncs%E2%80%9D-abuse.

Meister, Robert. *After Evil: A Politics of Human Rights*. New York: Columbia University Press, 2010.

Miéville, China. *Between Equal Rights: A Marxist Theory of International Law*. London: Pluto, 2006.

Mignolo, Walter. "The Geopolitics of Knowledge and the Colonial Difference." *South Atlantic Quarterly* 101, no. 1 (2002): 57–96. https://doi.org/10.1215 /00382876-101-1-57.

Mignolo, Walter. *Local Histories/Global Designs: Coloniality, Subaltern Knowledges and Border-Thinking.* Princeton, NJ: Princeton University Press, 2000.

Mignolo, Walter. "Sylvia Wynter: What Does It Mean to be Human?" In *Sylvia Wynter: On Being Human as Praxis*, edited by Katherine McKittrick, 106–23. Durham, NC: Duke University Press, 2015.

Mignolo, Walter. "Who Speaks for the Human in Human Rights?" In *Human Rights from a Third World Perspective: Critique, History and International Law*, edited by José Manuel Barreto, 44–64. Newcastle-upon-Tyne: Cambridge Scholars, 2012.

Migone, Andrea. "Embedded Markets: A Dialogue between F. A. Hayek and Karl Polanyi." *Review of Austrian Economics* 24, no. 4 (2011): 355–81. https://doi.org/10 .1007/s11138-011-0148-2.

Mills, Catherine. "Undoing Ethics: Butler on Precarity, Opacity and Responsibility." In *Butler and Ethics*, edited by Moira Lloyd, 41–64. Edinburgh: Edinburgh University Press, 2018.

Monje Carvajal, Jhon Jairo. *Los planes de vida de los pueblos indígenas en Colombia: Una propuesta para su construcción desde la agroecología.* Bogotá: Corporación Universitaria Minuto de Dios, Facultad de Ingenería, 2014.

Montag, Warren. "Necro-economics: Adam Smith and Death in the Life of the Universal." *Radical Philosophy* 134 (2005). https://www.radicalphilosophy.com /article/necro-economics.

Montag, Warren. "War and the Market: The Place of the Global South in the Origins of Neo-liberalism." *Global South* 3, no. 1 (2009): 126–38. https://www. jstor.org/stable/40339252.

Moody, Kim. *Workers in a Lean World: Unions in the International Economy.* London: Verso, 1997.

Motta, Sara. *Liminal Subjects: Weaving (Our) Liberation.* London: Rowman and Littlefield, 2018.

Moyn, Samuel. *Not Enough: Human Rights in an Unequal World.* Cambridge, MA: Harvard University Press, 2018.

Moyn, Samuel. "A Powerless Companion: Human Rights in the Age of Neoliberalism." *Law and Contemporary Problems* 77 (2015): 147–69. https://scholarship .law.duke.edu/lcp/vol77/iss4/7.

Muppidi, Himadeep. *The Colonial Signs of International Relations.* London: Hurst, 2012.

Murdoch, Iris. *Metaphysics as a Guide to Morals.* London: Vintage, 1992.

Murdoch, Iris. *The Sovereignty of Good.* London: Routledge and Kegan Paul, 1970.

Murphy, Ann. "Corporeal Vulnerability and the New Humanism." *Hypatia* 26, no. 3 (2011): 575–90. https://www.jstor.org/stable/23016569.

Myers, Milton L. *The Soul of Modern Economic Man: Ideas of Self-interest from Thomas Hobbes to Adam Smith.* Chicago: University of Chicago Press, 1983.

Nair, Deepak. "Sociability in International Politics: Golf and ASEAN's Cold War Diplomacy." *International Political Sociology* 14 (2020). https://doi.org/10.1093/ips/olz024.

National Union of Students. "The Importance of Ethics to Students." Online video, 2010. Accessed August 17, 2020. http://www.nus.org.uk/en/Lifestyle/Ethical-Living/Going-Green/The-importance-of-ethics-to-students.

National Union of Students. "Motion on Coke Passed at NUS Conference in March 2006." Accessed February 2, 2009. http://www.nus.org.uk/About-NUS/Ethical—Environmental/Constructive-Engagement-with-suppliers/Constructive-Engagement-with-Coca-Cola/.

Nersessian, David L. *Genocide and Political Groups.* Oxford: Oxford University Press, 2010.

Newton, Richard. "Business and Human Rights." Speech at Amnesty International event, Birmingham, UK, November 1, 1997. Previously available at www.bp.com.

Norrie, Alan. *Crime, Reason and History: A Critical Introduction to Criminal Law.* Cambridge: Cambridge University Press, 2014.

Norrie, Alan. "Legal and Social Murder: What's the Difference?" *Criminal Law Review* 7 (2018): 531–42.

Norrie, Alan. "Simulacra of Morality? Beyond the Actual/Ideal Antimonies of Criminal Justice." In *Philosophy and the Criminal Law: Principle and Critique,* edited by Anthony Duff, 101–55. Cambridge: Cambridge University Press, 1998.

NUS Services Ltd. "Accusations of Human Rights Violations against Coca-Cola Workers in Colombia." First published January 12, 2004, last updated November 6, 2008. http://www.nus.org.uk/About-NUS/Ethical—Environmental/Constructive-Engagement-with-suppliers/Constructive-Engagement-with-Coca-Cola.

NUS Services Ltd. "Coca-Cola Enterprises Ltd.: Commercial Briefing, February 2005." Accessed February 2, 2009. http://www.nus.org.uk/About-NUS/Ethical—Environmental/Constructive-Engagement-with-suppliers/Constructive-Engagement-with-Coca-Cola.

NUS Services Ltd. "Coca-Cola—Key Arguments for Constructive Engagement, Not Boycott," March 27, 2005. Accessed February 2, 2009. http://www.nus.org.uk/About-NUS/Ethical—Environmental/Constructive-Engagement-with-suppliers/Constructive-Engagement-with-Coca-Cola.

NUS Services Ltd. "Summary of the Ongoing Constructive Engagement with Coca-Cola in Relation to the Accusations Relating to Colombia and India." April 1, 2004; updated January 14, 2008. http://www.nus.org.uk/About-NUS/Ethical—Environmental/Constructive-Engagement-with-suppliers/Constructive-Engagement-with-Coca-Cola.

Occhipinti, Marco. "Tensione e proteste anti-sponsor all'arrivo della fiaccola olimpica." *La Repubblica,* June 29, 2004.

Odysseos, Louiza. "Prolegomena to Any Future Decolonial Ethics: Coloniality, Poetics and 'Being Human as Praxis.'" *Millennium* 45, no. 3 (2017): 447–72. https://doi.org/10.1177/0305829810364876.

Offeddu, Luigi. "Empoli boicotta la Coca-Cola 'Sfrutta gli operai colombiani.'" *Corriere della Serra*, November 18, 2004.

Olarte, Maria Carolina. "Depoliticization and Criminalization of Social Protest through Economic Decisionism: The Colombian Case." *Oñati Socio-Legal Series* 4, no. 1 (2014): 139–60. http://ssrn.com/abstract=2358593.

Oliviero, Katie. "Vulnerability's Ambivalent Political Life: Trayvon Martin and the Racialized and Gendered Politics of Protection." *Feminist Formations* 28, no. 1 (2016): 1–32. https://doi.org/10.1353/ff.2016.0013.

Ó Loingsigh, Gearóid. *Catatumbo: Un reto por la verdad*. Bogotá: Comité de Integración Social del Catatumbo y Corporación Sembrar, 2007.

Ó Loingsigh, Gearóid. *La estrategia integral de los paramilitares en el Magdalena Medio*, 2nd ed. Bogotá: Anon, 2004.

Ó Loingsigh, Gearóid. "Peace Laboratories: Europe's Plan Colombia." *Frontline Latin America* 2, no. 3 (2006): 4, 20.

Ó Loingsigh, Gearóid. *La reconquista del pacífico: Invasión, inversión, impunidad*. Bogotá: Coordinador Nacional Agrario and Proceso de Comunidades Negras, 2013.

Ortiz, Astrid Martínez. "La política energética en Colombia durante los años noventa. ¿Neoliberal?" In *La falacia neoliberal: Crítica y alternativas*, edited by Dario I. Restrepo Botero, 231–48. Bogotá: Universidad Nacional de Colombia, 2003.

Osborne, Samuel. "Two Women Feared Dead in Grenfell Tower Were 'Threatened with Legal Action' for Questioning Fire Safety." *Independent*, June 19, 2017.

Oulton, Lucy. "Loving by Instinct: Environmental Ethics in Iris Murdoch's *The Sovereignty of Good* and *Nuns and Soldiers*." *Études Britanniques Contemporaines* 59 (2020). https://doi.org/10.4000/ebc.10237.

Oxfam. *Influencing for Impact Guide: How to Deliver Effective Influencing Strategies*. Oxford: Oxfam, 2020.

Palmer, Hilda, and David Whyte. "Health and Safety at the Frontline of Austerity." In *The Violence of Austerity*, edited by Vickie Cooper and David Whyte, 141–48. London: Pluto, 2017.

Parra Dussan, Carlos. "La regla fiscal configura una política económica del Estado." *La Republica,* June 21, 2013. https://www.larepublica.co/asuntos-legales/actualidad/la-regla-fiscal-configura-una-politica-economica-de-estado-2041170.

Pashukanis, Evgeny. *Law and Marxism: A General Theory*. Edited by Chris Arthur, translated by Barbara Einhorn. London: Pluto, 1987.

Patients4NHS. "The Health and Social Care Act 2012." Accessed June 19, 2017. http://www.patients4nhs.org.uk/the-health-and-social-care-act.

Pearce, Jenny. "Beyond the Perimeter Fence: Oil and Armed Conflict in Casanare, Colombia." Discussion paper, Centre for Global Governance, London School of Economics, 2004. http://eprints.lse.ac.uk/id/eprint/23438.

Pearce, Jenny. "The Case of Casanare, Colombia." Report for the Inter-Agency Group, London, UK, 1998. Photocopy in author's possession.

Pearce, Jenny. "Oil and Armed Conflict in Casanare: Contemporary Conflicts and Contingent Moments." In *Oil Wars*, edited by Mary Kaldor, Terry Lynne, and Yahia Said, 225–73. London: Pluto, 2007.

Perraudin, Frances. "Tories Reject Move to Ensure Rented Homes Fit for Human Habitation." *Guardian*, January 12, 2016.

Petersmann, Ernst-Ulrich. "How to Promote the International Rule of Law? Contributions by the World Trade Organization Appellate Review System." *Journal of International Economic Law* 1, no. 1 (1998): 25–48. https://doi.org/10 .1093/jiel/1.1.25.

Petersmann, Ernst-Ulrich. "The WTO Constitution and Human Rights." *Journal of International Economic Law* 3, no. 1 (2000): 1–25. https://doi.org/10.1093/jiel/3.1.19.

Polanyi, Karl. *The Great Transformation: The Political and Economic Origins of Our Time*. Boston: Beacon, 2002.

Policante, Amedeo. "Of Cameras and Balaclavas: Violence, Myth and the Convulsive Kettle." *Globalizations* 8, no. 4 (2011): 457–71. https://doi.org/10.1080 /14747731.2011.585848.

Pollock, Allyson. *NHS Plc.: The Privatisation of Our Health Care*. London: Verso, 2004.

Povinelli, Elizabeth. *Economies of Abandonment: Social Belonging and Endurance in Late Liberalism*. Durham, NC: Duke University Press, 2011.

Prentis, Dave. "Sharing the Benefits of Globalisation." In *Trades Unions and Globalisation*, edited by Tony Pilch, 26–31. London: Smith Institute, 2007.

Pring, John. "Welfare Reform and the Attack on Disabled People." In *The Violence of Austerity*, edited by Vickie Cooper and David Whyte, 51–58. London: Pluto, 2017.

Proceso de Comunidades Negras. "Entrevista con José Santos Caicedo." *Renacientes,* January 28, 2018. https://renacientes.net/blog/2018/01/28/entrevista-con -jose-santos-caicedo.

Procuraduría General de la Nación, Fiscalía General de la Nación, Defensoría del Pueblo, Consejaría Presidencial para los Derechos Humanos, Asociación Nacional de Usarios Campesinos, and Fundación Comite de Solidaridad con los Presos Políticos. *Informe de la Comisión Interinstitucional sobre la situación de derechos humanos en los departamentos de Casanare y Arauca*. Human rights report by various government agencies, Bogotá, 1995. Photocopy in author's possession.

Pugh, Michael. "The Political Economy of Peace-Building: A Critical Theory Perspective." *International Journal of Peace Studies* 10, no. 2 (2005): 23–42.

Quinn, Ben. "Air of Discontent around Cerrejón Mine Deepens as Colombians Cry Foul." *Guardian*, October 26, 2016. https://www.theguardian.com/global -development/2016/oct/26/discontent-cerrejon-coal-mine-colombians-cry -foul.

Radical Housing Network. "Justice for Grenfell Tower." Accessed June 19, 2017. http://radicalhousingnetwork.org/grenfell-fire-warnings-fell-on-deaf-ears.

Rajak, Dinah. *In Good Company: An Anatomy of Corporate Social Responsibility*. Stanford, CA: Stanford University Press, 2011.

Rancière, Jacques. "Does 'Democracy' Mean Something?" In *Dissensus: On Politics and Aesthetics*, edited and translated by Steven Corcoran, 45–61. London: Continuum, 2010.

Rancière, Jacques. "Who Is the Subject of the Rights of Man?" *South Atlantic Quarterly* 102, nos. 2–3 (2004): 297–310. http://muse.jhu.edu/article/169147.

Raynor, William. "A Lethal Brew of Oil and Blood." *Independent on Sunday*, August 31, 1997.

Raynor, William. "Shadowy Trail That Leads to London." *Independent on Sunday*, August 31, 1997.

Raynor, William, and Richard Halstead. "Colombia's 'Dirty War' Embroils BP." *Independent on Sunday*, June 22, 1997.

Rice, David. "Human Rights Strategies for Corporations." *Business Ethics* 11, no. 2 (2002): 134–36. https://doi.org/10.1111/beer.2002.11.issue-2.

Rist, Gilbert. *The History of Development: From Western Origins to Global Faith*, 2nd ed. Translated by Patrick Camiller. London: Zed, 2002.

Rivera Cusicanqui, Silvia. "*Ch'ixinakax utxiwa*: A Reflection on the Practices and Discourses of Decolonization." *South Atlantic Quarterly* 11, no. 1 (2012): 95–109.

Roberts, Christopher N. J. "From the Evolution of the State of Emergency to the Rule of Law: The Evolution of Repressive Legality in the Nineteenth Century British Empire." *Chicago Journal of International Law* 20, no. 1 (2019), article 1. https://chicagounbound.uchicago.edu/cjil/vol20/iss1/1.

Rodríguez, Carlos, and Boris Montes de Oca. *La CUT y las empresas multinacionales*. Bogotá: Central Unitaria de Trabajadores de Colombia, 2005.

Rodríguez Garavito, Cesar, ed. *Extractivismo versus derechos humanos: Crónicas de los nuevos campos minados en el Sur Global*. Buenos Aires: Siglo Veintiuno/Dejusticia, 2016.

Rojas-Páez, Gustavo. "Understanding Environmental Harm and Justice Claims in the Global South: Crimes of the Powerful and People's Resistance." In *Environmental Crime in Latin America: The Theft of Nature and the Poisoning of the Land*, edited by David Rodríguez Goyes, Hanneke Mol, Avi Brisman, and Nigel South, 49–85. London: Palgrave Macmillan, 2017.

Rojas-Páez, Gustavo. "Whose Nature? Whose Rights? Criminalization of Social Protest in a Globalizing World." *Oñati Socio-Legal Series* 4, no. 1 (2014): 1–12. https://ssrn.com/abstract=2386597.

Romero, Federico. *The United States and the European Trade Union Movement, 1944–1951*. Translated by Harvey Ferguson II. Chapel Hill: University of North Carolina Press, 1992.

Romero, Mauricio. "Los trabajadores bananeros de Urabá: ¿De 'súbditos' a 'ciudadanos'?" In *Emancipación social y violencia en Colombia*, edited by Boaventura de Sousa Santos and Mauricio Villegas, 249–80. Bogotá: Norma, 2004.

Rose, David. "The Firm That Hijacked the NHS: MoS Investigation Reveals Extraordinary Extent of International Management Consultant's Role in Lansley's Health Reforms." *Mail on Sunday*, February 12, 2012.

Rowe, James K. "Corporate Social Responsibility as Business Strategy." In *Globalization, Governmentality and Global Politics: Regulation for the Rest of Us?*, by James K. Rowe and Ronnie D. Lipschutz, 130–70. London: Routledge, 2005.

Rudqvist, Anders, and Fred van Sluys. *Informe final de evaluación de medio término Laboratorio de Paz del Magdalena Medio.* Brussels: European Commission, 2005.

Rütters, Peter, and Rüdiger Zimmermann. *On the History and Policy of the IUF.* Translated by Rhodes Barrett. Bonn: Bibliothek der Friedric-Ebert-Stiftung, 2003.

Sachs, Wolfgang. "Introduction." In *The Development Dictionary: A Guide to Knowledge as Power*, edited by Wolfgang Sachs, 1–15. London: Zed, 1992.

Sanders, James E. *Contentious Republicans: Popular Politics, Race and Class in Nineteenth-Century Colombia.* Durham, NC: Duke University Press, 2004.

Santos, Boaventura de Sousa. "Human Rights as an Emancipatory Script? Cultural and Political Conditions." In *Another Knowledge Is Possible: Beyond Northern Epistemologies,* edited by Boaventura de Sousa Santos, 3–40. London: Verso, 2007.

Santos, Boaventura de Sousa. *Toward a New Legal Common Sense: Law, Globalization and Emancipation.* London: Butterworth LexisNexis, 2002.

Santos, Boaventura de Sousa, and Mauricio García Villegas. "Colombia: El revés del contrato social de la modernidad." In *El caleidoscopio de las justicias en Colombia*, vol. 1, edited by Boaventura de Sousa Santos and Mauricio García Villegas, 11–83. Bogotá: Siglo de Hombres, 2001.

Sarmiento Anzola, Libardo. *El Magdalena Medio: Un modelo piloto de modernización authoritaria en Colombia.* Barrancabermeja, Colombia: Corporación Regional para la Defensa de los Derechos Humanos, 1996.

Schwöbel-Patel, Christine. *Marketing Global Justice: The Political Economy of International Criminal Law.* Cambridge: Cambridge University Press, 2021.

Scott, David. "The Re-enchantment of Humanism: An Interview with Sylvia Wynter." *Small Axe* 8 (2000): 119–207.

Selwyn, Benjamin. "Social Upgrading and Labour in Global Production Networks: A Critique and an Alternative Conception." *Competition and Change* 17, no. 1 (2013): 75–90.

Serje, Margarita. *El revés de la nación: Territorios salvajes, fronteras y tierras de nadie.* Bogotá: Publicaciones Uniandes, 2005.

Shamir, Ronen. "Between Self-Regulation and the Alien Tort Claims Act." *Law and Society Review* 38, no. 4 (2004): 635–64. https://www.jstor.org/stable/1555086.

Shamir, Ronen. "The De-radicalization of Corporate Social Responsibility." *Critical Sociology* 30, no. 3 (2004): 669–89. https://doi.org/10.1163/1569163042119831.

Shilliam, Robbie. "Enoch Powell: Britain's First Neoliberal Politician." *New Political Economy* 26, no. 2 (2021): 239–49. https://doi.org/10.1080/13563467.2020.1841140.

Shilliam, Robbie. *Race and the Undeserving Poor: From Abolition to Brexit.* Newcastle-upon-Tyne: Agenda, 2018.

Sikkink, Kathryn. "Human Rights: Advancing the Frontier of Emancipation." *Development* 61 (2019): 14–20. https://doi.org/10.1057/s41301-018-0186-1.

Simpson, Derek. "Globalisation—Trade Union Scourge or an Unprecedented Opportunity for International Labour?" In *Trades Unions and Globalization*, edited by Tony Pilch, 32–41. London: Smith Institute, 2007.

SINALTRAINAL (Sindicato Nacional de Trabajadores de la Industria de Alimentos). *Complaint to the International Labour Organization against the Colombian Government for Violating* SINALTRAINAL's *Rights of Trade Union Freedom.* Bogotá, September 18, 2007.

SINALTRAINAL (Sindicato Nacional de Trabajadores de la Industria de Alimentos). "Genocidio en Carepa: Empresa Coca-Cola." Submission to the Food and Agriculture Hearing of the Permanent Peoples' Tribunal, Colombia sess., Bogotá, April 1–2, 2006.

SINALTRAINAL (Sindicato Nacional de Trabajadores de la Industria de Alimentos). "El hambre: Un crimen de lesa humanidad." *La Red Voltaire*, October 15, 2004. http://www.voltairenet.org/article122608.html.

SINALTRAINAL (Sindicato Nacional de Trabajadores de la Industria de Alimentos). "Martires." Accessed July 27, 2016. http://www.sinaltrainal.org/index.php/home/martires.

SINALTRAINAL (Sindicato Nacional de Trabajadores de la Industria de Alimentos). *Report to* UN *Special Rapporteur on the Rights to Freedom of Peaceful Assembly and of Association and to* UN *Special Rapporteur on Extrajudicial, Summary or Arbitrary Executions*, Bogotá, September 2, 2014.

SINALTRAINAL (Sindicato Nacional de Trabajadores de la Industria de Alimentos). "SINALTRAINAL 38 años de lucha." News release, January 24, 2020. http://sinaltrainal.org/web/index.php?ecsmodule=frmstasection&ida=131&idb=338&idc=551.

SINALTRAINAL (Sindicato Nacional de Trabajadores de la Industria de Alimentos). "La transnacional Coca-Cola y el paramilitarismo en Colombia." Submission to the Food and Agriculture Hearing of the Permanent Peoples' Tribunal, Colombia sess., Bogotá, April 1–2, 2006.

"Sindicalismo de derecha: A la sombra del paramilitarismo." *Correo de Magdalena*, June 6–13, 2009.

Slobodian, Quinn. *Globalists: The End of Empire and the Birth of Neoliberalism.* Cambridge, MA: Harvard University Press, 2018.

Smith, Adam. *The Theory of Moral Sentiments.* New York: Augustus N. Kelley, 1966.

Sommerlad, Nick, and Martin Bagot. "Deathtrap Towers as 87 Blocks Face Enforcement Orders over Fire Safety Rules." *Mirror*, June 16, 2017.

Spivak, Gayatri Chakravorty. "Righting Wrongs." In *Human Rights, Human Wrongs: Oxford Amnesty Lectures*, edited by Nicholas Owen, 168–227. Oxford: Oxford University Press, 2002.

Suárez-Krabbe, Julia. *Race, Rights and Rebels: Alternatives to Human Rights and Development from the Global South.* London: Rowman and Littlefield, 2015.

Tapsfield, James. "John McDonnell Says Grenfell Deaths Were 'Social Murder' as He Uses Marxist Phrase Describing How Rich Oppress Proletariat." *Daily Mail*, June 16, 2017.

Tasioulas, John. "On the Foundations of Human Rights." In *Philosophical Foundations of Human Rights*, edited by Rowan Cruft, S. Matthew Liao, and Massimo Renzo. Oxford: Oxford University Press, 2015. https://doi.org/10.1093/acprof:oso/9780199688623.001.0001.

Tate, Winnifred. *Counting the Dead: The Culture and Politics of Human Rights Activism in Colombia*. Berkeley: University of California Press, 2007.

Taylor, Diana. *¡Presente! The Politics of Presence*. Durham, NC: Duke University Press, 2020.

Taylor, Jerome. "Alfie Meadows Calls on IPCC to Re-open Investigation into Student Protest." *Independent*, March 11, 2013.

Tepe-Belfrage, Daniela. "The Intersectional Consequences of Austerity." *Political Economy Research Centre* (blog), posted April 27, 2015. http://www.perc.org.uk/project_posts/the-intersectional-consequences-of-austerity.

Thomas, Owen. "Blind to Complicity? Official Truth and the Hidden Role of Methods." In *Exploring Complicity: Concept, Cases and Critique*, edited by Afxentis Afxentiou, Robin Dunford, and Michael Neu, 161–78. London: Rowman and Littlefield, 2017.

Thomas, Owen. "Good Faith and (Dis)honest Mistakes? Learning from Britain's Iraq War Inquiry." *Politics* 37, no. 4 (2017): 371–85. https://doi.org/10.1177/0263395716688488.

Thompson, E. P. *Whigs and Hunters: The Origin of the Black Act*. London: Breviary Stuff, 2013.

Thomson, Benjamin. "Was *Kiobel* Detrimental to Corporate Social Responsibility? Applying Lessons Learnt from American Exceptionalism." *Utrecht Journal of International and European Law* 30, no. 78 (2014): 82–98. https://utrechtjournal.org/articles/70/#.

Tilley, Lisa. "'A Strange Industrial Order': Indonesia's Racialized Plantation Ecologies and Anticolonial Estate Worker Rebellions." *History of the Present* 10, no. 1 (2020): 67–83. https://doi.org/10.1215/21599785-8221425.

Tombs, Steve. "Undoing Social Protection." In *The Violence of Austerity*, edited by Vickie Cooper and David Whyte, 113–40. London: Pluto, 2017.

Tombs, Steve, and David Whyte. *The Corporate Criminal: Why Corporations Must Be Abolished*. London: Routledge, 2015.

Tribunal Permanente de los Pueblos. "Empresas transnacionales y derechos de los pueblos en Colombia, 2006–2008." *Sentencia*, July 23, 2008. Accessed October 10, 2021. http://permanentpeoplestribunal.org/wp-content/uploads/2016/07/Colombia_VII_TPP-Es.pdf.

Tribunal Permanente de los Pueblos. "Genocidio político, impunidad y los crímenes contra la paz en Colombia." *Sentencia*, June 2021. Accessed October 10, 2021. http://permanentpeoplestribunal.org/wp-content/uploads/2021/06/TPP-SENTENCIA-COLOMBIA-2021-DEFINITIVA-CON-ANEXOS.pdf.

Tsantsoulas, Tiffany N. "Sylvia Wynter's Decolonial Rejoinder to Judith Butler's Ethics of Vulnerability." *Symposium* 22, no. 2 (2018): 158–77. https://philpapers.org/archive/TSASWD.pdf.

Tzouvala, Ntina. "Neoliberalism as Legalism: International Economic Law and the Rise of the Judiciary." In *The Politics of Legality in a Neoliberal Age*, edited by Ben Golder and Daniel McLoughlin, 116–13. London: Routledge, 2017.

United Nations Human Rights Council. *Report of the Special Representative of the Secretary-General (SRSG) on the Issue of Human Rights and Transnational Corporations and Other Business Enterprises.* Report A/HRC/4/035, February 9, 2007. https://media.business-humanrights.org/media/documents/files/media/bhr/files/SRSG-report-Human-Rights-Council-19-Feb-2007.pdf.

United Nations Office of the High Commissioner for Human Rights. *Guiding Principles on Business and Human Rights.* New York: United Nations, 2011. Accessed July 19, 2018. https://www.ohchr.org/Documents/Publications/GuidingPrinciplesBusinessHR_EN.pdf.

United Nations Office on Genocide Prevention and the Responsibility to Protect. "Crimes against Humanity." Accessed June 16, 2022. https://www.un.org/en/genocideprevention/crimes-against-humanity.shtml.

van de Sandt, Joris, and Marianne Moore, eds. *Peace, Everyone's Business! Corporate Accountability in Transitional Justice: Lessons for Colombia.* Utrecht: Pax, 2017.

Van Schaack, Beth. "The Crime of Political Genocide: Repairing the Genocide Convention's Blind Spot." *Yale Law Journal* 106, no. 7 (1997): 2259–91. https://doi.org/10.2307/797169.

Vázquez, Rolando. "Translation as Erasure: Thoughts on Modernity's Epistemic Violence." *Journal of Historical Sociology* 24, no. 1 (2011): 27–44. https://doi.org/10.1111/j.1467-6443.2011.01387.x.

Vega Cantor, Renán. *¡Sindicalicidio! Un cuento (poco imaginativo) del terrorismo laboral.* Report, Bogotá, February 25, 2012. Accessed June 27, 2016. http://www.rebelion.org/docs/147552.pdf.

Veitch, Scott. *Law and Irresponsibility: On the Legitimation of Human Suffering.* Abingdon, UK: Routledge-Cavendish, 2007.

Veltmeyer, Henry, James Petras, and Steve Vieux. *Neoliberalism and Class Conflict in Latin America.* London: Macmillan, 1997.

Vij, Ritu. "The Global Subject of Precarity." *Globalizations* 16, no. 4 (2019): 506–24. https://doi.org/10.1080/14747731.2019.1600287.

Viveiros de Castro, Eduardo. "Perspectival Anthropology and the Method of Controlled Equivocation." *Tipiti* 2, no. 1 (2004): 3–21. http://digitalcommons.trinity.edu/tipiti/vol2/iss1/1.

Wade, Robert. "Showdown at the World Bank." *New Left Review* 7 (January–February 2001): 124–37.

Waldron, Jeremy. "Is Dignity the Foundation of Human Rights?" In *Philosophical Foundations of Human Rights*, edited by Rowan Cruft, S. Matthew Liao, and Massimo Renzo. Oxford: Oxford University Press, 2015. https://doi.org/10.1093/acprof:oso/9780199688623.001.0001.

War on Want. "The Importance of Language." Accessed September 20, 2021. https://waronwant.org/about/importance-of-language.

War on Want. *The New Colonialism: Britain's Scramble for Africa's Energy and Mineral Resources*. London: War on Want, 2016.

Waterman, Peter. *Social Movements, Globalization and the New Internationalisms*. London: Mansell, 1998.

Waterman, Peter. "Social Movement Unionism: A New Union Model for a New World Order." *Review (Fernand Braudel Center)* 16, no. 3 (1993): 245–78.

Waterman, Peter. "A Trade Union Internationalism for the 21st Century: Meeting the Challenges from Above, Below and Beyond." In *Labour and the Challenges of Globalisation*, edited by Andreas Bieler, Ingemar Lindberg, and Devan Pillay, 248–63. London: Pluto, 2008.

Webber, Jeffrey. *Red October: Left-Indigenous Struggles in Modern Bolivia*. Chicago: Haymarket, 2012.

Weiler, Peter. "The United States, International Labor, and the Cold War: The Breakup of the World Federation of Trade Unions." *Diplomatic History* 5, no. 1 (1981): 1–22. https://www.jstor.org/stable/24911249.

Wenar, Leir. "The Nature of Rights." *Philosophy and Public Affairs* 36, no. 1 (2005): 223–52. https://www.jstor.org/stable/3557929.

Wheyler, Rex. "Chevron's Amazon Chernobyl Case Moves to Canada." *Deep Green*, September 9, 2017. https://intercontinentalcry.org/chevrons-amazon-chernobyl-case-moves-canada.

Whyte, David. "The Autonomous Corporation: The Acceptable Mask of Capitalism." *Kings Law Journal* 29, no. 1 (2018): 88–110. https://doi.org/10.1080/09615768.2018.1475847.

Whyte, David. "Naked Labour: Putting Agamben to Work." *Australian Feminist Law Journal* 31 (2009): 57–76. https://doi.org/10.1080/13200968.2009.10854427.

Whyte, David. "The Neo-liberal State of Exception in Occupied Iraq." In *State Crime in the Global Age*, edited by William J. Chambliss, Raymond Mikalowski, and Ronald C. Kramer, 134–51. Abingdon, UK: Routledge, 2013.

Whyte, Jessica. *The Morals of the Market*. London: Verso, 2019.

Whyte, Jessica. "Powerless Companions or Fellow Travellers? Human Rights and the Neoliberal Assault on Post-colonial Economic Justice." *Radical Philosophy* 2, no. 2 (2018): 13–29.

Winter, Yves. "Violence and Visibility." *New Political Science* 34, no. 2 (2012): 195–202. https://doi.org/10.1080/07393148.2012.676397.

Wynter, Sylvia. "Ethno or Socio Poetics." *Alcheringa* 2, no. 2 (1976): 78–94.

Wynter, Sylvia. "Unsettling the Coloniality of Being/Power/Truth/Freedom: Towards the Human, after Man, It's Overrepresentation—an Argument." *CR: New Centennial Review* 3, no. 3 (2003): 257–337.

Žižek, Slavoj. *The Courage of Hopelessness: Chronicles of a Year of Acting Dangerously*. London: Penguin, 2018.

Žižek, Slavoj. *Violence: Six Sideways Reflections*. London: Profile, 2008.

Zwehl, Philipp. "Nestle Worker and Union Activist Killed by Paramilitary." *Colombia Reports*, November 12, 2013. https://colombiareports.com/nestle -worker-union-activist-killed-receiving-threats-paramilitary-western -colombia.

index

102–3, 196n74, 197n102; comprehensive reparation demands from, 128; corporate impunity of, 114; crimes against humanity alleged against, 125; forced resignations of employees by, 29, 43, 97, 125, 183n105, 183n108; impunity of, 107–8; IUF and, 88–91, 138; legal strategy and tactics in campaign against, 119–22; negative publicity for, 118; War on Want allegations against, 93–94, 196n56, 204n20

Coca-Cola–Fomento Económico Mexicano, 43

Cohen, Stanley, 138

Collingsworth, Terry, 99

Colombia: austerity constitutionalization in, 52; British Petroleum links to military in, 58, 64–65; capitalism and violence in, 23–24; civil war in, 45–47; coal mining in, 112–13; constitutionalization of violence, 46–47, 50, 184n124, 184n129; economic opening in, 41–44; grassroots organizations in, 17–23; human rights in, 3–4; labor unionism in, 86–88; militarization of regions in, 146–49; neoliberal economics in, 28–29, 50; peace laboratories in, 55–56; Permanent Peoples' Tribunal and, 123–24; *planes de vida* (plans of/for life) in, 142–49; racist nationalism in, 41; rule of law ideology in, 36; state genocide claims against, 129–30, 202n87; state legal structure and violence in, 45–47; states of exception in, 66–67; student mobilization suppression in, 48; union solidarity in, 194n55; US support of state violence in, 45–47; violence of BP oil extraction in, 62–65

Colombian Air Force, 29

Colombian Food Workers Union, 18, 24; anti-impunity discourse and, 106–8; *buen vivir* concept in, 158; Coca-Cola and, 29–32, 43–44, 84–88, 98–100, 102–3, 196n74, 197n102; corporate impunity and, 114; feel-good ethics and delegitimation of, 135–41; forced resignations in, 29, 43, 97, 125, 183n105, 183n108; IUF and, 83–85, 88–98, 103–4, 193n29; legal strategy and tactics of, 117–22; paramilitary targeting of, 94; Permanent Peoples' Tribunal and,

123–24; public people's hearings held by, 127–28; reparation demands of, 96–97; social partnership and, 91–92

Colombian Oil Workers Union, 107

Colombia's Killer Networks (Human Rights Watch), 184n124

colonialism: capitalism and, 18–20, 86–88; corporate human rights whitewash and, 60–62; cosmopolitanism and, 76–78, 172; counterlegalities against, 126–27; development policy-speak and, 70–74; ethics and, 24; human rights and, 7–9, 154, 170–71; impunity and, 79–80; Indigenous rights and, 15; legal structures of violence and, 45–47; neoliberal defense of, 11, 40–41; resource extraction and, 33–34; United Kingdom and, 102

Colonial Labour Advisory Committee, 102

Comité de Integración Social del Catatumbo (Committee for the Social Integration of Catatumbo [CISCA]), 142–49, 157

commodified responsibility, corporate accountability and, 114

compañerxs, research and relations with, 21–23

comprehensive reparation demands, 128

Condition of the Working Class in England in 1844, The (Engels), 33

confidentiality agreements, corporate accountability and, 114

conflict, development policy-speak concerning, 71–74

constructive engagement, advocacy of, 61, 68, 88–90, 100, 104, 136, 138

Construyendo nuestros planes de vida (Building our plans for life), 144, 205n37, 206n41

controlling mind, corporate accountability and establishment of, 111, 113–17, 124, 200n53

Cooper, Vickie, 32

Coordinador Nacional Agrario (CNA), 142–44, 156–57, 160

Cornelissen, Lars, 40

Corporación Social para la Asesoría y Capacitación Comunitaria (Social Corporation for Community Advice and Training [COSPACC]), 29, 61–64, 70, 74–75, 78, 119–22, 128–29 corporations: accountability of, 4, 113–17; chain of causation in litigation against, 200n46; code of conduct for human rights and, 24; human rights and, 57–62, 171–72; impunity of, 24–25, 79–80, 106–8, 113–17, 130–31; IUF engagement with, 95–100; personhood of, 113, 116, 201n55; social responsibility and, 57–58, 76–78, 187n11; violence against labor by, 28–29; whitewash by, 49–60

Correa, Javier, 84, 90–91, 97

cosmopolitan ethics: colonialism and, 76–78; human rights and, 172

Coulthard, Glen, 15

counterinsurgency policies: corporate support and involvement in, 63–65; labor violence and, 45–47

counterlegalities: corporate criminality and, 123–30; human rights advocacy and, 172–73

crimes against humanity, legal strategies involving, 123–30

criminal law: corporate crime and, 113–14, 120–21; counterlegalities and, 122–30; crimes against humanity and, 123–30; impunity and, 105–8, 110–13; individualism and, 110–13; rule of law and, 35

critical theory, human rights and, 5

cruel optimism, feel-good ethics and, 138–41

Çubukçu, Ayça, 167–68, 202n88

Danewid, Ida, 211n55

Darwin, Charles, 9

Decent Work Agenda (ILO), 100–102

decolonization: grassroots activism and, 19–23; human rights and, 7–8, 10; romanticization of Indigenous thought and culture and, 140–41, 158; union role in, 84–85

Decree 3398 (Colombia), 46

Defence Systems Limited, 29, 64, 76

De la stratégie judiciare (Vergès), 126–27

Delgado, Ana Carolina Teixera, 158

democracy: neoliberal framing of, 56; social fascism and hollowing out of, 52–56

Denning (Lord), 200n53

denuncia, social movement use of, 118

Derrida, Jacques, 209n41

developmentist intervention, communities' resistance to, 144–49

de Vitoria, Francisco, 7–8

devoir de vigilance (duty of vigilance), 115

disavowal, feel-good ethics and, 138–41

distant view, Foucault's concept of, 21

Dowling, Paul, 115–16

Drainville, André C., 101

D'Souza, Radha, 79–80

due diligence, corporate accountability and, 115–16

Dunford, Robin, 15–16

Dussel, Enrique, 7

duty of care, corporate accountability and, 114–15

Eagleton, Terry, 150–52

Eco, Umberto, 93

economic development: civil society linked to, 74–75; humanness and, 153–54; human rights and, 1–2, 19–23, 60; immanent critique of, 127–28; labor violence and, 45–47; law and, 23–24; violence of, 62–65; virtual reality of policy-speak and, 69–74

Economies of Abandonment (Povinelli), 132

Ecuador, landmark judgment against Chevron in, 199n41

Ejército de Liberación Nacional (National Liberation Army), 46, 64, 72–74, 208n25

El Morro Association of Community Action Groups, 68–69

engagement: BP engagement with NGOs, 61, 68; with Coca-Cola, 89–90, 104; human rights mobilization and, 15; IUF advocacy for constructive, 88, 136, 138; with neoliberalism, 100

Engels, Friedrich, 33

English Factory Acts, 113

Enlightenment: human equality and, 11; human rights law and theory and, 14

equality, necroeconomics and reduction of, 39

equity, law and logic of, 14, 131

Escobar, Arturo, 19, 62, 157–58

Estado Social de Derecho, 182n101. See also Social Rule of Law ideology ethics: feel-good, 135–41; human rights and, 4–6, 17, 168; logic of deferral and, 133–35; necroeconomics and, 38; normative judgments and, 133–35; obligations of, 161–66; social fascism and subversion of, 53; transnational cosmopolitanism and, 172; of vulnerability, 164–66

ethnodesarollo (ethnodevelopment), 205n37

Europe: anarchist thought in, 146; Colombian Food Workers Union campaign in, 118–22; Colombian grassroots activism and social movements in, 18–23; neoliberalism in, 50–51, 54–56

European Commission, 51

European Union (EU), 51–52, 55–56

exceptionalism in law: normalization of, 65–67; state violence and, 47–49

extractivism, in Latin America, 60–62

extraterritorial litigation, corporate impunity and, 117–22

Fanon, Frantz, 151, 154

Feierstein, Daniel, 203n99

Ferreira, Marcelo, 203n99

Fiscal Responsibility Act (2010, United Kingdom), 51–52, 185n160

Fisher, Mark, 104, 135–36

forced resignations of employees, Coca-Cola and, 29, 43, 97, 125

foreign investment, extractivism and, 61

Foucault, Michel, 21

France, corporate accountability in, 115–16

freedom, illegal rule of law and, 49–52

Fresh Del Monte Produce, 97–99

Freud, Sigmund, 129, 138

Friedman, Milton, 50, 58–59

Fuerzas Armadas Revolucionarias de Colombia (Revolutionary Armed Forces of Colombia [FARC]), 46, 56, 106

Fundación Amanecer (Dawn Foundation), 75

Galindo, Pedro, 74

García Márquez, Gabriel, 45

García Villegas, Mauricio, 52, 66, 96

gender, hierarchies of, 10

General Agreement on Tariffs and Trade (GATT), 40–41

Geneva School neoliberalism, 11

genocide: Colombia paramilitary, 29, 45–47, 129–30, 146–49, 202n87; criminal law and accountability for, 123–24; of Indigenous peoples, 123–24; reorganization, 203n99; of union members, 28–29, 87–88

geopolitics, of knowledge, 19–20, 177n74

Gil, Isidro, 193n29

Gill, Lesley, 118

Gillard, Michael, 77

Glencore, 31

Global Campaign to Dismantle Corporate Power and Stop Impunity, 121

Global Coca-Cola Workers' Alliance, 193n40

global financial crisis of 2008, neoliberalism and, 51

global framework agreements, workers' rights and, 83–85

globalization: extractive-export model and, 60–62; human rights and, 10–11; illegal rule of law and, 49–52; workers' rights and, 82–85

global justice: human rights and, 6; marketization of, 109–13

global unions: labor rights and, 24, 82–85; multinational corporations and, 91–100; pernicious optimism and, 139–41

Golder, Ben, 5

Gómez, Guillermo, 30

good intentions, assumption of, 133–35, 137–38

Gordon, Lewis, 4

Gordon, Uri, 146

Graeber, David, 156

grassroots organizations, human rights and, 17–23

Greece, EU bailout of, 51

Grenfell Tower fire (United Kingdom), 32–33

Guatemala, union activism in, 97–99, 196n78

Guevara, Ernesto Che, 163

guilty mind, corporate accountability and establishment of, 111, 113–17, 124, 200n53

Guzman Daza, Carlos, 64–65

Habsburg Empire, 11

Hale, Charles R., 44

harm, responsibility for, 112, 131, 139–41

Allied Workers' Associations (IUF), 83–85, 88–98, 103–4, 134, 137–41, 192n27, 193n29, 193n40

Italian activists, Coca-Cola boycott and, 89–90, 194n43

Jiménez, Asdrubal, 77–78

journalists, corporate allegations against, 77–78

justice: agreement as, 137–41; impunity and, 108–13

Justice, Dwight W., 83

Justice for Colombia (British NGO), 89, 90, 93

just war theory: human rights and, 7; neoliberal defense of, 40

Kennedy, Roddy, 77

Khoury, Stéfanie, 3

King, Zak, 49

Klein, Naomi, 2

knowledge production, human rights activism and, 21

Knox, Robert, 51, 117, 120–21, 204n20

Kochi, Tarik, 37

Krever, Tor, 109

labor: Colombian legislation on, 42–43, 183n105, 183n108; commodification of, 12–13, 24; conditions in nineteenth-century England for, 33; deaths at work and, 41–42, 112–13; multinational corporations and, 85–88; pernicious optimism and, 139–41; privatization of human rights and, 24; sweatshop labor, 57–58; violence against, in Colombia, 28–31, 45–46, 183n108; welfare state advocacy by, 81–85. *See also* unions

Labour Party (United Kingdom), 52, 55

land rights: Colombia elite abrogation of, 44; of Indigenous peoples, 7–8, 31, 44; post-conflict restitution proposals, 56

la Red de Hermandad (Network of Brotherhood/Sisterhood), 17–23, 142–49, 157

Latin America: citizenship in, 9–10; extractivism in, 60–62; rule of law in, 35–36, 45

law: atrocity in context of, 65–67; British state exceptionalism and, 47–49; capitalism and, 13–17; corporate accountability and, 115–17; critique of the present and, 130–31; economic relations and, 23–24; social movement strategy and tactics using, 117–22, 204n20; social relations and, 12–13

Law 10 (Colombia, 1989), 42–43

Law 48 (Colombia, 1968), 46, 184n126

Law 50 (Colombia), 183n105

Law 70 (Colombia, 1993), 44

Law 189 (Colombia), 183n105

Lear, Jonathan, 150–51, 163

Legislative Act 3 (Colombia), 50

Le Guin, Ursula, 132–34

les damnés, Fanon's concept of, 151

Levinas, Emmanuel, 165

liberal individualism, human rights and, 2, 10–11

liberationist Christianity, *buen vivir* concept and, 158–59, 208nn25–26

Liberty (human rights organization), 3

López, Oscar, 30, 87

Lorde, Audre, 13

Löwy, Michael, 208n25

Lyotard, Jean-François, 209n41

Maastricht Treaty of 1992, 51

MacIntyre, Jody, 48

Madhok, Sumi, 15

Magna Carta, 34

Maldonado-Torres, Nelson, 154

Mandinga, Naka, 157

Marín, Álvaro, 1–2, 22–23, 28, 56, 95, 153–54

market economy: feel-good ethics and, 137; human rights and role of, 5, 12, 134–35; mythology of, 28; necroeconomics and, 39, 181n71; pernicious optimism and, 139–41; social responsibility and, 59; workers' rights and, 102–4

market Stalinism, 104

Martínez, Carlos Daniel, 146

Marx, Karl: on capitalism, 14; on labor, 9; labor violence and, 30–31; on law, 121; on liberalism, 53; necroeconomics and, 37

Marxism, self-determination and, 19–23

Mattei, Ugo, 34, 36, 49–50

Mbembe, Achille, 7
McKinsey & Company, 32
Meadows, Alfie, 48
Meister, Robert, 202n98
Mendoza, William, 205n33
Mendoza gang (Guatemala), 97
mens rea, corporate accountability and, 111, 200n53
Mignolo, Walter, 8, 19
Mills, Catherine, 165
modernity: atrocity and, 65–67; austerity constitutionalization and, 52; colonial violence and, 7
Montag, Warren, 38–40, 133
Mont Pèlerin Society, 11, 39–40, 56
morality, feel-good ethics and, 136–41
Mora Sanabria, Gustavo, 141
Mora Sanabria, Jefer, 141
motive, criminal responsibility and, 110–12
Movement for the Survival of the Ogoni People, 58
Moyn, Samuel, 10–11
multinational corporations: human rights and, 1; impunity of, 200n47; social impact of, 58–59; social responsibility of, 76–78, 187n11; unions and, 85–88, 95–100, 196n74
Múnera, Adolfo, 29–30, 44, 87–88
Muppidi, Himadeep, 78
Murdoch, Iris, 26, 163–64, 167–68, 209n41, 210n45

Nader, Laura, 34, 36, 49–50
Nandini Sundar et al. v. State of Chhattisgarh, 127
Nasa Indigenous group, 7
National Association of Hospital and Clinic Workers, 31
National Constitution (Colombia), 42, 44, 184n129
National Health Service (NHS) (United Kingdom), humanitarian crisis in, 32, 55, 186n177
National Union of Students (NUS) (United Kingdom), 89, 135–36, 197n102; feel-good ethics and 135–36
natural selection, rationality paradigm and, 8–9
necroeconomics, 37–44

negligence, corporate accountability and, 114
neoliberalism: in Colombia, 28–29; colonialism defended by, 29–30, 39–41; constitutionalization of, 50; contractualism and, 52; development policy-speak and, 72–74; human rights and, 2–3, 10–12, 170–72; illegal rule of law and, 49–52; mythology of, 28, 41–44; as social fascism, 52–56; social partnerships and, 91–100; social responsibility and, 58–59; state exceptionalism and, 47–48; in United Kingdom, 32; wealth protection and, 100–103
Nestlé Corporation: Colombian Food Workers Union campaign against, 29–30, 85–88; workers' rights and, 84–85
new humanism, 164–66
New International Economic Order, 10–11, 40, 59
New York Times Magazine, 58
non-disparagement clauses, corporate accountability and, 91, 114
nongovernmental organizations (NGOs): British Petroleum and, 61–62, 67–69, 137–41; corporate ties with, 58, 75; economic development and, 56; feel-good ethics and, 135–41; good intentions assumption by, 133–35; human rights advocacy and, 4, 23; impact on peasants' demands of, 69–74; paramilitary groups' formation of, 186n183; "rights-proofing" of violence by, 76–77; union alliances with, 99
normalization of violence, 65–67
normative judgments, ethics and, 133–35
Norrie, Alan, 112, 125
Nuremberg Trials, 109
NUS Services Limited, 89–90, 197n102

Occidental Petroleum, 29, 64
Ocensa (BP pipeline company), 69, 115
Odysseos, Louiza, 154–55
Office for Budgetary Responsibility (United Kingdom), 52
Oil Justice campaign, 119–20
Olaya, Carlos, 106–7, 109–12
Ó Loingsigh, Gearóid, 55, 143, 158